W9-BYB-199

The Femme's Guide to the Universe

The Femme's Guide to the Universe

Shar Rednour

alyson books
los angeles | new york

MANUFACTURED IN CANADA.

THIS TRADE PAPERBACK ORIGINAL IS PUBLISHED BY ALYSON PUBLICATIONS,
P.O. BOX 4371, LOS ANGELES, CA 90078-4371.
DISTRIBUTION IN THE UNITED KINGDOM BY TURNAROUND PUBLISHER SERVICES LTD.,
UNIT 3, OLYMPIA TRADING ESTATE, COBURG ROAD, WOOD GREEN,
LONDON N22 6TZ ENGLAND.

FIRST EDITION: AUGUST 2000

00 01 02 03 04 ▉ 10 9 8 7 6 5 4 3 2 1

ISBN: 1-55583-461-2

LIBRARY OF CONGRESS CATALOGING-IN-PUBLICATION DATA
REDNOUR, SHAR.
   THE FEMME'S GUIDE TO THE UNIVERSE / SHAR REDNOUR.
   ISBN 1-555583-461-2
   1. WOMEN—MISCELLANEA. 2. WOMEN—PSYCHOLOGY—MISCELLANEA.
3. WOMEN—LIFE SKILLS GUIDES—MISCELLANEA. I. TITLE.
HQ1233.R44 2000
305.4—DC21   00-038043

CREDITS
• HAIL MARYS LYRICS © JACKIE STRANO. REPRINTED BY PERMISSION OF JACKIE STRANO.
• "NEED" © 1972 BY MARCY SHEINER. REPRINTED BY PERMISSION OF MARCY SHEINER.
• COVER AND TEXT DESIGN BY B. ZINDA.
• COVER PHOTOGRAPHY BY PHYLLIS CHRISTOPHER.
• CARTOONS BY MELINDA GEBBIE.

Contents

Acknowledgments and Cast Credits!

I know this part is for thanking folks, but frankly, it also reads as my cast of characters. If you're one of the few people who actually read acknowledgments, you can say "na na na" to those who don't because you'll have insider information.

Here we go…. This book took several years to complete. Granted, I was splitting my Diva time between my productions, my wife Jackie's productions, *our* productions, personal crises, family crises, making rent, and raising animals. I have a lot of people to acknowledge 'cuz those years involved a lot of folks. I figure if I win an Academy Award for screenwriting (one of my goals in this lifetime), they will cut me short, so I better get most of it in here. (P.S. Many of my friends share their brilliance, humor, and charm with the world in ways other than through me, so type their names into your favorite search engine and see what comes up.)

My editor, Angela Brown, arrived on the scene with my book half written. She responded openly to my direct nature and made a commitment not to desert my project (which happens in publishing all the time these days). She's smart, funny, and damn good at her job. I thank her for working above and beyond the call of duty just like an editor from the olden days.

I thank Gerry (formerly of Alyson) for signing me. I thank Scott Brassart and everyone at Alyson for wholeheartedly believing in this book. (Get this—one publisher rejected *The FG*, telling me, "Femme is a passing trend, Shar, and you missed it." All I have to say is, "HaHaHaHa!")

I really don't know how to begin to thank Bruce Zinda, Alyson's fabulous art designer, for working his fingers to the bone to make this book a dazzling, sparkling, gorgeous reality. Just thumb through and you'll see what I mean! Thank you, Bruce!

Jackie gave her patience and dedication—she went to work for the man—all so I could finish this book. She keeps me balanced, thinking, informed, laughing, coming, happy. Her songs fill my ears and my heart. She sings our life. She's my family, my rock, my inspiration, my true love.

Steve Mounce and Brian Wood are my gay brothers, my court and best friends for more than 15 years. (Steve is also my humor editor). We've gone through so much; they've not only known me when *all* of my hair was the color of my roots, but they've also experienced the roots of almost every chapter in this book. To know, hard-core, that they would do anything for me is a gift that no words can begin to show thanks for. Also, they make fun of me and keep the Queen humble.

Scratch, scratch, kiss, kiss, and big thanks to Susie Bright for her love, thoughtfulness, support, and for all those times she comes home from touring and calls me to dish about what all the femme dykes across the country are doing or saying. (P.S. Thanks also to her fans who articulated the phrase "butch flight." We'd all talked about it, but no one knew what to call it.)

I thank hottie, redhead, "where's the dolls?" Phyllis Christopher and bad boy, "where's the femme tops?" Karen Everett for being witness to our "good ol' days" and continuing to document the fucking great new ones. They always saw the Queen in me.

Besides Jackie's, Marcy Sheiner's eyes were always the first to behold the pages of *The FG* and the first to edit them. I could never have completed *The FG* without her emotional, intellectual, and pharmaceutical support.

Melinda Gebbie, who has fondly become more to me than "the striking woman in the hat" (a famous photo by Honey Lee Cottrell), worked across the Atlantic and against the clock to ensure that this book held fabulous cartoons.

I thank Honey Lee for her tremendous support in all my crazy projects as a designer, confidante, and friend. She helped generate Mel's cartoons and acted as liaison. She has also given me priceless insider butch info.

Kent Taylor loaned his studio and pink backdrop to my cause. Kiss, kiss, darlin'.

I thank Stephanie Rosenbaum for starting this book with me, not to mention for being a hottie femme and witty writer. She's got savvy. I can't even remember how many years ago we handwrote the outline for this book in my notebook. I always say I've been writing this book my whole life, but doing stuff with a friend makes it so much more fun. If Steph and I hadn't started the ink flowing together, who knows if the book would have happened. She gave me her blessing and told me to go forth and birth *The FG* so the world would be saved.

Mike Ford is one of my generation's best writers. Lucky for me he thinks I'm a doll, and I thank him for pressuring the powers that *were* at Alyson into seeing *The FG* through his fuschia lens.

Christina Vickory gave me loads of tips for the book, but that's not why I'm thanking her. As always, I thank her for her incredible chest—I mean inspiration. Just knowing that Christina exists makes me feel better. She always thinks too much about things like sexual politics, makeup, how long frosted lip gloss will be in fashion *this time* around.... She's a drop-dead gorgeous, smart Virginian who offers up, without reservation, girl-sistergirlfriend understanding and validation yet wholeheartedly nurtures and perpetuates the femme mystique. Only a Southern belle can maintain that balance like it's nothin' harder than sippin' iced tea on a hot day.

Shoshana "Crem" Rosenfeld created the movie *Scent Uva Butch*. During any low, "why am I even writing this anyway" days it was her demanding assertions that "This book is needed *now*" that got my fingers clicking again.

Denise, oh Denise. Denise Macias is a muse. Yes, she's been one of my muses, but she's also one of those few-and-far-between beauties whose depth of mystique has kept more than a few of us tripping over ourselves in wonder. As a real per-

Me and the Queen Mommy Mavis

son, she's plumped me up when I was feelin' down, whether that was physical (like the time I fell and broke my elbow) or emotional. She's another one who would return from the field with adamant orders that the girls on the front line needed this book. She always offered to listen or advise as much as I needed it.

Tina D'Elia showed up with insightful quotes and well-thought-out tips at Marlena's Bar just when I needed them.

Carol Queen and Robert Lawrence I thank for their sophisticated contributions to the glossary and for their love and support, as always.

I thank the voluptuous brunette Billie Mandel (who makes the best of nonmonogamy ideals come to life) for sharing her 'Dess babe secrets.

I thank the staff at Good Vibes (Angus, Terry M, Karlyn, Ray, Violet, Cheryl, Janelle, Jules, Priscilla) who worked there when I temped. They all pondered many a question about femme/butch relationships, sex, and nonmonogamy. And Laura Wiede, who's the coolest example of a rioting, activist femme: miniskirts and industrial boots all in one.

Special kiss to Karlyn "Fairy Butch" Lotney for all our fun convos at 4 A.M. You *must* read her story in *Virgin Territory 2*.

Debbie, Vickie, Toby, and Veronica are a part of the Hail Marys family. Debbie's guitar-playing butch fingers have inspired many a femme. I like her 'cuz she always loved it when Jackie put her on surrogate husband patrol. Vicki's another hottie Southern belle—'nuff said. Toby's a hot butch from Queens—'nuff said. And Veronica I thank for her butt, not to mention her smarts and her love of the weird (some of my favorite traits).

My brothers in fabu-queerdom: Steve on the left and Brian on the right

I thank Lynn Breedlove for letting me quote her story.

I thank Ann Whidden for speaking so frankly about living with repetitive stress injuries (RSI).

Justice Howard shot photos of me after a die-hard party weekend in Vegas. Thank you, Queen o' Babes, for all your contributions.

I thank Dan Nicoletta for scoring us the current Lust Palace, not to mention his commitment to documenting fabulousness. (Pissed fabu, celebrating fabu, and fabu flying to heaven—he gets it all.)

My gratitude goes to David de Freschville Torrey for all his help and skill with my original

Shartopia Web site plus his current assistance. I thank Joani Blank for her patience and financial assistance while I worked on *The FG*.

The two following women are the creators and producers of the infamous spoken word show/group/tour, Sister Spit. I toured with them and ten other women in summer 1998. Mark my words, these two women will be canonized one day. We're all in each other's bestest-fan club: Aquarian Michelle Tea does non-monogamy counseling according to your air sign. She's a punky femme who is *the* reason Fudge hair color made Blueberry. She's me only more air and less Girl Scout. (P.S. She's a fuckin' killer writer as well.) There are very few poets who speak to me and give me comfort when I'm spinning in madness—the number one person on that list is Sini Anderson. She's also a great hugger (you know those goo-oo-ood butch hugs).

Sash is a boy cutie who should basically wait on me all the time, but she's so smart that she's always off doing math or producing the Spoken Word night K'Vetch or drinking beer with SF's fabulorati that she doesn't have enough hours in the day to take care of me and Jack as well.

I caught the fabulous photographer Phyllis Christopher in front of the camera for a kiss!

I just want to mention that Ida Acton and Sash Sunday both shared their baby butch stories of what it's like to come out butch in the big city these days. I thank Amy Anner and Sally Carter and *all* the butches who shared their feelings and perspectives with me.

Youme Landowne is the kindest person on this earth as well as a remarkable artist. Youme always saw the Queen in me, and I always saw the Princess in her. She's like flowers, angels, and chocolate all in one living, breathing creature.

Laurie Sirois is from Maine. With a heart as big as the state, she's a quirky, smart beauty. Orange.

Jenny, the curly-haired muse, in her absolute loveliness, inspired me in many ways. She and

Shoshana von Blankensie acted as my baby femmes and let me grill them on how they see relationships, butches, and babes.

Lissa Ivy is beautiful to behold. Pink.

Kiss, kiss to Elle.

Air kiss to Downtown Donna for all those comps.

I thank Jennifer and Ursula Bruckman for being my straight-girl femme informants.

I thank my models: Simone, Veronica, Denise, Stephanie, Tina, and Christina.

My gratitude to Mom Lynn for her support and all those coffee talks.

Aretha Bright is my soul sister. Her beauty, curiosity, and love of the arts has inspired me many times over.

Jon Bailiff is a curly-headed love who has nourished me with thoughtful conversation and good cooking more than a few times.

I thank Dan Dean for being a sweetie and coming through when we needed him.

I thank Alison Austin for all the advice and savvy contributions to the glossary.

I thank both of my grandmas: Pearlene for her influence of high drag in camp, attitude, and costume and Lilian for showing me how to act with class and sophistication.

I thank Daddy for raising me to know how to do everything myself. I didn't realize that was unusual growing up, but I sure learned otherwise when I hit the world.

I've got some terrific aunts. I particularly thank Aunt Mary for passing down her love of the story and Aunt Connie for cutting my hair in seventh grade and sharing all her makeup tips.

Mom, I don't even no where to begin. Mavis is my premiere muse. Besides that, she raised me with the confidence to ask questions, the humor to not care if I looked like a fool when asking, and she *tried* to give me the patience to wait for the answers. She and Dad both raised me with the sense of importance of sharing what we learn, have, and think.

The Foundations of Femmehood

Kick off those crystal slippers and prepare for your guided Shar-tour through the realm of femmedom.

Welcome to Shartopia

The Shartopian Credo: Get What You Want and Nobody Gets Hurt

I believe everyone can get what they want. I believe in "win-win" situations. I believe in orgies. I believe in love hangovers. I believe nonmonogamy can work. My shorthand reference to getting what you want, to making your dreams come true, to never thinking you're stuck, is "Shartopia."

In Shartopia you sleep on *your* schedule and still make enough money to pay the rent.

In Shartopia you get fucked regularly and receive foot massages like clockwork.

In Shartopia there are always enough strawberries, chocolate, shrimp, and avocados to go around.

As you read this book, when you come across a "Shartopia," let your mind stretch to the farthest horizon. Dream of endless possibilities.

In Shartopia references to fashion, makeup, and style are literal as well as symbolic; there's more to an eyebrow than a natural curve. If you aren't already living in Shartopia, just remember: No one is stuck. We're all creative and smart (or we find creative and smart friends to tell us what to do), so we create our own possibilities. Of course, not all our days are going to be glimmering Shartopian slices of life. But when we do make it to the Shartopian suburbs, we can all discover ways to tackle our challenges and locate opportunities where we had previously only seen obstacles. Then, once we hit the city limits, lipstick stays on like cement and looks and feels like velvet. Perfection.

If you let it, *The Femme's Guide* will help you stake out and settle your own Shartopia and create *You*topia. The tips in this book provide a practical map by which you can create your own Youtopian Femminesto. For those of you who think you know what you want in this world, in another person, or in yourselves—in other words, for experienced femmes—this book will remind you of essential elements that will enhance your life.

Often, the realizations I come to from reading what I call "those woo-woo, New-Agey books" are not new for me, but simply things I've forgotten. We know so much when we are three years old, but somewhere along the way some of it gets stolen or so mushed around with untruths that we lose sight of our precious internal knowledge. Perhaps this is why folks flock to New Age books: They ring true somewhere in our hearts. Why? Because their words are familiar, something we *already knew,* and we trust ourselves most of all. *The Femme's Guide* offers this kind of experience for the royal femme who's been around the kingdom a few times. Whether you need validation concerning your latest dating experience or are searching for new ways to revel in marabou boas, this guide will take care of you from head to toe more completely than a latex-clad naughty nurse.

For new princesses and their fans, *The Femme's Guide* makes the entire femme experience fun and easy. Why should you lose an eyelash when I've already tested the curler? I've never bought the advice, "You have to make your own mistakes." Being a young or new femme in some parts of the Milky Way can be downright scary. Baby, let me tell you how to make your lipstick stay put, let me give you the definition of *ecru*. Do you want to know what to do about those troublesome, studly butches, or how to get between the knees of a leggy femme? Would you like to be a femme for a day or a lifetime? No matter, princess. Whatever it is, we'll take care of it.

Femmes and aspiring femmes of all genders and sexualities, as well as our fans, are official citizens of Shartopia. Although I address all femmes and refer to all femmes, this is not a how-to-be-a-just-any-femme handbook. *The Femme's Guide* lays out a royal map for the Queen in all of us, and I will slink you, slowly but surely, down that red carpet to femmehood. Sweetie, I don't mean femme as in *femmer than butch*. I mean a heel-slinkin', lipstick-printin', chickie-vampin', nail-rippin', lust-purrin', divaluscious, high as in *ozone-piercing-high* femme.

When a high femme glides through a space, everything halts as the experience is absorbed. Traffic stops, breaths are held, conversations falter. In our multitasking world, future and past fall away until there is only one moment, and that moment is *her*. You think I'm going too far? Just watch it happen. I didn't say the whole night will be stolen by her presence (although it will be for some souls), but I promise that everyone who experiences her will be wholly captivated, if only for a moment. That's more attention than our kids or bosses get most of the time.

Shartopia is an equal-opportunity domain where folks of all incomes can reside. You'll notice that in *The Femme's Guide* I often tell how to make things happen if you're financially downtrodden. I very much welcome readers who make the dough, but I want my tips, ideas, and lifestyle to be accessible to everyone, no matter how much money is available. Believe me, I have lived on very little, so this advice comes from experience. Remaining a Queen against most odds has become my specialty. I also have friends who possess plenty of cash and love to spend it, so, luckily, I get to witness both lifestyles. Have you noticed that people who have money buy things they can't make, and broke folks make things they can't buy? See, the grass is always greener.

The Femme's Guide is all about camp and attitude, yet filled with hands-on advice. There's nothing in here I haven't experienced or felt vibrantly through a close friend. You'll also learn all my friends' names and habits as you read. Sharing stories advances our femme experience with human delight and discord. Ultimately, I hope my stories and theirs will help you to revel in your new (or rejuvenated) femme identity. So choose a comfortable yet luxurious throne, prop those royal feet up, and prepare for your guided Shar-tour through the realm of femmedom.

JUSTICE HOWARD

This is me being a post-30 babe for the famous fine art photographer Justice Howard.
She makes the video series Hell Cats in High Heels. Need I say more?

Sharstory:

How I Collected My Femme Power and Lived to Tell About It

"I'm standing on the horizon looking for somebody recognizing that I might have been queen."
—Tina Turner

Being an only child meant I didn't get just stereotypical girlie presents on holidays. Since I had no brother to receive gifts of cars and trains, I got them. I played both sides of the fence—with Matchbox cars, a racetrack, and two go-carts, plus baby dolls, stuffed animals, and Barbies. Lots of Barbies. I dreaded sports and flunked phys ed, but I have to thank my dad for at least making sure I could shoot a basket and hit a softball. My mom, Mavis, played dolls with me and even made dresses for my babies. I donned fancy skirts with bells sewn into the ruffles and groovy pantsuits that matched Mom's. As far as I was concerned, I had the best of both worlds.

Still, I was always getting into trouble because I didn't pick up on the sexist socialization pervading our culture. In fact, it missed me by a long shot. To my teachers' dismay, I constantly took off my shirt on the playground. My Barbies also went topless in their free-love communes where they shared Ken *and* each other. I must have been a wonder to Mavis, a factory-working, water-skiing, bar-b-quing redhead, who would watch in awe as I acted out my "strange" ideas.

All children are born innocent, but some pick up on social mores faster than others. I was definitely driving in the slow lane when it came to understanding cultural expectations. In fact, I thought women surely must rule the world. After all, Barbie was leaps and bounds beyond Ken. Mommy was smarter than Daddy. And the boys at school never did their homework. They just blew spit wads and smelled funny. *Clearly, women must reign supreme.*

I was raised in a blue-collar, working-class family, the stuff honky-tonk songs are made of. Cheatin' and drinkin' men. Multiple marriages. It was from the women in my family that I began to collect my femme power—persevering Southern women who weren't treated like Queens but who certainly acted like royalty. They always offered charm, humor, or leadership when needed and, of course, dolled themselves up through it all. Forget the romantic version of the South. No *Steel Magnolias* here. Instead, imagine Aunt Naomi with a cigarette dangling out of her mouth as she holds a bleeding steak to her daughter's black eye while her boyfriend (whose wife doesn't know where he is) goes out to kick the ass of the ex-boyfriend of my cousin. Aunt Naomi provided leadership: "Jeanine, sit down and put this meat on your eye. Leonard, if you're gonna kill him, don't get caught because we don't have money for

MELINDA GEBBIE

My throne is a circa-1966 crayon-pink hairdresser's chair.

bail. And don't get a black eye neither 'cause we can't afford another steak." And charm: "Baby, on your way back would you get me some cigarettes?" She'd wink at Uncle Leonard to imply his reward. And humor: "Jeanine, don't you worry none. We'll just smudge liner around your other eye and tell everybody you've gone punk rock."

I learned I had an impact, that I counted. I realized my words, attitude, and presence made a difference in other's lives. While other people sat around feeling sorry for themselves, my family did something about bad situations, even if "doing something" meant making a lemon icebox pie and a joke. Sometimes it meant just pouring a cold Pepsi and listening.

My mom's mom, Pearlene, who had a rough life, always wore fabulous shoes with a matching pocketbook and sparkling costume jewelry, absolutely demanding to be respected despite her social or marital status. If she could sparkle in working poverty, I could surely dazzle.

I was out of my element after we moved from Arkansas to Illinois. My cousin Natalie was the only saving grace in this mundane, dreadful place. A sassy blond who shared my sense of humor and priorities, she saw the necessity of making mud pies *and* writing poetry *and* chasing snakes *and* scouring catalogs to circle each and every outfit we would buy if we ever got rich. Alas, Natalie was not enough in this new land. We were blue-collar city folks who somehow ended up in this *field* surrounded by Republican farmers. No one appreciated our fast cars and fine bar-b-que. None of the other girls wore go-go boots and groovy A-line dresses. And the teachers treated me like a sinner for doing so. Clearly, I had to find a new court to worship me.

Tuffy and me in the back of my dad's GMC four-by-four. Note the CB antenna. My folks and I are all about communication.

It didn't happen until high school, but it came with a boom. My friend and neighbor (*neighbor* meaning 1.5 miles away) Dawn validated that we were both indeed in the wrong place and had to get out. My best friends, Brian and Steve, saw the Queen in me, which infused me with the confidence to be me when others tried to shoot down us queers (*queer* in the truest sense: "odd or unusual"). Brian and Steve loved my dark purple lipstick and Tina Turner hair as much as they were drawn to my philosophical maxims. My ideals—and their faith in me—gave us all hope, and hope kept us alive.

Then came college and those 1980s high-fashion years, when I came out. As gay people, when we say "when I came out" we hear "when I grew up" because that's what it means to us. Most of us are taken under wing by older queers and taught lessons that we will, in turn, teach others. I learned some stuff I'd instinctively known but had never seen in action. One of the most important lessons I learned was that "feminine" does not equal "weak."

I befriended drag queens who took little high-heeled me as their pet project and protected me, since I didn't have a big butch to do the job. Vanessa and Chloe taught me how to transform bedraggled thrift-store pumps into bedazzling high heels with glue and a broken strand of 50-cent pearls. Another queen, Stacy, led me through some of my darker lessons. One night I witnessed her slam a drunken, homophobic asshole against a wall and hold him by his neck as she pulled a knife from her cleavage and put it to his throat. The guy was quite shaken; frat brat wasn't so tough anymore. I learned you gotta have some brain and/or muscle behind your skirt because the world isn't as squeaky-clean as it is on sitcoms. These queens protected me, but at the same time they had complete faith that I could do anything on my own (not *alone*; no one would wish that even on Stacy—but that I had something to contribute and would be a fine soldier in any ugly situation).

Later I trekked from small-town-everybody-welcome Carbondale to small-city-thinks-it-knows-something Indianapolis, where I lived through years of

Me on the property line of my parents' field. Barbed wire can really do a number on stockings, so step high if you're taking shortcuts through the neighbor's field.

people despising me for being femme. Women thought I either purposely sold out to the patriarchy, so therefore I was a traitor, or that I was stupid because I didn't realize I was selling out. But whatever disgust they projected, once I slipped a tequila shot past those criticizing lips, many of them wanted to sleep with me. There were quite a few, though, who got to know me for me, despite themselves.

Meanwhile, in San Francisco, publishers Debi Sundahl and Nan Kinney, along with editor Susie Bright, were putting butches and femmes back on the map with *On Our Backs*.[1] They took fat pink scissors, cut us right out of the history books, licked our backs, and stuck us into the present. Now the whole country knew we existed.

I moved to SF, hooked up with the *On Our Backs* gang, and began to live the single-femme high life. The few drinks I actually paid for were bought with dollars earned from baby-sitting.

I made friends with Susie Bright through her baby Aretha. We rarely talked business. Our conversations were consumed by two topics: babies and butches. I knew a lot about one and she knew a lot about the other. Susie's daughter, at the age of three months, was delivered to my arms at the infant department of the preschool where I worked. Eventually I took care of her during Susie's many gigs. Susie always insisted I arrive early so she could try on her many outfits, then make me choose the best. As a result, I got a fabulous preview of California fashion. Susie knew all the secret finds of our fine city: private designers' warehouses; Piedmont, the high-drag store that also equips the Sisters of Perpetual Indulgence; fetish stores—all of it.

In Susie I also found a willing ear for my dating tales. She put everything in perspective, so I no longer felt I was lost in a strange land without a translation book. Susie slurped up my sex details as though they were fine oysters, asking all the right questions to keep me talking. Although I had practiced writing erotica behind closed doors, I honed my talent by retelling my stories to Susie and the boys. Susie would also stop me dead in my tracks whenever I'd beat myself up over some psycho butch. I'd be convinced I was living some unique nightmare when she'd interrupt and tell me the details of my date as if she'd just read my diary. It had all happened to her! Different names and places, but the games—the good ones and the bad—were amazingly similar. We published one of our conversations in *Dagger: On Butch Women*, edited by Linnea Due, Roxxie Rosen, and Lily Burana. I got feedback from femmes all over the country confiding that our words could have come from their own journals. Debi and Susie both validated me and taught me a lot about being femme. Honey Lee Cottrell (Susie's former lover and now godmom to Aretha) gave me the butch inside scoop, providing insight that saved more than a few of my relationships. Susie, Honey

Lee, and I grew into a queer family as our love deepened and matured. It helps to have someone you can tell anything to, no matter how foolish you feel, who has been there and has also felt foolish at one time or another. My strongest piece of advice for you, reader, is to find a girlsistergirlfriend if you don't have one already.

As a child, I had perfected the art of making my mom and aunts tell me stories. I now turned my craft on to Susie, Honey Lee, Nan, and Debi. I made them tell their personal accounts over and over from every angle. I considered them war stories, heeding the wisdom that if you can learn from history, maybe you won't repeat the bad parts and can even prolong the good ones.

I wanted to know if Susie had always been femme and, if so, had she been ostracized like I had. Did Debi really teach all the Mitchell Brothers strippers to fist in latex gloves? Had Honey Lee, a motorcycle-riding, crew-cut sporting bulldagger, ever guessed she'd be pushing a baby carriage through Noe Valley? And I wanted to learn to dress to knock 'em dead. My first fetish closet contained gifts from Susie, who loves to try the latest in any style, and Debi, who passed on some fabulous hand-me-downs from her stripper days.

I learned how to model from Debi (hold your breath and stretch) and how to court from Honey Lee. Susie found me as a little wavering flower in the sidewalk crack, took me in, watered me, and taught me how to stretch my roots and leaves and find water for myself. Their stories injected me with 110% high-femme octane that to this day keeps my motor revving.

I've dated gals from all walks of life, from stone foxes to stone butches. I lived in the "Den of Perpetual Indulgence," where "Don't come home 'til you've got a good coming story" was our motto. My high school pals, Brian and Steve, had followed me to SF sight unseen, and together we made the city our candy dish. We'd begin our nights together getting ready, frothing at the mouth with all our plans, then spend the end of each escapade confiding the details. In the middle we often went our separate ways, me trailing the gals and them the meat.

As the assistant editor at *OOB*, I became close friends with photographer Phyllis Christopher and filmmaker Karen Everett. Their cameras documented our experiences in the early gay '90s. We fucked for the lens during the first days of women's sex clubs, when they were just ramshackle flats or warehouses. I also hooked up with two high-femme friends, Christina and Stephanie. Everyone called us "Charlie's Angels," as we dolled up in vintage dresses and sashayed around Downtown Donna's club, Faster Pussycat, like we owned the place. I could always make an extra buck there go-go dancing. As people came and went, lines between friends and lovers blurred into one big lubed-up experiment—our second coming of age.

In 1993 I met my true love, Jackie, who became my wife in 1996. She's a flamboyant rock-and-roll butch with old-fashioned manners and new-fashioned expectations. The night we met, I was a hostess at Club Cream and she had decorated the place to get a free pass. When we kissed I told her, "You make my knees weak. I have to sit down." I did, right on her lap. Not only did we have out-of-this-world chemistry, but we were also compatible *and* she isn't crazy. Wow. A miracle. She was a sex educator and I was a sex writer. Our worlds came together in an explosion of love, passion, value of life, and the force to live it fully.

I'll talk a lot in this book about being single, married, and in between—I've done it all. I'll also reveal many of my handy tips and sayings that get me through the day. I wasn't rambling on about Mavis and drag queens for nothin'. These are the people who influenced me, who taught me the wonders of eyelash glue or let me try out my ideas on them. (Not everyone will let you sit her up on a pedestal and proceed to create duct-tape and shelf-paper halter tops right on her skin, if you know what I mean. Granted, it *was* leopard-print shelf paper.) Anyhoo, that's my story. Onward, darlings, onward.

1. *On Our Backs* is a magazine featuring pictures, stories, and essays on lesbian sex that thrived in the late 1980s and was revived in the late '90s.

Chickies of a Feather Flock Together

The (Un)Common Denominator of Femmes

What I absolutely do not want to do is put femmes into a box or to perpetuate, in any way, the silly notion that gender identity is rigid. I think women are so used to the whole fucking world trying to contain and define us that we get defensive and see opposition where there often is none. Girlfriend, you're welcome here even if you're a *boyfriend* tomorrow. So, with that said, allow me to sexplain....

Femme dykes come in a cornucopia of sexualities. We are not all bottoms, vanilla or otherwise. Nor are we all whip-wielding, corset-wearing dominatrixes. Some femmes are high femme, some medium. Some look corporate, some punk. Some live quiet and some loud. Some make quiche and others make noise. But I've found that whether we like to put a butch over our knee or another femme between the sheets, we're all objects of desire. You might think that I just misspoke, that I should have said, "We all love *being* objects of desire." No, I wrote what I meant.

The phrase "object of desire" (OoD: pronounced "oo" as in coo-oo-ool and "dee" as in de-e-eli-cious) usually refers to a person being the subject or object of another person's lust, obsession, and desire.[1] I have determined that "object of desire" is its own class of sexual orientation, the way the terms *fag* or *femme* or *dyke* or *S/M* are often used. OoDs get their rocks off independent of others' reactions to them. This is *my* turn-on, no matter who I'm with or even if I'm not with anyone. Being an OoD means our levels of arousal rise when someone gets excited by being with us or looking at us. We get turned on simply from turning on others.

Being an OoD is a self-contained sexuality. Everyone—men, women, straight, gay—may find someone more attractive if s/he knows the other person likes her/him. But for OoDs it isn't a conscious thing. It's chemical. I've felt attracted to people who I thought didn't even know I existed, then found out later they had been lusting heavily for me from afar. My body had responded. If you find me desirable, my mind may not realize it, but my body will grow aware and react.

This doesn't mean we get wet over any Joe Blow who wolf-whistles at us; we *do* exercise powers of discernment.

Most people consciously react to others who lust after them. One person may love it, one may run, another may scoff. But with OoDs, being adored and wanted plays an integral part in our sexuality. Still, OoDs can be superhot on our own. We don't require someone else's attention to be sexual. We can be our own OoDs.

To understand what I'm talking about, try this: Set up a mirror so you can see your body but not your face while you assume your favorite masturbation position. Now talk dirty while you have sex (with yourself). Call yourself a slut or princess, whatever words are charged for you. Depending on your position, you may see fingers on pussy, titties bouncing, a mouth moaning. Someone is watching you. Feel the heat of her passion. You may be surprised to find that your arousal rises, even though that someone is only you.

Girlsistergirlfriends Are a Girl's Best Friend

Until my third year in college, all my femme friends were high-drag straight girls. They were great, but it was nice to finally meet someone like me, a Drag-Diva-Queen-Dyke. Elle was that only femme in all of Indiana and I'd been that only femme in Illinois. At the time, of course, we didn't call ourselves femmes. But we did wear makeup and skirts instead of succumbing to peer pressure to wear those baggy pants from the Limited. We looked like we did for the same reasons we'd liked Boy George when we were teenagers: to let our identity shine through to a world of dull-eyed clones. And we found each piece of information about each other fascinating: "You use *that* brand of eye shadow? So do I!" and "Your girlfriend says that about you? So does mine!"

We began our relationship by relating our life stories for hours on end. Everyone does that when they make new friends—I know that—but with Elle, it was like finding a twin sister I'd lost at birth. We had no idea there were even more like us. (Elle stayed back in

Indiana with a UPS man, insisting she'd "flunked as a lesbian," so I don't know if she ever found out.)

Femme friends offer you a mirror in which to view yourself. They understand your situation *from experience*. They keep you sane, reminding you that, yes, sometimes it *is* the rest of the world and not you. Femmes can also talk to each other honestly. To whom else can you say, "God, I need to wax these pubes ASAP!" or "You know, she just didn't fuck me long enough"? You can cry for hours on end or pluck eyebrows together. And who's easier to shop for? Forget trying to figure out where to get a blabbity-blah knife, you can just whip out the latest shade from Chanel and she oohs with delight.

I had one of my first S/M experiences with my friend Christina. She laid me down on her kitchen floor and, while holding my spread legs down with hers, smeared wax over my bikini line, then ripped off the strips to the piercing din of my screams. Now *that's* sisterhood.

Femmes, too, are able to switch from raving bitch to concerned friend at the drop of an ear-ring. All she needs is to hear you're upset. Frankly, I feel a little sorry for those nonfemme pals of ours because, sure, if there's a serious problem, we'll stop and listen. But when we see another *femme* upset, we instantly give her the benefit of the doubt. We know her situation is *serious* and that she's hurting, even if we find out she's just having a fugly day and needs to hear

FUGLY: fuh·glee, adj.: (1) being fucking ugly; (2) feeling one's body is fucking ugly; (3) staring into a mirror and perceiving oneself to be fucking ugly, as in *to have the fuglies*.

THE FUGLIES: thuh fuh·gleez, noun: a severe case of: (1) being unable to get dressed as a result of being or perceiving to be fugly; (2) refusing to leave one's domicile because one feels fugly (see *fugly*). Usually occurring in women, often as a part of, but not solely limited to, their monthly period.

POSSEXIBLE: pos·sex·eh·bull, adj., noun: possible opportunity for sex, as in *a possexible date* or *this van has possexiblities*.

you'll still like her if she cuts off all her hair or sets her entire wardrobe aflame. Even though you know she probably *won't* do the drastic deed, you're not wasting your time and breath. She knows someone understands and feels unconditional love for her. And unconditional love from you is almost the same as her having unconditional love for herself. Your loyalty and friendship gives her the freedom to be herself, which is all she ever wanted.

See? Girlsistergirlfriends are beyond great; they're *necessary.*

Honor your girlsistergirlfriends and certainly don't lose them over possexible dates. It's easy to be catty in our misogynistic world, but remember that while dates come and go, girlsistergirl-friends last longer than waterproof mascara.

You may be tempted to steal another gal's lovefix, especially if you live in one of those areas where it seems there aren't any choice women to date. *Don't do it.* Losing a friend over fucking the same chick isn't worth it. First of all, it's tacky. Second, it gives the wanna-fuck-ables too much power. Finally, the way dykes re-create relationships, there's absolutely no need to step on painted toenails, because sooner or later that couple will (most likely) break up, and your babefriend won't even care if you do her old thing. Even if your friends date for a "long" time, what's that? Three, four, five years? If you want to marry your friend's ex, that's a different story. You could just be non-monogamous and have a three-way with them.[2] Don't scream. It *is* possible. My friend Christina used to say, "We're environmentalist femmes 'cuz we recycle." Back in the day, you couldn't find many butches who would fuck femmes. So we had to share as much as we could.

Femmes do much more than try on lipstick together. We talk. We talk and listen a lot. And more than that, we plot, plan, and strategize our relationships. We don't ever admit it to anyone else, but that's what all that talking and listening is about. It gives us fuel when we need it; it calms us down when we don't; it helps us figure out how to get something through her (the lover's) thick skull; and it makes us feel we're not alone when we don't succeed (because our femme friends always understand and have numerous examples of communication breakdown with their own lovefucks).

Some of my best femme friends have not been strictly femme lesbians with biovulvas. Femme sisters come in a vast array of sexualities. Some femme women are attracted to masculinity whether it appears in a man or a woman. Some femme women were born with male bodies. The range is endless. But *you* know who your sisters are. Never take them for granted, and demand the same from them.

Chances are you're already aware of how dates who disrespect us affect our egos and our fun.

When you pick up a femme friend and dust her off—whether that means holding her hand or putting her *on* your hand—you're being a good Femmeinist and keeping our gender going strong.

Sometimes I need to be around another Queen just to see my own reflection, to know I'm not alone, that I'm not imagining things; we *are* here in this crazy solar system. I remember I'm strong by sharing my strength when it's needed and helping a girlsistergirlfriend when she's down. Conversely, I find comfort in an equal when I'm not feeling strong, letting my friends pick me up, knowing there are no head trips because of my blue moments.

1. OoD can also stand for "Out of Drag," but we will only use it for "Object of Desire."
2. "How to Have a Three-Way, Four-Way, or More-Way" is a pamphlet available from Shartopia.

Part II

The Queen and Her Domain

Velvet, lemons, and candles...lots of candles. These are just a few of the props you'll need to complete your castle—to make your surroundings as incredible and marvelous as you are.

Just Add Velvet:

How to Turn Any Shack Into a Royalty-Ready Love Den

"My command stands firm like the mountains, and the sun's disk shines and spreads rays over the titulary of my august person, and my falcon rises high above the kingly banner unto all eternity."

—Hatshepsut, Egyptian Pharoah, 1400s B.C.

The Royal Touch

A femme is the Queen, matriarch, empress, or princess of her world. She not only has control over her Queendom but also holds responsibilities. She may hand some of her power over to a king or another Queen now and then so she can relax, but it is *her* power to give up.

Some people hate references to royalty. It's gotten a bad rap somewhere along the way, probably from that uptight Victoria or maybe those rolling heads of Henry's. But a Queen is not an inherently bad person. In fact, being a Queen is something to take pride in. Many Queens in history were amazing. In *The Dinner Party: A Symbol of Our Heritage*, Judy Chicago writes about many great women leaders such as Theodora, a Byzantine empress who turned one of her palaces into a refuge for prostitutes and actresses (who were basically enslaved by pimps or theaters). Or Hatshepsut, the only female pharaoh we really know anything about, who fostered military strength and a prosperous economy.

A good Queen possesses finely tuned diplomatic skills. She behaves with class in both delightful and dreadful situations. Her followers look to her for strength and guidance in hard times and as a model of achievement in prosperous times. She brings charity and resources to those low on hope, her leadership to those floundering, and her dazzle to the dull. Often just her gaze, touch, or kind word will lift the spirits of the most downtrodden. When necessary, she slices her power through her Queendom with a firm and precise hand. Yet, when possible, she wields her power with such thought, charm, wit, and grace that it's as smooth as milk chocolate and as subtle as a slow moon rising.

Like diamonds in the rough, Queens aren't born polished and ready to go. Preparation is necessary. A diamond needs to be cut, carefully prepared, polished, and placed into a fabulous setting. Accordingly, a Queen needs to claim her royal identity, polish her skills, care for herself, and take *her* place in a fabulous setting.

The Queendom: Creating the Lust Palace Brick by Brick

"You don't chase the glittering life. You lay a trap for it." —Helen Gurley Brown

Do you understand? We are creating your set. We are setting the scene where *your* script will come to life. You might want to skip ahead to the sex-toy section or the how-to-get-under-a-butch-belt chapter. No, no, my dear royal sisters. You must first lay the groundwork for your love lair. As I said earlier, you must mount your throne in a fabulous setting. So let's create that setting.

Chances are, if you're a natural femme your space is already screaming YOU, and that's what it's all about. But maybe you're like me: so-o-o busy that you overflow with all these great ideas and never take time to implement them. Nike your ass and just do it. You will love bringing a date back to your home and reveling in Youtopia. It reveals the real you. Nothing kills a mood faster than your date discovering your Debbie Gibson poster in the bathroom (even if you were just trying to cover an unsightly, crack in the wall). A good lust den makes getting it on smooth and delectable.

If you can't possess an entire palace, at least create a throne. If you share a home where your personality is kept mostly in one room, let that room be your court. This is where you will be worshiped and adored. This will be your regal love lounge.

Dazzling on Dimes: Thrifty Decorating Tips

As I mentioned earlier, not everyone can afford Lalique vases or crystal chandeliers, but that doesn't mean you have to settle for Broyhill or even Target's Furio collection. For pennies on the dollar you can create a lust palace that will be the envy of every other Queen on the block. All it takes is one part innovation, one part perspiration, and a dash of the *Shartiste* in all of us.

Let's start with the walls. Did you know you can buy used paint? Actually it's unused, but the can of paint has already visited someone else's house, and they didn't need the entire can to finish the job. These already opened cans cost about half as much as new paint. Most stores that sell it new also sell it used. Just call around and ask. Unfortunately, your selection will be significantly narrowed, so pick out a shade close to the color you want, then ask the nice folks at the paint store to add pigment until it's the hue of your desire. They usually charge another couple of bucks for this, but use your charm or tale of woe to talk down the price. (Mutter to yourself within the hearing range of a sales clerk, "This is close to the color I need. I guess the kids at the day care center won't care that much that their Barney mural will be the wrong shade of purple." Follow with a loud sigh. I swear it's worked for me.)

Have you always wanted mosquito netting hanging from the ceiling but can't fork over the cash to Pier 1 or IKEA? That netting your grandma used for her hats and underskirts is about 70 cents a yard, sometimes less, at most fabric stores. Buy yards and yards of the stuff. It's not as soft, but you're not rolling in it, so who cares! How do you hang it from the ceiling? Forget those fancy hanging thingies. They require too much hardware for gals like us who are thrifty not only with cash but also with our time. Just grab some tacks and borrow a ladder. Also, never forget the convenience of a staple gun.

Love velvet? Just look, look, look for sales, not only for velvet, but also hunt through thrift stores, rummage sales, and estate sales for old velvet curtains. Depending on your needs, velveteen or velour might do. Jackie and I were lounging on the cloud (our bed) with two delightful chickies one night when my friends Carol and Robert burst in and unrolled yards and yards of pink satin on top of us. Satin of every shade of pink! Those two are big estate-sale freaks, and they always come home with loads of fabulicious stuff that is ridiculously cheap.

Find a good place for inexpensive candles. Taper candles are often the cheapest at spiritual shops, but sometimes the opposite is true, so compare prices. If you've got a date coming and need ambiance *now,* buy a package of "emergency candles" (four small white stick candles for $2). They sell them at drugstores and supermarkets. If your town has a 99-cent store, you're in luck. You can get at least half a dozen there for under a buck.

Don't trouble yourself over trying to plan the placement of every picture in the house. If you do that *naturally,* go for it, but I know so many empty-walled homes because the Mistress can't make up her mind about where to put things. Just toss it up there and move it when/if you decide you don't like it. Matching pictures is so out of style and was *never* in for me. Thrift stores sport some of the best frames around. Granted, they're usually surrounding some faded '70s sunset string-art, but you can toss that out and replace it with whatever you wish. On second thought, never throw out string-art.

Is your space small or with few windows? Use reflective colors for your paint and hang up as many mirrors as possible. Mirrors open up a room and reflect even the tiniest light. Candlelight reflected across the room by a mirror makes anyone look like a dream.

If you can, save your pennies and invest in good furniture one piece at a time. Your furniture needs to reflect your personality, but not the you that's suffering with bills and PMS—the inner *La Reina* you. No one likes a hodgepodge pileup of filthy furniture, but an eclectic mix of "finds" can transform your pad into a palace as long as you take care of these orphans. Every piece needs to look welcomed to your home and made to belong. You do *not* get a brown couch because it was a hand-me-down from a friend and because "Well, I needed a couch and this was *free-e-ee.*" Cover it with fabric that matches the room, repaint it, strip it, glitter-glue it, decoupage it. Whatever. You can do it or cajole a friend into doing it for you. You don't need a couch that says "you" but one that says "Youtopia." A couch that screams, "My Queen sits here when she's not on her throne!"

Cooking, cleaning, mending: What is it about putting on a skirt that makes people suddenly assume you're Donna Reed? Personally, I know plenty of femmes who couldn't darn a sock for all the MAC lipstick in the world. Fix your carburetor, hook up your computer, sure. However, there are lots of ways to fake it, and nothing will make a girl offer to marry you (or at least stay for breakfast) than good home cooking.

If you can drink a latte, put on mascara, and drive your car at the same time, you can make muffins. Trust me. Muffins are a snap to make from scratch. But if you need a dry run before you get out the sifter and measuring cups, go to the store and pick up a couple boxes of Jiffy cornbread mix. They cost about 35 cents a box, they don't have too many weird chemicals in them, and besides being completely idiot-proof, they're tasty. Get a bag of pancake mix while you're at it, and you're set for either a quick coffee-and-a-muffin

Faking it in the Kitchen By Stephanie Rosenbaum

morning or a lazy, make-pancakes-for-everyone brunch. Most pancake mixes are pretty bland, so feel free to add some cinnamon or what's generically sold as pumpkin pie spice, a mixture of nutmeg, allspice, and cinnamon. You can also add finely chopped fruit, nuts, or raisins.

If you bake, even a little, everyone will assume you're a fabulous cook. Even very simple things will convince most people. Chocolate chip cookies, for example. Buy a package of chocolate chips, follow the recipe on the bag, and you'll get a pretty perfect batch of cookies—infinitely better than anything prepackaged—or use one of those cylinders of frozen dough. These are especially good to whip up when some studly babe is over at your house doing you a favor—putting together your big new bed, or fixing that leaky faucet.

For late-night, back-from-the-bar-at-2 A.M. eating, nothing beats a quesadilla. You can make these in the time it takes for your date to park the car. First, slip into something comfy—a robe over your lingerie, boxers and a baby tee, mules and just about anything. Warm up a skillet (grease lightly first), grate some cheese (cheddar, jack, anything fairly mild that melts well), and get out a jar of salsa. Throw a couple of tortillas in the pan, and flip them over once or twice to warm them through. Top each tortilla with a couple of tablespoons of grated cheese, fold over, and heat until cheese melts, turning over once or twice. Serve with salsa on the side.

But the one, absolutely foolproof, get-me-a-U-Haul-right-now trick? Bring her hot coffee in bed. Trust me. It works.

Kitchen Basics

When I first moved to San Francisco, my boys and I called our house the "Den of Perpetual Indulgence." Indulgence ruled. We often indulged in sex, cartoons, and a few drugs, but food was high on the list too. Indulge yourself in the art of wining and dining. You don't even have to know how to turn on the stove. I presented wine, avocados, chilled shrimp, and strawberries to Jackie her first time at my palace. I didn't want her eating a big meal—you know, getting weighed down early in the evening. With my fingers, I fed her shrimp by candlelight. She didn't complain one bit about the lack of courses.

You'll probably have your own particulars for your kitchen, but here are some of mine.

Space and Storage

Look at your countertop, honey. Are you utilizing space-saving items such as cup hooks and utensil racks? Cup hooks are *it* as far as I'm concerned. They can hang everything from a pot holder to a riding crop. Minimize machinery. A blender will do almost anything, including grind coffee beans, so unless you have proper storage, forget all those electric time-savers. They not only hoard counter space but also consume cleaning and psychic space. I don't know about you, but if my date gets so enchanted by a good dose of finger-fed shrimp that she wants to clam-dive on my countertop, I sure as hell don't want to worry about my hoo-hoo being impaled by a toaster oven! One exception to my no-machine rule is the food processor, which will open up your world to a whole new menu of sauces, soups, juices, and desserts—that is, if you actually use it. If you're not going to use it, send it to me and I'll find someone who will.

Do you have little critter problems? Mice, roaches, or ants? Save big jars to hold your rice, noodles, and cereal. Dog or cat food especially attracts tiny varmints, so keep it out of the way in a new trash container or pickle barrel (this will also keep the food fresh for your pet). In the end you'll have a very homey kitchen instead of a "store-bought" one hosting brand-name boxes.

Glassware

I must have the perfect glass for the drink. If you don't want to share my narrow view, remember that on-the-rocks glasses work for anything and champagne flutes work for everything else.

Most hotels have good on-the-rocks glasses: their water glasses. At the prices they charge, don't feel bad about taking some of their glassware compliments of the house. Many stores have basements or areas where they keep stemware that is more affordable than the stuff upstairs. I buy a set of glassware whenever I can afford it. I also pick up orphaned glasses at rummage sales or thrift stores. I can serve a formal drink in matching stemware or I can whip out a selection of mismatched wine glasses for guests to choose from.

Libations

The Shartini has earned a reputation of its own. Try one and you'll see why.

Shartini

Put exactly three drops of vermouth in a martini glass. Using a swirling motion, turn glass upside down, then with a dramatic and quick twist, flick the remaining drop and a half into outer space. Pour vodka over ice, strain into glass. Add two olives and you're done!

To order a Shartini:

Lean onto bar as if leaning in order to be heard, frame your breasts with your arms. Look deep into your barkeep's eyes. Say, "I'll have a vodka martini. (pause) Xtre-e-emely dry. (Do peace sign with one hand) Two olives (smile), up. Thank you." Don't order Shartinis unless you're sitting at the bar because a server will just not be able to get this across to the bartender. It's best to make eye contact with bartender when ordering or somehow get her/his ego involved in your drink.

Sharmonade

I once got all the tenants of a building of shotgun flats where I lived hooked on Sharmonade. The back half of the building on Guerrero Street was condemned by the city inspectors who said the whole staircase and landings could at any time just rip right off and crash to the overgrown lot below. It was so hot that day, and we all hated our jobs and hated those rotting flats, although we loved our neighbors. I can still see my friend Kevin carefully stepping over Walrus, a fat, fluffy cat with a broken leg in a cast, as he made his way down the back stairs with a pitcher of Sharmonade that I'd whipped up out of leftovers. Soon we were all feelin' fine.

Fill pitcher two thirds of the way with ice
Pour in vodka until it's a little over halfway mark
Squeeze three fresh lemons into pitcher.
Squeeze one or two limes into pitcher
Mix 1½ tablespoons of sugar into half cup of water. Stir until dissolved; pour into pitcher
Add one cup fruity white wine
Pour in more vodka until pitcher is full
With a ladle, push the top ingredients to the bottom, then pull the bottom up, just once. Don't swirl around and don't overstir. You want the flavors to cradle the vodka so that any given glass of Sharmonade has many flavors, not just one.

The Bounties of the Bedroom

The bed.

Oh, what better throne than your bed? A Prince throws open your bedroom door to see…what? What? Stand in your doorway and envision a bed made for Cleopatra. Imagine yourself looking out to the tall shadow in the doorway. What do you see? It's up to you to create the dream that is your bedroom. Do you want sheer white flowing curtains and light-reflecting walls? Do you want heavy red velvet coverings and gaudy gold sconces? Envision your setting down to the last detail. Then plug in what you can. Remember that stage sets are pieced together with anything from "real" props to one-dimensional painted backdrops. But all sets begin with the playwright's vision.

Let's begin with the bed itself. Beds are costly, but you'll need a good one. I'm referring to the mattress set, not the headboard. Headboards can be painted right onto the wall with flair and you won't miss a wink of sleep or that special thrust (if you know what I mean). But a bad mattress? Forget it. That thrust might be comin' from an errant spring, never mind the Prince hitting her target!

You *must* have something decent to love and lullaby on. No matter how great or bad your mattress is, egg-crate foam makes any bed better and a feather bed makes any bed its best. To buy egg-crate foam, measure your bed, buy the foam at a fabric store, then put it right on top of the mattress under your sheet. With just the fitted sheet, the surface will look funny, but who cares, because it feels great. After you've made up the bed with a spread or comforter, it'll look invitingly soft and fluffy, unlike the severe, Navy-regimen, hospital corners of yore.

A feather bed isn't a mattress at all. It's a bed of feathers gathered into a futon-like pad. Usually they're less than six inches thick, and some are just loose feathers between two pieces of sewn-together fabric. Others are contained in more structured pads. Feather beds keep you warm in the winter and cool in the summer. The bed smooshes up around you, supporting your body so you don't get kinks. If you have a down-filled comforter for the top, you're set as you nest among all those feathers. If you get allergic easily or loathe mites and dust, buy a cover that keeps those nasty critters away from you. Hypoallergenic covers are available for everything from pillows to mattresses. Or if you don't want to infringe on a critter's right to her own feathers, purchase one of the new "fiber beds," a hypoallergenic, fake feather bed. They're as good as the real thing, and nobody had to get plucked for your slumber.

Many chiropractors and orthopedic specialists highly recommend sleeping on Swedish foam or just a thick pad of dense foam. Swedish foam can be as expensive as a mattress set, but, once again, visit a few fabric stores because more and more of them now carry dense foam that can be cut to size. For it to support your back well, foam needs only a flat surface such as an oyster bed (you know, the ones that are kinda like water-bed frames, surrounding the mattress with drawers on the bottom), platform bed, piece of plywood on blocks, or the floor.

When I first moved to San Francisco, I had a trunk of shoes, my typewriter, and $100. My first cloud, my first bed, here in town, slowly evolved from many pads. The final pileup starting at the bottom: foam pad, thin futon, feather bed, comforter, flannel sheets, then a down comforter on top with my ex-girlfriend's grandmother's quilt at the foot. All this was on a frame made by my butch uncle, Honey Lee, that comprised a solid headboard, footboard, railings for drinks, and slats made of used redwood. It was so comfortable and was truly a cloud.

You may be able to afford a dramatic frame straight from the store. Many new beds nowadays look like antique wrought-iron beds. No matter how intense a bed appears, chances are it won't take a licking as is—that is, coming straight from the store. Reinforce connections at corners and between the four posters (if you have them). Believe me, when you've got a five-fingered astronaut exploring your fifth chakra and you're about to make *contact*, you don't want your bed crashing down around you à la earthquake. It's not a pretty scene.

Rather than go store-bought, maybe you'd prefer to find an old brass bed and build your muscles by polishing it, which takes hours upon days. Try antique stores or, better yet, rummage sales. Many people don't want the hassle of moving a brass bed, so they'll let go of them way underpriced. When buying any second-hand bed, get specific instructions on how to put it together. If possible,

Jackie and me on the original cloud. My hair looked pretty lofty that day as well!

get the name and phone number of the person selling it so you can call them if you need directions.

No matter what kind of bed you get, try hard to get *something* so you're not on the floor.

Besides the bed, you'll need storage for your clothes and sex toys. Much of what I said about living room furniture applies here. Just pick out pieces that scream "Youtopia!" Bedroom furniture is also necessary because you'll need many horizontal surfaces for candles. Regarding sex toys, read on....

Bedroom Accoutrements (i.e., Sex Toys)

Don't worry, darlin', you don't *really* need to keep your toys in the bedroom, but it's often where people go to be private, so I thought I'd start there. Your sex-toy box can be just that, a box or trunk, or it could be a special drawer in your dresser or an area on your shelf. Baby, just throw that terry cloth away—you don't want to use anything that attracts dust or lint. Though velvet linings sound luscious, they can be more trouble than they're worth. Satin, on the other hand, doesn't cling to your toys and presents them with a regal backdrop.

So what do you fill that toy box with? Everything! But sex toys can be expensive, so it might take you a while to build up your collection. Hey, that's OK, sweetie. Museums aren't created overnight. If you have the cash, head out to your local women-owned sex-toy store immediately. If you don't have a store near you, check out my resource page at the end of the book. Oh, BooBoo, you say you don't know what you want? Well, then educate yourself through books and videos. Buy some erotic fiction. The *Best American Erotica* series edited by Susie Bright and the *Herotica* series are both great starters. Also acquire reference books such as Carol Queen's *Exhibitionism for the Shy*.

Ask about the quality of the toys you want. Buy good stuff and it'll last for a long time. Ask how to take care of it. Investing in sex toys will reward you over and over again for a lifetime. If you feel you aren't getting quality information, buy *The Whole Lesbian Sex Book* by Felice Newman (or borrow from your local library), which tells you not only about sex but also how to care for yourself and your toys.

If funds limit your purchases, get toys as you can. You'll probably want an electric vibrator, a harness, and a dildo. Silicone dildos are by far the best. They retain body heat and can be sanitized again and again. Plus they can be used with oil lubricants (as long as you aren't using condoms, and you don't *have* to use condoms because they can be sanitized). It's no secret that I highly recommend dildos by Vixen Creations (www.vixencreations.com). If you don't want to drop a lot of dough on silicone, you can buy rubber dildos and cover them with condoms to keep them sanitary and to increase their longevity.

If you're dating, you'll want to have some safer-sex items no matter what your feelings are on safer sex (unless you won't do it period). You should always be committed to performing sex safe enough for the most conservative partner. Meaning, Jane may think safer sex means no oral sex without a barrier, but Daphne thinks oral sex with no barrier is OK. This couple is obligated to follow the safer gal's (Jane's) wishes; therefore they use barriers, such as plastic wrap or Glyde dams, for oral sex. Even if you don't want to wear latex gloves, you might bring home a gal who does want you to or who wants to wear them herself. Condoms are the easiest way to keep your dildos clean. Plus they're free in most cities at AIDS projects, queer community centers, and women's clinics. These clinics and projects may be a part of larger organizations, so investigate. Latex gloves cover up calluses, cuts, fingernails, and hangnails. They not only keep diseases such as hepatitis from flowing into your bloodstream, but also prevent pussy cuts from happening in the first place. And plastic wrap is useful when you don't know when a gal is having her period. Maybe it's obvious that she's not flowing heavily right now, but she might have been yesterday. HIV doesn't fall out of her pussy with a neon sign saying, HEY, DON'T LICK ME UP! You gotta have a microscope to see it, so teeny amounts of blood aren't any safer than big amounts. You or a sex partner may not want to lick up any vaginal juices at all, no matter what time of the month. Plastic wrap also makes rimming (licking around the anus) worry free.

Toy Box Checklist

Basics:

Roll of plastic wrap
Latex gloves (available from drugstores for about $6 for a box of 50)
Butt plug your size or smaller/larger for others
Dildo your size, and, if you like them on the big side, get a six-inch as a standby for any tricks you might bring home (the more choices, the better)
Finger cots (the finger part of the latex glove; great for ass play)
Harness for hands-free fucking
Lubricant without nonoxynol-9
Condoms without nonoxynol-9
Vibrators: electric for yourself, if you please, and a little battery-operated vibrator for guest (the silver bullet is perfect)

Luxuries:

Dildo with vibrator in base
Blindfold (could be new or could be your bathrobe sash)
Bondage cuffs (a.k.a. restraints, *not* handcuffs)
Butt plugs with fake horse's tail attached (makes a person into a horsie)
Flavored condoms
Heating oils
Paddle

Depending on your preferences, you might move some of the luxuries to the basics list. Customize your own Youtopian list; this is just a start.

The Powder Room

Oh, the bathroom! What a haven, especially if you have a bathtub. My friend Deborah takes a bath laced with essential oils every day. I remember being astounded by this because I always seem too busy for baths. "Shar," she told me, "there's always time for a bath." She said it so matter-of-factly, as if she were telling me ice cream comes in chocolate, and I took it like that, as a fact. You need to fill yourself up before you can take care of others or even yourself. A bath is one of the best ways to do this. Turn your bathroom into a sanctuary that submerges you into feelings of serenity. If clutter bothers you, stick to the basics. If seeing your favorite things helps you, fill your bathroom with flowers, pictures, or trinkets. Hang up a saying that reminds you of your true nature.

The most important thing about a bathroom—and all the rooms of your palace—is to keep it clean and smelling like a daisy. Cleaning tips, from sinks and floors to skirts and leather, follow in the next chapter. For what is a palace if it's not shimmering?

Grime, Begone!

(How to Make Your Castle Sparkle)

Oh, get in here, little lady, and read this chapter. I know you just want to skip ahead to the all the *sex* chapters, but this is important. I know you're asking, "A Queen cleaning?"

Of course! A sex-ready, smart, and savvy gal like you needs to be prepared for anything: guests, sex on countertops, finding your head shots in the blink of an eye. Having clean floors means you can pad around barefoot and still not fret when receiving a foot-licking. A sparkling counter means you can be plopped onto it without any panties and not worry about surface bacteria!

This book is about Shartopia, and in Shartopia you don't have to throw away your favorite baby tee because it's got blood on it. I *know* how to get out stains, so read on. I'm telling you my tips so you won't have to waste a minute reading *Woman's Day* (unless the ladies in the knitting spreads turn you on).

Basic Cleansers

You can buy cleansers marketed specifically for every nook and cranny. Just go to the store and

How to Remove Candle Wax

I'm not going to ask. I don't need to know how you got plum-violet candle wax on the appliqué Venice lace trim of your baby-doll teddy. Let's just get it ready for the next date, shall we? Put a brown paper bag over the spot and iron it on a light setting. Patiently repeat this process until the wax is absorbed into the paper. The whole point is absorption, so don't keep ironing over the same part of the bag. You'll need to move the bag repeatedly to get it all. (Oh, and for lace, put a bag *underneath* it as well.)

read the labels. I prefer more old-fashioned techniques that keep my money in *my* pocketbook, not some corporation's, and that have minimal impact on animals, the environment, and my lungs.

Baking soda is a nonabrasive powder that can be used much like Comet. Comet also has bleach in it, so follow up your baking soda scrub with a splash of bleach water as needed.

Never, ever mix bleach and ammonia. If you do, hold your breath, grab your cat, and run.

Vinegar and water, ammonia and water, and rubbing alcohol and water all wash mirrors and windows fantastically. Remember to use wadded-up newspaper instead of paper towels to avoid streaks. Ammonia mixed with water also works on countertops and toasters. Usually, soap and water alone will do the job.

To keep drains running freely, periodically pour boiling water down the drain.

Sprinkle salt in your sink, cut a lemon in half, then scrub the sink with the lemon as if it were a sponge. Lemon and salt makes an excellent polish for copper pots as well.

For toilets, pour a spot of bleach and one cup of baking soda into the bowl, let soak, then scrub.

Stains

Nothing's more of a dildo downer that having to be a priss about messes while you're in the throes of passion. Go ahead, knock over the wine, spill the shrimp cocktail sauce, and most importantly, don't stop the action just because it's that time of the month. I have worked as a nanny and a housekeeper, and have had to get out *a lot* of stains. I've had friends show up on my doorstep (not going to name names, *Michelle*) with her sister's Martha Stewart terra-cotta sheets covered not only with menstrual blood but Fudge Blueberry Hill hair dye as well. One night of lovin' had turned her sister's precious linen into a hippie's tie-dyed dream come true. Three bottles of Safeway brand club soda and a Laundromat later, the sheets were as good as new.

Wine, coffee, or blood: As quickly as possible, put a towel on the spot and soak up as much as you can by blotting. For clothes you are wearing or for carpets, pour club soda on the spot, wait a

PHYLLIS CHRISTOPHER

A clean countertop is always ready for special occasions.

few seconds, dab, then repeat until the stain is gone. If it's something you can soak, place the item into a bowl of club soda and forget about it. When you come back it will be clean. If the stain is tough to get out, you may have to rinse with cold water and repeat the soaking process. If you don't have club soda on hand, *do not* run hot water on the stain. This will cause it to set. Rinse with cold water, preferably running the water through the stain so as to not spread it, then go get some club soda. The bubbles are the key. Nurses swear by hydrogen peroxide. (Ever wonder how those outfits stay so white?) In a pinch, try sparkling water or tonic.

If you have light carpet, keep unopened (so it stays bubbly) club soda on hand at all times. Hide it under the bathroom sink with your other cleaners so your guests won't drink it.

For natural stains (blood, grass, dirt), i.e., not chemical such as ink: First of all, try club soda. Secondly, let me just say, "Oh, the joys of Era detergent." You know, the one that fights "protein stains with protein." They are not lying. I have gotten *years*-old bloodstains out of white sheets by soaking the stains in Era. This fabulous product has even taken bloodstains out of my plush white terry cloth robe. Safeway grocery stores in California do not carry Era for some reason, which really bugs me. It's hard to find in the Bay Area, but it's worth the hunt no matter where you live. I buy a no-name detergent for most of my wash and save my Era for stains. It works ten times better than any so-called stain remover.

Simply rubbing a spot with white hand soap then rinsing with cold water and repeating will take out many stains. Remember two points, though: (1) White soaps are not all alike, so don't use a moisturizing soap such as Dove, which will add oil to your problem; (2) Don't be afraid to scrub! Rub that fabric together! This gets the cleaning agent into the weave of the fabric—the next best thing to scrubbing it on a rock down in the river.

Chemical stains such as ink or dye: These are a bit more complicated. Spray the strongest hair spray you have, preferably Aqua Net, on the stain, then immediately rinse with cold water. Repeat until the stain comes out or until it doesn't seem to be getting any better. Then scrub with a toothbrush and spray Aqua Net again, rinse with cold water, repeat. Finally, rub with white soap and water while scrubbing as hard as garment will allow. Those "sold on TV only" stain removers stink to high heaven, but they do work on most stains. The remover itself sometimes leaves a stain because it contains chemicals.

✤   ✤   ✤

If you really must purchase ready-made cleaners and you're rich, I say buy those fancy ones from the natural foods store. You know, the ones named "Soleil de Douche"—you have no idea that they're even *for* cleaning. They have pictures of sunflower fields with happy old men lounging in the background; you think it's sunflower-seed pesto dressing, but it's actually bathtub cleaner. Although they don't even work, and you can crush your own sunflower seeds at home a lot cheaper, at least they don't kill any animals or hurt the environment. If you must buy ready-made cleaners and you're poor, I advise wrapping your elegant fingers around a few bottles of the generic knockoff products like Tileplex and Pine-doll at the 99-cent store when you're there picking up candles.

Above all else, get a house "girl" or "boy" who loves to wait on you in exchange for housing, loving, whippings, or you teaching her how to do something you know how to do (like produce shows or porn, put together mailing lists, be a rock star, etc.).

The Multifaceted Handy Queen

Just as a good CEO works her way up from the secretarial pool, a good top has bottomed; and just as a golfer has played caddy, a good Queen has been the handmaiden *and* the handyman. You mustn't always depend on others to do your chores. When hiring people, it's best for you to know what you're talking about even if you can't do it yourself. When asking a big hunk to help out, you may have to be the brain to her muscle. Finally, there's the adage, "If you want something done with majestic flourish, you might have to do it yourself!" Basically, if ya paint your nails, they're painted.

Between Mavis, my dad, and the Girl Scouts, I really am a Queen-of-all-trades. We rely on supposed experts too much these days. Sure, get professional backup for a flood, but if you need to retrieve an earring from the drain, save your moolah and do it yourself. It never hurts to know how to start a fire, a car, or a riot. Educate yourself and take the opportunities to practice when you can. The following sections relate some handy know-how for girls on the go.

Tools

Every gal needs a toolbox. You can buy one of those ready-made ones that have all the tools, but if you do, be wary of the quality. This is one area where cost does reflect craftsmanship. Rather,

STOPHER

...did I tell you I'm a
... is my wrench. Not

it's best if you collect good pieces individually. The box itself, even empty, can really cost a lot. I still don't have a good metal one. For some of my tools, I bought a used 1960s cosmetic case, the kind that matches a luggage set. I also have a cardboard box for bigger items—it is a tool *box*, after all. Metal lunch boxes make perfect toolboxes for traveling (but won't accommodate your hammer).

TOOLBOX CHECKLIST:
Hammer (good one with an industrial handle)
Pliers
Big wrench (large enough to go around a two-inch pipe)
Needle-nose pliers with a wire cutter built in
Phillips screwdriver
Flathead screwdriver
Huge flathead screwdriver
Black electrical tape
Clamps (big office clamps are fine)
Wood glue
Super glue
Tacky glue
Assorted screws (you can buy a box at most drugstores
    that says "assorted screws" or just collect them as you
    go)
Various nails (ditto)
Duct tape
Masking tape
Staple gun and staples
Tacks
Good measuring tape

If you can't or won't collect your own tools, at least get a Leatherman™, a hammer, and a measuring tape. A Leatherman™—that's actually the brand name—is a pocketknife and tool that most audio/video crews around the world find irreplaceable. It has needle-nose pliers, wire cutters, two different styles of screwdrivers, a file, a knife, and a small ruler.

The Violet and Corky Rendezvous or, How to Rescue an Earring That's Fallen Into the Drain

Supplies

A big crescent wrench or monkey wrench
Pipe threading (available at hardware stores and comes in a tube labeled "pipe threading" right on it)
Bucket or big soup pan
A little muscle

What to Do

If you have a standard sink, look under it. The pipe that leads down from the basin will make a dramatic U shape. This is the earring pipe. Its sole purpose is to save little things that fall into the sink. Put a bucket or pan under the earring pipe. Using your monkey wrench, loosen the pipe at both connections. Then gently lower it into your bucket and dump the contents. No telling what you'll find. Using your nails, scooch off any little hangers-on around all the pipe openings. Put some pipe threading around the threads and screw both sections of the pipe back on with your fingers. When you think you have it on evenly and threaded properly, use your wrench to tighten it.

How to Start a Riot: Bright Posters & Wheat Paste

OK, I don't know how to start a riot *exactly*, but I do know that to have a good riot, march, or party, all the Queendom must be notified. Everyone is ready to join your cause—they just have to know about it!

First step: Create outrageous posters with the where, what, and when in BIG, easy-to-read letters that can be seen from at least 20 feet away. Copy your posters on really bright paper if you can afford it.

Second step: Whether you're leading or joining a riot, there's nothing more irritating than someone tearing down your posters, and that's what happens if they are simply stapled onto telephone poles. Wheat paste is the answer. It's a bitch to remove, and it sticks to almost any surface. Note: In many communities, posting flyers is *not* considered freedom of speech, but vandalism, and is therefore illegal. Wheat-pasted flyers may be specifically targeted in your community. I'll leave it up to you to know your local laws. You can buy wallpaper paste at the hardware store. Most rioters I know, though, make their own. Look up the recipe on the Web or try this: Mix one cup of flour into 1½ cups water and stir until the lumps are gone. Heat until it boils, then let it thicken a bit. Add more water until it turns clear but is still a thick slime. Reduce heat. Cook for at least a half hour. Be careful not to burn it. Watch out; it expands and expands like a *Brady Bunch* science fair experiment.

Third step: Dress like a Bond Girl burglar (or Audrey Hepburn in the beatnik segment of *Funny Face*) wearing a black beret, turtleneck, and pants. Slather your eyeliner on thicker than ever. Carry a big black bag with the posters rolled up in it.

Fourth Step: You and a friend (preferably someone with a car) go out and paste up your posters. With giant paintbrushes, paint the back of your posters, making sure to get the edges, then stick them down. If you can, have a third person roll over them with a dry paint roller that'll smooth them out and make them stick even better.

Finally, you don't have to have a world crisis to pull out some wheat paste and let the world know you're here, you're queer, and you have no fear (or as I like to say, I'm present, iridescent, efflorescent, and certainly not apprehensent). Paste down your art, poetry, and orders for the universe to behold.

How to Start a Car (that won't start but should)

Older cars: If the engine won't turn over, check your battery cables and lights. Did you leave your lights on? If the battery is totally dead, the engine will not turn over. But maybe a cable is just loose.

Perhaps the engine is flooded. Say, for example, your battery was half dead and you kept trying to start the car. Now you have someone there with jumper cables, but the engine is flooded.

Most people will tell you to wait a while. Go right ahead if it's a babe holding those cables and you, um, want to prolong recharging your battery. But if you can't wait to hightail it outta there, simply floor the gas pedal and keep it pushed to the floor while you start the car. The engine will sputter. If you keep that pedal to the floor, it'll start.

If you think there's something wrong with the ignition (because you know the battery isn't dead, but the engine won't turn over at all while you're turning the key), try hitting the underside of the steering column near the ignition. If there's a loose wire, a good blunt hit works wonders. Brian and I were on the way to his prom in his Thunderbird, and we stopped at Huck's convenience mart for some gum. We were already running late. The car wouldn't start, so I ran around to the driver's side in my three-hoop dress, lying on the front seat with my legs splayed, and popped one to the steering column, which made her start right up. All the local farmers' jaws dropped as Brian, in his tuxedo, thought nothing of standing out of the way as I did my work.

If the car still won't start, make sure it has gas. And always keep a gas can in the trunk.

Also, if smoke or steam is coming from the engine, *do not* attempt to add water or anti-freeze until the car has been off for at least 30 minutes—even longer if it's a hot day. If water or coolant is leaking from the car, do not attempt to drive it. My editor, Angela, did this with her just-purchased '82 Volvo wagon, and she cracked the head gasket (a $1,000-dollar repair on a $700 car). Luckily, she used her charm, good looks, and tale of woe on the guy she bought it from, got her money back, and actually made $40 by selling the evil vehicle for scrap.

Newer cars: I don't have many "tips" other than going to the dealer for work *and* following the instruction manual regarding how often to go. Get tune-ups as often as they suggest. Do not get your oil changed at those ten-minute places. The 50 bucks you save in the short term will cost you $500 in the long run. New cars have so many computer chips that you must have the latest diagnostic equipment to even know how to set your clock.

Above all else, invest $40 in an AAA membership.

How to Save Your Ass (and the rest of you)

Many self-defense classes focus on physical tactics, while some give you a broader base of power. An example of the latter is Home Alive, based in Seattle; you should contact this type of group for support. The following are just a few tidbits I picked up along the way. May they keep you safe until you get to a class or support system that really gives you the 411.

If someone is about to invade your space, say calmly yet loudly, "Hey, buddy, step back now!" Repeat if necessary. Anyone sane will respond to this. If they don't, you'll have to go into a higher mode of protection. Say this to *anyone* invading your space, *period.* Don't let the person get closer and *then* decide if you like him or her. No. Directions, time, anything can be asked of you in a loud voice from a distance. No one needs to get close to you for any reason. They know what the world is about; you aren't offending anyone (even if you are, offend away!).

Walk in the middle of the street.

Pick your nose. Mutter crazy shit to yourself.

> **"She's strong as hell. Like a fucking machine. Like a sleek Chevelle, she's my dirty Queen...."**
> —"Sissybar" by The Hail Marys, lyrics by Jackie Strano

If shady characters are checking you out, but you don't want to act crazy, talk loudly to yourself in a sane way. I will say, "Shit! You have got to be kidding me! I can't believe this is the kind of day I'm having!" Maybe you're just thinking about your day, or maybe more. Dozens of times, by talking loudly, I've made *the other guy* cross the street. If you and a friend are walking and you feel even the slightest bit unsafe, talk loudly to each other. You can talk about whatever, but say it loudly. I start saying stuff like, "No way! She said she'd *kill him*? You gotta be kidding me. She's so crazy! Hell, my uncle killed that guy last year! Shit, I don't blame her." Think J*erry Springer.*

Remember that everyone has weak spots: kneecaps, groin, eyeballs. One of my friends, Veronica, never took self-defense but did that kind of wrestling that high school boys do. She weighs 100 pounds, but I've seen her knock down people twice her size. She does this crazy dive for the kneecaps, then runs like mad once they're down. If you go for anywhere a man can use his hands against you, he'll most likely win. Your assets are your legs, his weak spots, and your smarts.

If you want to carry a weapon, remember one thing: **A weapon does you no good if it can be taken away.** Meaning, do not arm yourself unless you have the skill to make sure no one can wrench the weapon from you and use it on you.

Never get into a car with anyone, no matter what weapon the assailant has. Some people do tell stories of being raped in a car, then surviving, but those examples are *so-o-o* rare. Usually, if someone puts a gun to your gut and tells you to get in a car, he wants to do much worse things to you than simply shoot you. I can't really tell you what to do in such an extreme circumstance, but crime experts say your best chance is to yell, "I won't go with you. Help!" as loudly as you can and try to get out of the person's grip and flee. One of my friends did this and got away. The guy was shocked at her response and ran. Ultimately, you'll have to follow your instinct.

Finally, if someone is pointing a gun at you, it's imperative to remain calm (unless someone wants you to go with them). The assailant is almost always nervous, and the last thing you want is a nervous person behind a gun. Your calmness and cooperation may keep them steady, and that's a good thing. Shaky fingers on triggers are a bad thing. Move very, very slowly. I've had both a gun and a knife pulled on me. Both times I moved slowly, telling the guy what I was doing as I did it: "Hey, man, it's cool, it's cool. I'll help you out. My wallet is in my pocket. I'm going to reach into this pocket, get my wallet, and give it to you. It's cool, dude. I'm just hanging slow tonight." I even got to keep my driver's license. It's not fair that you're the one on whom the crime's being perpetrated, yet you have to become the therapist, but your life is what's most important.

❖   ❖   ❖

Above all, remember that being self-sufficient is the key to being a Multifaceted Handy Queen. Sure, having servants and admirers to dote and deliver is fantastic, but when they're not around or have the day off, you'll need to know you can rely on your own brawn and smarts. That's what being a Queen is all about.

P.S.: About starting that fire: (1) send out a smoldering SOS with your eyes; (2) hold out a cigarette in classic movie-star style about three inches from lips; (3) choose from the many lights that are offered to you; (4) place cigarette cherry on whatever you wish to torch, your ex-girlfriend's Monet prints for example.

Part III

Beyond the Palace Walls

Out & About in the Universe

Darling, you can't hide under the satin sheets forever! You must take your brand of wonderfulness out into the Milky Way. Here are a few pointers for hitting the pavement.

The Working Girl

A Brief History

Femmes are all-powerful, and that means on the job too. Traditionally speaking, femme lesbians, as long as they stayed in the closet, could find work in the few places that welcomed women. Not so long ago, though, our butch sisters were complete pariahs in the work world. Employers weren't willing to hire them unless they suffered in skirts and feminine shoes. We're barely a generation from those days, but how quickly we forget. We don't realize what our foresisters went through and how attitudes of the past still affect us. A black or Jewish young person today can trace her ancestral patterns back through the challenges endured by her grandparents, great-grandparents, and so on. She can look at her family's past to discover how it affects the way she behaves today. With queers, examining our history becomes much more elusive because queer history does not run through bloodlines. It was most likely a stranger's blood that spilled so that I can now tread safely. Even though we can't trace those lines the way we can within our biological families, they've still had an impact on who we are today.

Decades ago, femme lesbians could find work as nurses, secretaries, or teachers, or did sex work to support their butch lovers. Just read any of Red Jordan Arobateau's[1] books to discover what butches went through attempting to make a living. A femme lesbian simply looked like a single straight woman to the world. She also appeared to be a woman without a man to protect her, who, therefore, was even more vulnerable than her married, straight sisters who could, implicitly or explicitly, threaten violent repercussions from an angry husband to avoid harassment on the job (though, of course, this didn't always protect her).

These days, a single woman in the work world isn't unusual. Many "soft" butches can get work anywhere, as long as they're not too bulldagger. But in general, a femme lesbian still has more mobility than her butch counterpart. When my wife and I were in our 20s and my income was increasing, Jackie felt trapped in retail sales at a progressive shop because she didn't want to have to downplay her butchness to enter another field. Many butch women earn the same salary at age 45 as they did at 25 because they stay in a field where they are accepted, whereas a femme can often pass in the workplace and change jobs or careers. Of course, none of us are immune to the problems all women face, but femmes still have it easier than butches (appearance-wise) when it comes to negotiating through the world of work.

With femmes there's always business going on.

PHYLLIS CHRISTOPHER

I point this out because awareness of our past helps us relate to others, to understand that we're not always responsible when we aren't offered promotions, to see where we're starting from so we can focus on where we're going. Looking at our people's past always helps us to be savvy navigators in the present and future. It also teaches us to feel good about our heritage. No one goes around bragging about us queers—what hard workers we are, what survivors we are. I'm very proud of our people as a workforce. I stand as free as I am today on the backs of brilliant, world-changing artists, writers, musicians, and designers. We are compassionate caregivers, doctors, and teachers. We led historical movements from communist uprisings to beat poetry to women's lib.

We are some of the best craftspeople, laborers, and servers in the business. So you too can take pride in continuing that legacy.

Working It

As femmes, it's important to show as much strength in the workforce as possible. We must maintain the advances made by our sisters and make even more. You don't need to take "seconds." If you choose to be a sex worker because the benefits of that job match your lifestyle, I'll be your biggest cheerleader as well as a fan. But you shouldn't *have to be* a stripper because you have no other choices. It's all about empowerment.

So you wanna take the world by storm? Here are some suggestions.

You've already read the definition of *Queen*. Well, behave like one on the job. I've always been a leader, but in one of my first jobs I stagnated, doing only what was asked of me and nothing more. I remember how I transformed into manager material while working as a hostess at a Ramada Inn restaurant. (And I still remember the pseudo-silk, polyester blouses we had to wear, cut to the sternum, and holding the '80s drape-bow between our breasts.) Unless I stood as straight as a rod, anyone could see down to my ankles, including everything in between. Anyway, my friend Laura was the night manager and moving her way on up the Ramada ladder. I was whining to her about something as usual while she half-listened as usual. Then she motioned for me to lean closer so she could speak quietly.

"You can keep whining like everybody else," she said, "or you can choose to make a difference."

Then I interrupted her with the beginnings of another whine about how everything is somebody else's fault.

"Managers figure out how to fix things, then let the right person know they fixed it."

Ah, the secret of moving up the corporate ladder. Is it brown-nosing or just getting the job done? Actually, it's a mixture of both. When a problem arises, don't ask yourself, "Whose job is it to fix this?" Ask yourself, "How much of this can *I* fix?"

Appearances account for a lot too. Move quickly but gracefully and don't show your sweat. That way you look busy but not frantic. Everything appears to be under control. And, well, isn't that all control is anyway? Yes, to a certain degree. When organizing an event I always say, "Do the best you can and know where the nearest KFC is." What I mean by that is, *do* organize the event you hope for. Hire the florist, plan the catering, buy the tents. Do it, then let go.

Events differ, but for the most part, having fun and connecting with people is most important. That's what you'll be remembered for. If you start running around frantically when things go awry, then you'll only stress others out more. So, if the caterer doesn't show up and it starts to rain and the tents fall down, instead of freaking out (sweating), send someone out for buckets of KFC and vegetarian egg rolls. Even folks in tuxedos will be happy. They love for you to "force" them to eat grease. Have everyone take off their shoes and dance in the rain. If the band doesn't show up, turn on a radio. Even in this cynical day and age, people are so ready to have fun. You just have to lead the way.

In any job, know how to delegate. Choose the best people to be on your team. Give a detailed list of your expectations with priorities and second choices marked, then let go. They'll know what you want; let them do their best. If you don't snap at folks, you won't have to make apologies. Be specific, direct, and clear.

At one of my jobs, I moved up to the position of sales team leader—but not because I was the best at sales. I sell well enough to keep a job, but I've never been the best. I got the job because I was the best *team leader* and always led my gang to the top. I know how to inspire people to be their best. I did everything from copying their memos on paper of their favorite colors to initiating creative rewards such as giving out gift certificates. Care such as this instills loyalty in your staff, and that loyalty is what saves your butt when a problem arises and a staff member is the only one there to fix it for you.

When working as someone else's right hand, do the same. Make sure you understand her needs in order—second choices if first can't be had—then do your job. Always confidently assert, "I'll take care of it." Period. Don't tell someone else, "Don't worry." Folks can't help worrying. Just tell her you'll take care of it, then do your damnedest to do just that. Come back with results, not excuses. If her plans are a complete no go, think of alternatives and suggest them. Have pros and cons thought out so you can present them, enabling her to make decisions more swiftly. Since she's the boss, she hopefully knows more than you. And if she knows more than you, she might correct one of your suggestions. Say, "I'm glad you pointed that out. Any other options?" Keep the focus on her brain. When she gets it, say, "Brilliant. I'll take care of it."

Look for opportunities to lead a project, even if it's something seemingly insignificant. Make it yours. Put your name all over it and present results yourself.

Ask for referrals. If you keep running into roadblocks as you search for something, ask each person who turns you down if they know someone who is the right person, has the answer, etc.

Don't take "just because" from a coworker as an excuse for doing things inefficiently. If you can see a better, faster, or easier way to do things, do it. Be sure, though, that there's not a darn good reason that your way isn't the right way already. Maybe someone else tried it last year and flunked miserably. Of course, if it's your boss's "just because," you'd better be extra careful.

Best thing I learned waitressing: Carry something each way you go.

Best thing I learned taking care of children: Ask people to "use their words." When a three-year-old gets frustrated she often reverts back to her baby ways by crying or screaming. When she was six months old, that was a surefire way to get fed or changed! But at three she knows how to express her frustration; she's just forgotten because her words, language skills, are new to her. So we remind her, "use your words." How many *adults* do you know who forget how to use their words? I don't say it that way to adults because it sounds condescending, but I sure as hell think it. I *do* ask for clarification, specifications, and demand that people represent themselves and not project their feelings onto others.

Another method preschool teachers maximize is voice control: the ability to send your voice through a noisy room filled with talking parents, playing kids, and busy teachers to reach one particular child so she knows what you need her to do. It requires vocal projection and modulation plus cultivating a voice that stands out among others. No matter how scary or irritating or nerve-racking a particular situation is, let your voice reflect the *best* of the situation: that cuts will heal, that it's actually funny when you get peed on, and that people learn to not bite. Surely you can see the universality in that advice!

I use the communication skills I learned doing day care in more jobs and relationships than any of my other skills.

Never show you're overwhelmed. If you're having problems getting everything done, don't act as though it's because of you or your skills. Instead say, "I need to check in with you about what our priorities are. Would you like this done first or this?" If you're faking it 'til you're making it and actually *don't* know what you're doing, just go to the Web. You can find out how to do anything there. Or have someone show you, but don't disclose exactly what you don't know. Say, "Could you go over your system with me? I don't want to take a shortcut and miss a step that's important to you."

Figure out who does know what they're doing and work with them. One of my bosses, Sam, had played basketball with an Arizona team, even though he was short by basketball's standards. He used to tell us, "I didn't get good by playing ball with the neighborhood kids my age who I could beat. I got good by *losing* to the older, taller boys who kicked my butt." Play with the best.

Be conscious. Stay awake.

Finding Your Desire and Staying True to Yourself

I've bartered for many necessities such as sex toys, laundry services, computer repair, massages, and more. Somehow making a velvet pillow or a beaded necklace for someone seems a better form of commerce to me. What are you good at? Don't underestimate others' desire for your skills. Transform your hobby into a business. You don't have to quit your day job and run up the credit cards right off the bat. Do it on the side for a while until you can make the move away from the daily grind. Having a stylin' price tag or brochure is really the key. Make anything and put a subtle yet fancy tag on it and watch it sell. If you can't stand making other people rich, why not exploit and cultivate your own talents? That way, you're not only doing what you love to do, but you'll also be working for one fantastic lady.

> **"The only courage you need is the courage to truly live the life of your dreams."**
>
> —Oprah Winfrey

Wrapped Around Your Little Finger, Not Your Boss's

Hands. Ooh, yum. I love hands. I love my hands. I love your hands. Soft hands seductively catch me off-guard, and rough hands shove me where I want to be. The lesbian hand flaunting lesbian fingers—our tool of love and lust wielded so precisely with sensual knowledge that only a woman can acquire. Who knows "just so" like a woman? The most poetic sexual organ, the most revered. Who can steal a heart right through a pussy but a woman with her firm yet delicate dyke grip? The magic tricks of Sappho's fingers have kept women bewitched for centuries. "How *do* you do that?" Sound familiar?

Honor your hands and fingers and the wrists and arms that support them. Don't lose your hands to a job. Fight for workers' compensation if you do. Advocate for yourself if you feel repetitive stress injury (RSI) such as carpal tunnel or tendinitis coming on. Don't settle for companies claiming they "can't afford" voice recognition computers. You can't afford to lose your hands. Will your company be between your gal's legs ten years from now? Will your human resource manager be holding your vibrator so you can see stars 20 years from now? Advocate for yourself. Don't accept "no." Be a part of changing the world and help end this epidemic. If straight men's penises were going numb, losing endurance and strength, and hurting from working at a computer all day, you can bet your bloomers that every workstation in the world would have voice-recognition programs.

Watch for symptoms early on and don't lie to yourself by ignoring you have them. Stretch your fingers, massage your hands, or have someone else do it. Wear orthopedic gloves that not only give support but also keep your hands warm. Use lots of lotion. Touch others. (For more information, see my section on RSI in Part V.)

I focus on RSI so much because lesbian hands are like gold to me. But our general health and well-being needs a watchdog too. Don't let your job take your back, knees, nerves, or immune system. Advocate for yourself. Don't think "victim." Instead (when possible), think creatively and figure out solutions to work problems with your employers. There *are* solutions. And when a situation really can't be resolved, get compensated and stick out your thumb 'cause it is time to *move on*.

✿ ✿ ✿

With femmes there's always business going on. I know many butches who are busy with business and activities day in and day out like most Americans, but in the lesbian world no one can compare to a femme when it comes to always being involved with some project. If she's not glue-gunning her own line of hats, she's decoupaging gift boxes for the whole family. If she's not running a magazine, she's peddling her own chapbook. If she's not pulling together the local poetry

reading, she's organizing a birthday party with a guest list of 200. Remember, though, stay smart and don't overdo it. The heavier the jewels, the longer the lobe—in other words, don't stretch yourself too thin. Prioritize spending time on personal projects, such as maintaining your beautiful skin, garden, spirituality, and candy-apple toenails.

1. Red's work is sporadically available through Amazon.com. You can always find it by writing to: Red Jordan Press, 484 Lake Park Ave., PMB 228, Oakland, CA 94610.

The Royal Decree: Flirt With the Whole Solar System!

There's a key element to being successful when out and about in the world. Remember, there's more to life than work and fixing your girlsistergirlfriend's car. As you glide through this universe, you'll want things to go smoothly, divinely, your way. There's a kind of person who has it easier than the rest. She's worked at it, of course; making it look easy is the point. Who is she? She's a flirt.

Flirts rule and are never short of a date. Now and then we may be short of a date who puts out, but just show me one flirt who doesn't have a date for the latest opening, reading, or picnic. Flirts always have an arm to hold on to. They're the first chosen to be surrogate trophy wives (or husbands—who said only femmes flirt?). That's because flirts make everyone feel comfortable and welcome, so there are plenty of folks around to return the favor when we need it.

Actually, flirts are simply friendly folks. There are two aspects of being a flirt. Yes, we are just friendly people, but on other hand we know how to pull our friendliness up out of our hearts when needed, the way some people pull out a $100 bill to pay the check. It's there for us when we need it to better our world, even if it means simply getting the tow truck guy not to charge.

Our friendliness is out there for others when they need it. A pretty woman's smile is worth a million bucks, especially to the downtrodden. I know this firsthand from the number of homeless people living on the streets of San Francisco. I'll apologize for not having money, then hear the reply, "From you a smile is enough." And they really mean it. So many people in our world are literally *overlooked*. People don't want to see them, so they look past them. Not just street people, but store clerks and coworkers too.

Never underestimate how much the tiniest amount of your attention and friendliness can mean to someone.

Is it manipulative to wield flirtation the way some wave a gun? (They can sometimes be of equal force.) Like a gun, flirting isn't bad; it just can be used by bad people sometimes.

For the longest time, I didn't even realize I was a big flirt. I've been one since I was born, according to

> ## *Reclaiming "Manipulate"*
>
> The term *manipulate* has been so overused to describe negative circumstances that people forget it isn't necessarily a bad thing to do.
>
> **MANIPULATE:** muh·nip·yu·late, verb: (1) to control or operate by the skilled use of the hands; handle; (2) to manage or influence shrewdly. (*shrewd:* having keen insight; astute, artful, cunning)

Mavis, that is. I was raised to be charming and friendly, to offer humor or sympathy with a twinkle in my eye. What I didn't learn at home I learned as a Girl Scout and a Christian. You read that right....

Grin and Share It

I was very into Christianity as a teenager. As with everything I do, I took many of the lessons I learned to heart and left the ones that didn't apply to me. In one of my Bible study workbooks,

I read a saying that I've thought about almost every day since: "If you see someone without a smile, give them yours." Having been raised on country music, I just love little phrases with double entendres, such as "Sleeping single in a double bed," so I remembered the saying easily. Now, when I get all citied out and angry walking down the street, I remind myself that I can change the city experience one smile at a time. I say my little saying in my head, then I smile at people.

The Challenge of Social Dependability

You may have heard of Girl Scout badges, but have you heard of the *challenges*? Challenges are difficult to obtain, and one must earn several badges first. Among the many challenges is the Challenge of Social Dependability. According to the Girl Scout Handbook, this challenge shows that "you have the understanding and skills to get along with people—older and younger, family and friends, boys and girls, those you already know and new people—and that you can bring them enjoyment and happiness in a social situation." Clearly this challenge underlines the importance of flirting with the whole solar system; it also touches on being a good hostess. What's the difference between a flirt and a hostess? Well, it's kinda like the difference between a square and a rectangle: You have to be a flirt to be a hostess, but not every flirt may be acting as a hostess all the time (although I will argue that point later).

How to Flirt

Be a Queen. Light up people's lives. Flirt with everyone, women and men alike. Think to yourself, "I am a light. This means I am noticed. This means I have the opportunity to brighten any corner into which I shine."

For example, let's say you walk into a party. Don't just run to whomever you know and gossip in a corner. Take a deep breath as you enter, straightening your back and thrusting your tits. Walk your walk. Smile at the first person you see. See each person as someone you might want to know. Pay attention to each person you talk to, but you only have to talk to each person for a few minutes. Keep moving, attracting some of the vivacious, charming, and most interesting people to your side. Soon you'll have your own group that others will cluster around to clamor for your attention. Remember, always make a big entrance and a teensy *au revoir*.

Flirting can happen anytime, anywhere. And it doesn't have to take up a huge amount of energy. When you go to the store, look the clerk in the eye, smile, then, when handed your groceries, say, "Thank you so much. Have a good night, OK?" The "OK?" gets them to respond. Besides making the world a more pleasant place, it never hurts to be remembered or noticed. Later, if you realize you left your laundry detergent under your cart, chances are the clerk will remember you if you call to inquire. As far as simply being noticed, well, that's a force unto itself.

You can always find a topic of conversation if you're talking to someone new at a dinner or party. Comment on a piece of her or his outfit. Don't just say, "I like that" or "Where did you get that?" That's boring and won't make you stand out. Reminisce about a cousin. Weave a whole story that comes back to their tie, earrings, etc., then end it with a provocative question. Don't say, "That's an interesting tie." Say, "Your tie brings me back to a New Year's Eve I spent on a boat on the Mississippi. What was your most memorable New Year's Eve?" This tactic is especially helpful if you were spacing out about

> ## Many doors have been opened with a bobby pin.

something and don't remember what the person just asked you. Something like, "I'm sorry. I *was* listening to you, then I got caught up wondering if your earrings are vintage or custom-made. They're really amazing. Do you have a lot of artisan friends?"

Are you painfully shy? If so, practice all this at home first. In public, finding your voice can be the hardest part. You open your mouth, but nothing comes out, or something does but just drips and hits the floor. Sing really loud around the house. That will open your lungs. Overdo it. Act out those bad late-night infomercials. Then practice more realistic lines. Stand in front of the mirror and make conversation with yourself. Give yourself a compliment, then act out your thank-you.

Reverse Flirting

So you've got a hanger-on you can't get rid of. There are many avenues of escape, my friend. Determining the most appropriate one depends on the person you wish to flee as well as your surroundings. Most importantly, remember you're not "asking for" anything by being kind to people, so don't feel obliged or guilty. Often you just need to be firm, but sometimes you'll have to be more outrageous.

Kinder Party Tactics

"Sorry to interrupt you, but I have got to get back to my wife" (even if you don't have one). That alone usually works because people are so assuming regarding marriage that it's gross. But for fun you can add, "You know our friends call her 'Amy Fisher' 'cuz she'd kill for love. Isn't that sweet? Bye."

"I haven't seen Jane in three years. She needs some attention. Bye."

"Oh, my God, I just started my period. I gotta hit the women's room. See ya."

Kinder Party Tactics for Slightly Rude People

In a nice fake voice say, "I'm sure you don't know how rude you're being right now. We'll talk some other time." If the person tries to apologize, say, "Apology accepted. Bye." If they try to apologize more, say, "You are once again demanding my attention. Others want my attention too. Our conversation is over now."

Or try saying, "I'm sure this is interesting to someone other than me."

For People Making Rude Comments About Your Outfit or Body

If you feel like giving them one more chance (because it's the husband of your cousin or your girlfriend's ex, whatever), say, "I'm sure in that (tiny) head of yours that was a beautiful compliment. Would you like another opportunity to flatter me in a more appropriate way?" Every time I've said this, the person has blushed in embarrassment and straightened themselves up.

Or a shorter version is to say, "It was not OK to talk to me that way. Do you want to try again?"

Finally, there's "You're really rude. You need to step away." If they persist, throw your arms into the air and say, "STEP AWAY FROM THE QUEEN, INTRUDER! STEP AWAY FROM THE QUEEN!" This is really obnoxious, so save it for the really obnoxious. But it *will* garner attention, and someone will sweep him/her away from you.

Final Suggestions for the Shy

When going to parties, bring a Polaroid camera with you. Everyone loves having her picture taken. And picture takers are always attracted to the area with the most action, so you'll be in the heart of it all. You can wander around and ask people if they want their picture taken, but soon enough they'll be hunting you down. You don't want people to like you just for your camera, so heads-up, doll, be fun and charming when you get their attention so that'll be what they remember about you.

When going to potlucks or events where a dish is welcome, whip up an unusual recipe (or buy something exotic and creative). Everyone will wonder how you got marshmallows to look like cell phones, and soon enough you'll have a captive audience for hours on end.

Nonsmoker alert. Did you know that smokers meet new people all the time? They do. A smoker can always bum a cigarette off a not-yet-but-soon-to-be-friend. They can pull out a Zippo to light a hovering cigarette. Since you often have to go outside to smoke, people who hardly know each other will grab the arm of a smoker heading outside, saying, "I'll join you." Whether you smoke or not, everyone needs to step outside now and then. If you don't mind kissing a smoker, volunteer to give her some company while she indulges in her nasty habit. Or ask a nonsmoker you like if she wants to get some fresh air. If you're being really romantic, you can ask for a walk under the stars. If you're not that serious, go ahead and make a little joke about how smokers aren't the only ones who get to step outside now and then.

✲ ✲ ✲

Flirting with the whole solar system is easy. You just gotta wear your friendliness on the outside. Some people dole out niceties like politicians remembering promises—it happens only if they want something from you. Of course there'll be times that you'll reel in your flirtatious line hoping to avoid the great white shark. But overall you'll want to empower strength and friendliness 24/7. Flirts rule.

Hostess to the Glitterati

Darling sweetie, sweetie darling. Did you actually think you could mete out your fascinating and dazzling self like you measure out bath beads? Oh, no no no. Now that you've cultivated it, all those around you will gravitate to the remarkable, efflorescent garden that is you. Your court will implore you to attend each soiree; every party thrower will breathe a sigh of relief when you walk through her door, and every partygoer will burst forth with, "YAY, *you* came!"

Naturally, you will be pressed upon to entertain. They can smell the velvet and roses a mile away. And they'll want to behold your famously potent love pad.

First off, you need some guidebooks. I suggest *In the Royal Manner: Expert Advice on Etiquette and Entertaining from the Former Butler to Diana, Princess of Wales* by Paul Burrell and *Guests Without Grief : Entertaining Made Easy for the Hesitant Host* by Paula Jhung. From the titles alone, I bet you can tell these books come from opposite ends of the spectrum. That's my Libra-influenced balance at work. If it's not fries and gravy, it's caviar!

The good thing about guidebooks, ahem, is not only do they teach you new stuff so you're not reinventing origami, but they also make you feel all validated and provide some authority to your social agenda. When a baby butch is setting your place at the table all wrong, you can sugar up to her ear and purr, "Ooh, tsk tsk, my baby stud. Princess Diana would never have been served that way. Now what do you think your punishment should be?"

Shar's Surefire Party Tips

Prepare for your gala wa-a-ay in advance. Flying through the house like a hummingbird on crack while your guests are having to meet and greet on their own makes your party a downer for everyone. Prepare your food in advance, clean the house a week before, put all the drinks in a cooler or set them out in a serve-yourself style. Don't serve what you can't afford in *time* or money. My friend Christina is known for her tater-tot hors d'oeuvres. At the first tot party, she featured them simply because it was a last-minute affair, and she grabbed the one thing she knew how to prepare from the corner store. Everyone loved them, and guests lent a hand in making them. Simply pour the frozen taters onto a tray, pop into the oven, wait 15 minutes, then serve. After success like that, her guests demanded a tot affair every year. (She's never short of volunteers to carry a serving tray through her soiree because everyone knows it's a fabu way to meet the guests of your choice.)

When reprimanding those you like, it's imperative to purr the reproach in your best Eartha Kitt voice.

Don't refuse any offers for assistance. At almost every party you'll find a kind soul who picks up stray cups, empties trash, or replenishes ice. At our parties Jack and I have found that having a blender ready to go brings out the bartender in everyone. I begin the evening as the Margarita Madame but soon pass my secrets (this much tequila, this much lime, etc.) onto the next blender tender. Shy tip: All single folks, listen up. Acting as barkeep means you'll meet most everyone at the event. Speaking of shy girls, they are the very people to put to work at your event. Hand a shy babe a tray of strawberries, and push her out into the crowd to fend for herself.

Can I just say, CHILL OUT! Please purchase your beer, wine, and sodas 24 hours before party o'clock and put them in ice or the fridge. You are nothing but immature and thoughtless if you try to serve your guests warm beer.

Set up ashtrays where you want people to smoke, even if it is outside. No one likes walking through cigarette butts, and it makes tidying up easier. When possible, burn big scented candles near the area to help cleanse the air.

Set out pitchers of water and cups for those who don't want to liquor up and to encourage those partaking of the spirits to pace themselves.

Buy a 24-pack of toilet paper and store it in an easy-to-find place in the bathroom.

Encourage guests to pick up after themselves by putting out as many recycling and trash cans as you can without ruining your palatial decor.

Place serving spoons in a big container on the food table so that guests who bring food can plop one down into their dish without your assistance.

Provide the public basics. Neatly arrange hair spray, hand lotion, emery boards, clear nail polish, and tissue on the bathroom counter. Leave a roll of paper towels out as well for hand drying. Much better than everyone using the same towel.

Provide the private basics. You know people are going to look in your medicine cabinet, so remove any personal items you don't want becoming gossip material. Instead, stock the cabinet with aspirin, ibuprofen, Tums, bandages, tampons, pads, dental floss, and other urgent items your guests might require.

Buy colored lightbulbs in bulk. Screw them into every socket in the house! For small gatherings, of course, I recommend candles, but for real parties, colored lights are the safest way to make everyone look beautiful.

Remember that club soda cleaning tip! Buy your bottle of bubbles before the party and stock it far away from the mixers so that when that red wine spill happens you'll be prepared.

Put taxi numbers beside the phone *and* the door. You may also choose to make a tasteful yet easy-to-read sign: WHY DRIVE DRUNK WHEN YOU CAN TAXI? Then list numbers. Of course, you'll keep your eye out for friends drinking too much, but be realistic. You can't be everywhere at all times. Before your party even starts, ask your closest friends to help you keep an eye out for anyone showing poor judgment, and have them stop the person and/or notify you immediately. Beware of friends who say they are only going to the car to sleep it off. Ask a handy butch to walk them to the car, unlock the door, put them in, then deliver the keys right back to you! I know everyone always says, "It's not cool or macho to drive drunk," but some people just don't get it. They think *everyone else* thinks they're pansies for giving up the keys. Like we're an after-school special or something. Let me spell it out for the drunk dunceheads out there. Do you know what everyone says behind your back? They do *not* say, "Hey, what a responsible chick; she can get home alone." No, sorry. They snarl, "God, what a stupid asshole." There, that's the truth. That's actually what people say about you, so just hand over the keys and stop the gossip from starting—not to mention that you're taking the opportunity to save someone's life. OK, dismounting soapbox. Onward.

Wear patent leather shoes so that when you get splashed on, you'll simply have to make the transgressor lick up her mistake.

Have a guest book for folks to sign. You may feature it grandly and encourage partygoers to autograph it, or you may keep it in a discreet corner available for guests you'd like more info on. Instead of fumbling with jotting down numbers and dates or dealing with business cards, you can simply point to your book and say, "Oh, would you be a doll and write your number (event, etc.) in my book? You can tuck your card in there as well. Then I'll be sure to find it in the morning."

Hire a DJ or pile up all your music beside the stereo so that when you get tired of changing the beat you can ask someone else to. If your musical tastes are limited—meaning you *only* listen to Michael Bolton—I implore you, invest in some other choices. Sound tracks work the best for parties because they feature many artists in one compilation.

Maintain techno-pagan-rave-stoner friends. They love to volunteer to shine their psychedelic, watercolor, acid, Lava lamp, slide-show thingies on your wall. It makes for warm ambiance. Not to mention those interesting brownies they bring.

Re-outfit as many times as you wish. Plan for at least three changes. Do not, however, pick changes that will keep you away from your party for more than a few minutes. Plan your outfits beforehand.

Be snag free. No, I'm not talking about kicking

SNAG: Sensitive New-Age Guy, noun: Sometimes a realistic description with no judgment attached, but often used in a derogatory manner to describe touchy-feely guys who are just a bit too sensitive and understanding of the woman's plight and who give you the creeps.

HASBIAN: has·be·in (pronounced with the same cadence as *lesbian*) noun: An ex-lesbian. I first heard this from my friend Thea. She's a self-proclaimed hasbian whose been with women in the past, and is instinctively bisexual, but is currently long-term mating with a boy.

out your neighbor the *hasbian's* new Wiccan boyfriend! I'm referring to clothing snags. Hugging and kissing is one of your main duties. Wear jewelry that won't get caught on guests when you're XOing.

PHYLLIS CHRISTOPHER

You are always the Queen of the party.

For Dinner Parties

You sit at the very center of the table, not at the end or "head." Your guest of honor, cohostess, or other most fascinating person sits across from you in the center. That way y'all are most accessible to everyone at the table.

Have vases washed and discreetly waiting. Surely your lovely guests will be bringing you flowers.

Don't wear flowy sleeves; you'll inevitably dip them into the fondue.

If your party is small and your courses few, you may choose to serve up each person's plate to control its presentation as well as the amount of food each person gets. If your party is larger or you've got plenty of food, I encourage setting up the serving dishes buffet style and letting everyone serve themselves.

Have your coffee and water measured into the coffee maker so that after dinner you only have to press "start."

Now that the basics are out of the way, let's talk about you at the party. Employ the party skills I discussed in the previous sections on flirting. Talk to everyone for at least five sincere minutes. It is your job to introduce everyone and make them feel comfortable. Ask your more outgoing friends to help you with this task. If at all possible, feature cleavage.

As a Guest

It's easy to be the perfect guest. Simply remember that the most exquisite guest is always a co-hostess. You know what it takes to make your events run smoothly, now it's your turn to play lube and help keep the night loose.

First off, RSVP or send regrets promptly when they're requested.

Bring an offering to your hostess. At BYOB parties a bottle of your favorite wine is not an offering, it's mandatory! I often choose an elegant but inexpensive gift such as truffles. Who said you have to buy the whole store? I choose two or three, which most chocolatiers will delicately wrap in a fancy but tiny box. Don't have a chocolatier in your neck of the woods? Grab a bag of Hershey's Kisses and place them in any decorative bowl, cup, or fine fabric, then wrap with a ribbon. One last suggestion for a present that I've found is always welcome: a gift certificate for a pedicure scheduled the day after the event.

Lend a helping hand if it's needed, but don't be a martyr. Your hostess benefits more from you charming everyone with your cultured tales in the living room than she does from you sweating away over her stove.

One of the best ways you can aid your hostess is by introducing everyone as you float through the room and by helping to keep the stream of the affair moving. Don't just introduce people by names; instead tell them what they will like about each other or mention a common interest. Be aware that this can come across as so-o-o staged, leaving all involved uncomfortable. The way to make it natural is to be extremely earnest about whatever it is you are saying. Not: "Kim, this Minnie. She has blond hair." To Minnie, "Kim only cruises blonds." Instead: "Minnie, this is my friend Kim. We had to talk to you because you have the insider information!" Minnie says, "I do?" You say, "Yes! We were just reading this *wild* exposé about how many hours academics have put into studying whether blonds have more fun. I mean (pause), Kim definitely has spent a few of her hours admiring the fair-headed (smile). What do you think?"

Offer a ride to guests who've partied too hard, even if you're not driving. Maybe you've noticed that someone else is going that way, or offer to call a cab.

Cruise through the party at least once, throwing away empty cups, bottles, plates, etc.

Not everyone is Girl Scout–trained, but I usually have a corkscrew, Band-Aids, and drugs somewhere on me, so when the hostess is lacking I'm prepared. The corkscrew has been a welcome surprise countless times.

Remember, make your grand entrance at a time when you will have an audience so:

•Forty-five minutes late for two-hour cocktail events, such as art openings running from 5 to 7 P.M.

•Two and one half hours late for "early" parties—ones that supposedly start at 8:30.

•Hit late-night parties around 1 A.M. Folks will still be sober enough to know you came.

•Formal dinner parties are trickier. For dinners that have cocktails before sitting down, you will arrive 12 minutes late (cocktails at 6:30, dinner at 7, so you arrive at 6:42). Unless, of course, you want to engage in intimate conversation with another guest or your hostess. For dinners where everyone else is arriving ten minutes early, you arrive exactly on time.

And of course, you'll make teensy-weensy *au revoirs*. It's gauche to stand around with your coat on your arm. Also, you don't want to steal the show—if everyone knows you're going, they might go as well. Don't yell from the door, "Hey, when you blow Snoresville, I'll meet you at the Martini Factory." If you do want a few choice people to know where you're headed, tell them your next stop one-on-one as you drift through the gathering.

Send a thank-you card. Your hostess went to a lot of work to ensure your fun; the least you can do is stick a note in the mail. Always have notes and stamps handy so you won't have to go shopping before hitting the post office. Also, you're more likely to send one if you aren't a perfectionist. A quick note is appreciated more than the perfect thank-you card that never gets sent.

Concluding Gala Thoughts

When the masses are begging for your attention, it's easy for your ego to swell like a bee-stung toe. You must take the good and leave the bad. What I mean is, great, treat that attention like pure femme octane and fill up on it. BUT do not take it seriously. The friends and family who love you for you are the ones who will always be there. Are those party revelers going to be buttering up your bagels when you break your arm? Are they going to be the ones feeding you soup when you've got cold sores on your mouth and snot running out of your nose from the latest flu? I think not.

Remember who your real friends are. If you wear yourself out party-hopping, then you won't have energy for yourself or your genuine, true-blue comrades. Not good.

A genuine Queen prioritizes self-attentive hours of pedicures, baths, spiritual health, and rest as well as quality time for her faithful loved ones. Lastly, select the events that are the most fabulous or given by the most thrilling folks to attend, then leave the rest. Not enough hours in the day? Take a bath with a friend.

Part IV

Galaxy-Wide Glamour for the New Millennium

A single crystal or a stained-glass—adorned cathedral can be a place of worship. Whether it's oiling up your birthday suit or adding sequins to your power suit, there's always a femme secret to help you be your best.

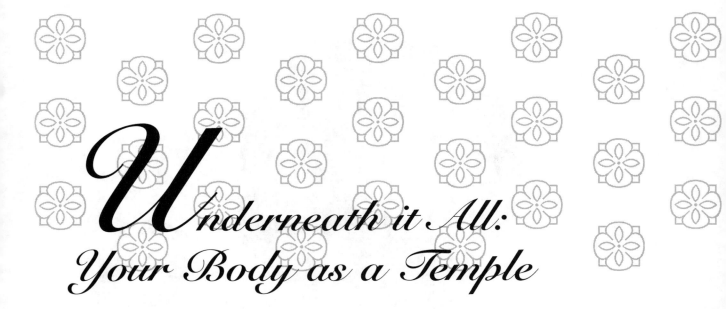

Underneath it All: Your Body as a Temple

Inner Space

Too many people label gender according to outer accoutrements such as skirts or pants. How rude! Gender is so much more than clothing. No matter what gender you doll yourself up in, you must take care of your body first. With all the wonderful books and magazines out there, I'm not going to detail every facial and conditioner on the market. I'm betting that if you're hip enough to read this book, you're hip enough to take care of business and learn about hair, makeup, skin, and fashion on your own. But I will offer some important tips, trade secrets, and nuances that separate the femmes from the females.

Diet and Exercise

Good nutrition and healthy living are beauty's foundations. No amount of cosmetics, designer clothes, plastic surgery, or attitude can make up for poor eating and exercise habits. Appearances are all well and good, but what use is a shiny apple if it's rotten on the inside? Granted, we all have different metabolisms, body shapes, and lifestyles that affect our body size and energy levels. Still, the following dietary guidelines work great for many women. They won't make you lose weight if you're looking to shed a few pounds. Nor will they help you gain weight. What this regimen will do is help you to maintain your ideal weight. (Don't argue until you try it, and remember, there might be a big difference between what *you* think you should weigh and what the Goddess, I, or your doctor might say is your "ideal weight.")

In our culture, women are completely obsessed with being thin, which is ridiculous. First of all, this mania doesn't even work. Our models are *skinnier* than ever (no, Twiggy was not skinnier than models nowadays), yet as a nation we are *bigger* than ever, and Goddess help American children because they're the least physically fit kids on the planet. My mother lives in the Midwest where the average size must be at least a 14, yet all those people talk about is who would be prettier if she only lost some weight. Why don't they look around and say, "Hey, we're all size 14, so size 14 must be OK"?

Remember in the movie *The Misfits* when Clark Gable says to Marilyn Monroe, "You're a size 12, right?" She nods, without a worry over why he's asking.

Then there are those with eating disorders. I'm not even going to touch the whys and where-fores around that one. So, don't listen to anyone *out there*. Listen to me: Have sex, stretch, take a brisk walk every day, and add dancing, hiking, or swimming now and then. This will keep you healthy and happy. The number one rule, however, is: Real girls eat real food.

The Shartopian Eating Plan

Sweeten foods with honey, maple syrup, or sugar if you have to—unless you're diabetic—but under no circumstances consume fake sweeteners.

Eat real butter unless you're a vegan. Don't eat "I wish you were…" (anything fake).

Don't eat all that fat-free stuff unless you know what every ingredient on the box is. Fat-free food is either all sugar or really strange stuff that isn't even food. Contrary to most fad-diet philosophies, calories are what put on weight, whether those calories are from sugar or fat.

Don't eat flesh (meat) unless you killed it yourself and know where it was before you killed it and thanked it for dying for you and were solemn about the moment. Flesh rots inside you and has no real nutritional purpose. Have you ever seen day-old roadkill? That's happening to the flesh inside your 98-degree body instead of on the 98-degree pavement. If you quit eating meat for a year, your brain will become deprogrammed, and it will all smell like a rotting slaughterhouse and you won't want it. That's right: A sirloin steak will smell like liver. It's wild but true. If you must eat flesh, try to get meat from animals that were raised free-range before being killed.

Eat carrots, broccoli, and a banana every day.

Consume whole-grain products, including rice, pasta, and cereal. Complement them with legumes to create complex proteins.

Avoid processed foods and refined sugars whenever possible.

Drink water all the time. Carry it around with you the way people used to carry around cigarettes. Make your coworkers and friends wonder what you'd look like without a glass of water in your hand. Caffeine robs your body of water, so if you have coffee in the morning, compensate by drinking extra water throughout the day.

Sometime in the morning do some brisk walking or exercise, even if it's only for 12 minutes (the minimum time to get the heart pumping at an aerobic level). This will get your metabolism going, increase your circulation, and boost your energy level.

Always stop eating the second your stomach feels full.

Have tea and two cookies at 3 P.M.

Always keep a big glass of water and carrot sticks around 'cuz that tea will make you thirsty and hungry in a little while.

Don't make dinner early. Eat veggies (you can have them with dip if you want—pick a healthy dip), drink water, and play loud music and do something. Exercise is ideal, but just picking up around the house is good too.

Go ahead and have dinner late—just don't eat a gigantic amount. Time differs depending on when you get up.

Sit for a while, then have tea and a cookie after dinner.

In the day or at night (if it's safe), walk everywhere possible. Be snobby about cars. Look at them and think about how filthy they are and how beautiful and pristine your lungs and skin are. Say things such as, "People pay hundreds of dollars to drive to a gym to work out when they could be walking or riding a bicycle around this lovely town/city/neighborhood." (For the record, I absolutely *love* cars and was raised bouncing around the seats of Cadillacs and Corvettes, but it never hurts to scoff at cars if you're trying to walk more because, after all, there's so much you can be snobby about regarding cars.)

Taste as many things as possible on your plate and your neighbor's. Don't eat just one thing until you're full.

Don't spend money on soda pop to drink at home. If you have PMS, go to a convenience mart and buy a big drink with ice and a straw—and a candy bar of your choice—and tell anyone who questions you that they can fuck off 'cuz you drink lots of water. After you've finished your soda, drink a bottle of water.

If you're not having active sex (I don't just mean with a partner; single sex *is* sex. But if masturbation for you is lying on your back vibrating off that counts as "not active"), then exercise as though it were sex. Moan and talk to yourself or your equipment like it's your lover. Say "Oh, yeah" a lot; aggressively attack your exercise like it's your lover. Really move and sweat. Go dancing once a week for two hours, stopping only to take drinks of water. Dance even to the bad songs. Now *that's* challenging exercise.

Whether your sex partner is yourself or someone else, add more positions and have sex longer on purpose.

Stretching is important. Say "I love you" in a singsong voice to yourself while you do it. This undoubtedly seems mushy to some of you, but just try it a few times. It can change your heart rate and make you more present in your body.

To Gain Curves: Are you just a slinky thing and want to gain weight? Maybe you have had health problems, leaving you without much meat on your bones. First of all, *see a doctor* to investigate any unexplained weight loss or inability to gain weight. The following plan is loaded with calories that come from *fat*. So if you have heart disease or any reason to worry over cholesterol, this program is not for you. If you know what's up and are ready to add a little flesh, try the following (obviously, avoid foods you are allergic to):

Pick three of the suggestions below and add them to your diet immediately!

Put butter in or on everything.

Substitute real whipping cream, heavy cream, or evaporated milk for regular milk when possible. Add cream to anything that could possibly host it: strawberries, tea, potatoes, etc.

Always have whipped cream or ice cream with cake or pie.

Eat tons of bread. Wheat products have lots of calories compared to rice, for example, so have toast alongside any meal. Eat cinnamon toast or toast with peanut butter and honey for snacks.

Enjoy a good-size piece of real cheesecake with cherry-pie filling on top as often as you can.

Slap a thick slice of cheese onto anything that'll have it.

Eat lasagna.

Eat lots of salt to stimulate your thirst, then drink beer.

Pour gravy on everything. Have it over bread with breakfast, dip French fries into it, pour it over baked potatoes, dip green beans into it, pour it over pasta and mushrooms as a stroganoff sauce. The possibilities are endless.

Prepare your veggies healthily (e.g., steam them), then at the last minute sauté them for just a minute in olive oil or butter.

If you have a superfast metabolism, chances are that adding a bunch of sugar won't help you because your body will just burn those calories right up. Instead, focus on heavy foods that slow you down: pasta with cream sauce, lasagna, big burritos, etc.

Make smoothies with lots of milk and fruit, and add protein powder.

If you eat fish, then eat fish.

Smother hollandaise sauce on your broccoli, fish, eggs, or anything you're eating.

Eat an egg with every meal. They can be added to sauces, deviled eggs make a fine between-meal snack, and a hard-boiled egg can go into your salad.

Eat lots of Miracle Whip or mayonnaise. For sandwiches, slather each piece of bread, then add mustard or pesto on top of the MW. Use MW. in dips, mashed potatoes, and biscuits. Dip french fries into MW.

Do be careful not to eat too many foods with high cholesterol content, and stay on this plan only until you've reached your ideal weight.

To Lose Curves: It seems only fair that if I include a section on gaining curves, I should make suggestions for losing them. The previous section is largely motivated by the fact that, due to illness, I and too many of my friends have found ourselves too skinny at times. If your doctor has checked you out and found no other health problems, then it's safe for me to make weight-gaining suggestions. By contrast, if you're unhealthily overweight, it's too unsafe for me to make diet suggestions. I do have one suggestion, though: Do not follow diet books. Those are for healthy people who wish to lose weight for cosmetic reasons. If you're unhealthily overweight, you must seek medical help.

"SHAR! SHAR! IT'S FOR COS-METIC REASONS. I ADMIT IT!"

OK, OK, stop begging. I do have a few tidbits for shedding an inch or two to get into an old dress. I promise the weight will come back. This is for fun and a short time only.

Do not eat *extra* salt. Eat only one pickle a day (as opposed to three).

Drink nothing but water or iced caffeine-free tea with no sugar. (Iced green tea works great as a short-term diet aid.) Do not drink diet sodas. No hot tea, either, because hot liquids stimulate your digestion, which could make you hungry.

Do not consume a lot of coffee. Caffeine may suppress your appetite for a bit, but in general it stimulates your appetite.

Eat carrots or other fruits and vegetables throughout the day. Eating, and doing aerobic exercise (for at least 12 minutes), will raise your metabolism, so eating is the thing to do. Your body has to work hard to digest, and this work will boost your metabolism by leaps and bounds, as long as you stick to veggies and fruits or other healthy snacks.

Fattening Gravy

Decide what fat you're going to use. It can be animal fat (if you must have it, use drippings from a cooked chicken), butter, olive oil, or vegetable oil. Heat your fat in a skillet. Stir in flour, salt, and pepper until a paste is formed. Slowly add a liquid. Milk is best for fattening gravy. Water or vegetable broth is OK if you don't want milk. Keep stirring over medium heat. The gravy will thicken as it heats. Add more liquid if necessary. The key to lumpless gravy is to *not* add flour to the gravy after you've already added your liquid. If you calculated incorrectly and your gravy is not getting thicker, you can do one of two things: 1) Dissolve some cornstarch (about one tablespoon into a half-cup of warm water) then add that. Cornstarch thickens any broth quickly; 2) You can add flour. To do this, reduce the heat under your gravy. Dissolve some flour into warm water. Make sure you have no lumps, then add this mixture *very slowly* to your gravy, gradually turning up your heat again. Even if the flour and water wasn't lumpy in the cup, it may lump in your gravy, so adding it slowly is imperative. If it lumps, maybe you'll get away with just a few instead of riddling the whole batch with them.

Do not starve yourself. Whenever you feel hungry, eat. But be sure to choose something sensible.

Do not eat meat.

Do not eat dairy products.

Do not drink alcoholic beverages. At all.

Eat whatever you want for breakfast and lunch as long as it follows the above guidelines, but eat only soup for dinner with a few low-calorie corn chips or rice chips on the side. If you do this for a few days, you'll lose a pound or two. You'll also look less bloated and your complexion will improve. Don't follow this plan for more than a week.

How to Have a Killer Ass: Avoiding LBS (Long-Butt Syndrome), Pimples, and More

You gotta work your assets.

What is a killer ass? Some like 'em round and wide. Some like high bubble butts. Some like tight muscle butts. It all depends on who you ask. That alone is my point. Personally, I like the supple butt. An ample posterior with a little jiggle thrown in, that's my favorite. We say, "Pull up to the bumper, baby," not "Pull up to the brick wall." Bumpers have give. As much as I chase after the round behind, I know plenty of folks who chase those little bony butts. And for those gymnasts reading this, if I were you, I'd say, "Pull up to the steel" at that opportune moment because it sounds so fierce and provocative.

The basics of achieving and maintaining a killer ass are simple: Take the hills. Wear high heels. Fuck. A lot. (Don't necessarily do them all at once. Umm, maybe two at a time....) San Francisco isn't called the "City of Fine Asses" for nothing. We've got all these hills to climb and all that fucking going on.

Straining, fighting, and worrying over getting a killer ass is not the way to a killer ass. Workout videos won't do it either. Butts are not supposed to be rocks. When you go on a picnic, do you sit on a pile of rocks or a nice bed of grass? Honey, asses are made for sittin' on, so it's nice if they're soft as can be. Softness on top of a firm foundation. Personally, I hate striving for anything physical. The only way I'd get tennis elbow is from talking on the phone. So, if that's your thing, by all means do the *Buns of Steel* workout. As for the rest of us, just try to do things in a more natural fashion instead of using modern conveniences. Examples: Walk through the airport, use the stairs wherever you go, walk where you can instead of driving. When you go to the mall, don't fight other drivers over the close parking spaces. Pull up to the far end of the lot and spend your time walking instead of circling.

> ## "Freud asked, 'What do women want?' Women want to dance!"
> —Bette Midler, in an interview with Charlie Rose, where she revealed that her funnest time performing was as a go-go dancer

If you want to take an exercise class, I'd recommend a fun dance class instead of a workout one. Dancing keeps the ass fit and the heart light. If ballet interests you, you're in luck because it works the butt the most. All dancing is fine-assing. Pick a dance that you love or have always wanted to try. Are you shy? Then do *Dancercise* videos at home. Some of us are too embarrassed to dance and sing even alone at home! That's crazy. Do it, girl. Don't get so hung up that you don't even dance with yourself. That's one of the pure joys of life.

SHAR BUTT EXERCISE NUMBER 1: Stand up and maintain a straight posture. Hold phone with right hand. Flex butt muscles, then relax. Flex, relax. Repeat 50 times. Hold phone in left hand. Repeat butt flex and relax another 50 times.

SHAR BUTT EXERCISE NUMBER 2: (This is also great for balance and grace.) Put your stocking and high heel on right leg while standing up. Repeat on left side.

SHAR ULTIMA-BUNS BUTT EXERCISE 3: Sex. Yes, sex gets you into interesting positions, thus working different sets of muscles. Sitting on a face strengthens those thighs, lying down coming into a mouth tightens up the tummy and inner, lower butt. Still, nothing like nothing works that ass more than fucking, whether you're on the receiving end or the giving end. Strapping on a dildo and working those hips as you pleasure your lover will keep your butt high and tight. One night of this and you'll definitely feel the workout the next day. Receiving a dyke dick while you're on your back or standing works your outer thighs and cheeks, keeping your ass from leaving its domain. Receiving on all fours actively, meaning really moving back and forth, works the entire area. These positions just cover the basics. What about wearing a strap-on, having a babe in front of you while you have one knee down and one knee up? That's a more strenuous workout for each leg. Of course, you'll have to switch legs for an even workout.

Pimples on the Butt—Yick!

The most fabulicious butt in the Milky Way won't look great if it's covered with zits. OK, I know it's gross to acknowledge it, but as a video producer and gal about town, I know asses, and quite a few asses sport a blemish or ten. Your ass *can* be zit free. First of all, treat your butt as you do your face. Wash it twice daily. Yes, twice daily with a gentle cleanser. Just hike your heinie over the edge of the bathtub or sink and do a quick wash. Pat dry, you're done. Secondly, wear underwear or wash your pants before wearing them again. Would you rub your face up against some oily cloth all day, then put that same cloth on your face the next day? That's what happens when you wear the same boxers, jammies, jeans, etc., without cleaning them. If you have them really bad, read my section on bad skin in the following section. Finally, put zit cream on the pimples on your butt. Get in the habit of feeling your butt everyday, and if you feel a pimple coming on, zap it right away. But don't try to squeeze them, as this may cause scarring. And don't put oily lotions on your ass. My ass is as soft as a duck's, and I smooth my lotion on my thighs and lower back but leave my ass lotion free.

❀   ❀   ❀

Remember, your body is *your* temple, and, above all, if you feel good, you'll look good, to yourself and others. Your confidence in yourself, and your body, will shine through to others whether you're a size 16 or a 0; whether your butt is a big as a house or merely a breadbox. Although I'm the last one to espouse the slow-and-steady route, when it comes to your body, moderation is crucial to your well-being and self-esteem. Queens come in all sizes, but it's the size of your mind and heart that truly count.

The Naked Surface: Skin and Nails

Sinsuous Skin

My friend Leah (the world's sexiest woman at the cultured age of 21) taught me a lot about vamping, girls, and leopard prints (way before they were in fashion). We'd take showers back to back, and as we dried off she'd say, "Sharlene, do you know what all of my dates say to me? Leah, you are *so-o-o* soft."

She delivered her wisdom like a magical incantation that only she had ever heard. "Always put on lotion right after the shower, Sharlene. It makes you very soft." I slathered on lotion from that moment forward, right after showering, just as she'd instructed. Of course, after I'd traveled around the block a few more times, I found out that many women hear sweet whisperings about how soft they are, not just Leah. Still, maybe I do hear "You are *so-o-o* soft" a little more often because of her sage advice.

There's no big secret to being extra soft. Just use lotion often. Gob lotion on and rub it in all the way. If you don't, it will dry on top of your skin, making it feel crusty and dry. Add a touch of oil to your elbows, heels, and knees. Olive oil or massage oil is perfect.

Don't wait until your skin is feeling dry to moisturize, or you'll be heading down a one-way road to Desert City. Once skin gets all reptilian with flakes and scales, it becomes difficult to bring it on back to supple and yummy, so moisturize every day.

Lightly stroke baby oil over your pubic area. It conditions your hair, keeping it its silkiest. (Even if you have coarse hair, this will give you your highest rating).

After nighttime showers, rub lotion into your feet, then oil them around the rough spots and your toes. Sleep in loose, soft socks.

Don't put alpha hydroxy creams on your eyelids, or they'll puff up like blowfish.

The Shartopian Extra-Softening Ritual

Heat your bathing room so that you're hot, almost to the point of sweating. We want open pores! Hopefully, you have a tub. If not, try to use a friend's or put lots of towels on the floor (you'll need to lie on them at one point).

Play relaxing music. Stand nude in the tub, pour a little lavender massage oil (not pure lavender oil, which is too strong) into your hands, then slowly massage into your shoulders and neck. Put the oil on your fingertips and massage it into your scalp at the center point of your hairline (a straight line from your nose) and on the crown. Massage your neck and ears. Then rub oil into your pulse points, slowly, one at a time. Be in the moment. Feel your skin, really feel the curves, bumps, veins, muscles, the nuances of you. Don't think about your day. Just feel you. Finally, massage your hands. Firmly rub oil around each fingernail, massaging along each muscle and bone. If you have that much time on your hands everyday, great. I don't, so I use the lavender massage as a part of my softening bath ritual, which I indulge in only once or twice a month.

Shower for a few minutes or soak in the tub for a while, until your skin softens. Get out of the water, and with big handfuls of sea salt or Epsom salt, rub your skin vigorously. Rub everywhere, but pay extra attention to any rough spots you happen upon.

Rinse off all the salt and wash with a gentle body soap as you drain the tub. Partially dry off, then lotion your entire body. If you can afford it, I highly recommend Zia Natural Skincare's all-over body lotion, available by calling (800) 334-7546 or logging on to www.ziacosmetics.com. If you can't afford Zia right now, I recommend Suave Vitamin E lotion.

Special Treatments

The best home facial I've found is Zia's Papaya Enzyme Peel. If you have sensitive skin like I don't use gritty washes (those made with ground nuts such as almonds, for example). They'll scratch your skin right off and irritate it. The Papaya Enzyme Peel won't irritate your skin and won't scratch it *at all,* yet removes all those nasty dead skin cells, revealing the beautiful skin underneath. You know how you'll do a mask and get all into it—woo-hoo, I'm doing a facial, playin' music 'n' all—rinse it off, then look into the mirror. Crash. You and your skin may *feel* better, but it doesn't *look* like it's changed one bit. Zia's Papaya Enzyme Peel has acquired so many fans because after you do it you look in the mirror and are staring at new skin. It's fabulous.

If you're a peel nut, you can go for it even more with their Citrus Nighttime Reversal cream. This stuff reverses free-radical damage, rejuvenates, and tightens. It's a miracle. I wholeheartedly recommend Zia products. They're all-natural and not tested on animals. (Oh, by the way, they didn't pay me for this endorsement. Try their products and you'll be an instant fan too.)

Abused Stripper Feet

Oh, my. Do your sexy pups really take a thrashing as you work your butt off putting caviar on the table? Have corns and calluses made permanent residence on your footies? No matter what the cause of your ped ailments is, can you say, "I'm not a stripper, but my feet play one on TV"?

Suffer no more. Do foot soaks, salt rubs, lotion slathers, then massage Bag Balm into your feet and cover them with socks. Bag Balm is just that, a balm for cow teats. Bag Balm relieves pain, draws moisture to the problem areas, then locks it in. I promise you will have baby-soft feet soon. It's available at most drugstores or at www.bagbalm.com. Remember, though, there's a fine line between pleasure and pain. Calluses or corns that honk so big they shove into your bone cause pain and permanent damage. Yet those *average* calluses are the reason you can stomp in stilettos like nobody's business. You don't have soft spots to weaken your stride. You don't want them to say good-bye completely. You just want those unsightly things to hide behind the curtains when company comes. In other words, not to be so repulsive they scare away an eager tongue.

Pedicures are a cheap treat that many of us can afford, usually costing $10 to $15. Talk about feeling like a Queen—just sit in that chair and tell me you don't. Pedicured feet make any gal fancy.

Working girls who need a royal pampering treatment at home: Put a loved one on her knees before you and have her apply a mint mask on your feet. Yes, your feet. It cools and soothes them. After eight hours of torture your tootsies deserve it.

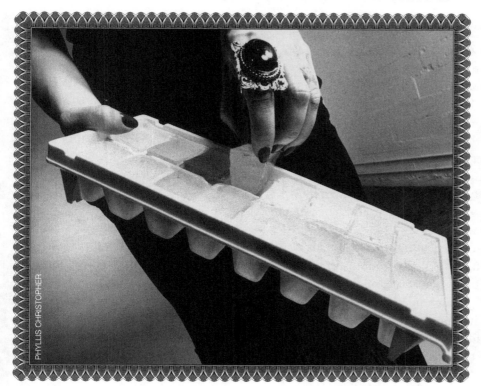

PHYLLIS CHRISTOPHER

Not just handy, sexy to boot! Long finger-nails can melt a lot more than ice.

The Queen's Claws: The Femme Fingernail

My fingernails and toenails have had their own fan club for years. My first fan was my cousin Yana. But since she's older than me, acting mostly like a big sister, and since I was her fan in every other way, for years she kept her nail worship closeted. To aid her own distressing nails, she resentfully tried to eat more onions, which our Grandma had told her would make her nails stronger. I happily report she now has beautiful nails—acrylic and beautiful.

But Jill A. was my first real fingernail-fan-club president. She declared so my sophomore year of high school. She bit her nails just awfully, down to bloody scraps of skin. When we became friends she admired my nails so much that she vowed (I signed on as witness) that she would have nails like mine. And she succeeded. Now she has wickedly long nails that are hard and gorgeous.

Your Own Fingernail Fan Club

"How can you do anything with those nails?" Folks have actually asked me that. Can you imagine? It's funny how some people wonder this and a number of others wonder the opposite. What can you do with nails?! You can clean your ears and scratch them really deep inside (ooh) without cotton swabs. You can open CDs, battery-operated vibrators, and soda-pop cans, *and* you can neatly scratch smoogie off the table, TV, glasses, etc. You can remove all those perforated, plastic safety coverings from water-bottle lids, salsa, etc. You most certainly can type. It would probably be difficult to type on an old-fashioned typewriter with long nails because you have to pound the keys, literally. Luckily, I never use an old typewriter.

Nothing but nothing points to jewelry in the case better than a well-manicured long nail. Tap, tap, tap. "I want to see that one."

One of the most fun things to do with long nails is to give tickies: Trail your nails lightly down a lover's or friend's skin, raising goose bumps until they scream. You can also give excellent back scratches—long strokes down her back or short, hard, back-and-forth scruffy scratches.

Second only to back scratching, the most coveted reason to have nails: You can carefully select just one ice cube from its home without disturbing its neighbors.

I recently cut my nails very short. You know, as an experiment. Brother, was that ever awkward. Without some kind of bumper, my hands kept running into things…like my *eyebrows*. I'm accustomed to being able to do a flick flick here and teensy scrape there. You can be so specific with long nails. I'd try to delicately flick off an eyelash and the stub of my finger would clumsily ram into my face. *Not* OK. Not to mention, I couldn't do any of the things listed above.

Of course, many women lament not being able to have long nails because they're in professions such as massage, graphics, or baking, or perhaps they feel oppressed because they don't want long nails and feel society is judging them for not being "feminine." To you I say, appreciate beautiful nails on other women. You can take a gander at them all you want. Not only that, but ask for nail assistance. We'll most likely share our nails whether it's back scratches or soda-can opening. Love your nails and the reasons you have chosen the nails you have. Personally, I love a good massage and a freshly baked loaf of bread.

Healthy nails begin on the inside. Taking care of our insides is the number 1 influence on our outsides. As with skin and hair, nails reflect our diet and sleeping habits. But let me tell you here what those articles in women's magazines won't: Healthy nails *are* created partly from what we eat, but also from how we absorb and utilize vitamins. Taking Vitamin E, calcium supplements, or flax seed oil daily can improve the texture and strength of your nails, but individual results will differ. Eat right, but if your nails don't respond, don't beat yourself up. For some reason your body may not take good nutrients and make good nails out of them. I could eat (and have) ramen noodles for weeks and my body will find that tiny bit of calcium and put it right into my nails and hair. Of course, I faint from hunger, hitting the floor and breaking the nails. Nevertheless, my nails and hair both grow off the charts. Um, 'scuse me, Miss-Diet-Rite-and-a-candy-bar, I didn't say you could eat carrot sticks for one day and expect change. Weeks, months, or years of good nutrition can improve your nails, but they might never be perfect. You may need some external help.

Nail Care Tips

Always wash your hands and dry them with a clean towel before doing manicures or any work on your hands or nails. Infections to the cuticle can pop up lickety split just from old lotion, dirty orange sticks, etc. That said, use lotion on your hands and feet often. Every now and then take time to rub it into your cuticles vigorously. Then, using your own nails, push your cuticles back. You can use an orange stick if you please, but your nails will do the job. Do the same for your toenails. In addition, vigorously scrub them with a quality nail brush in the bath or shower.

On doing-your-nails-day, before you remove your old polish, massage petroleum jelly into the skin around your nails. This will protect your skin and cuticles from the drying agents in the remover.

To grow your own nails, you will need the following supplies: fiber strengthener, smoother, color, top coat (optional), orange stick, polish remover, cotton swabs. Buy one of those two-part nail kits with the fiber for step one, then the smoother for step two. Follow the instructions and use a coat of both. Let the first coat of fiber dry at least ten minutes before applying the smoother, then let nails dry at least 20 minutes (even if they feel dry).

Apply color. Spoil yourself with a few expensive brands, but remember that no nail polish sticks like the cheap brands do, so have plenty of those around. Let nails dry for at least 20 minutes between coats. Remember that nails take six full hours to dry completely, so no doing laundry, scrubbing floors, and, to avoid those hideous sheet-prints, no sleeping. Polishes that claim to dry nails in 90 seconds don't. At first they seem to do the job. When you do that gentle brush against the nail to see if it's dry, they feel dry. But they get smudged, just like any other nail polish, the second you try to do *anything.*

Load up one side of the brush with polish and wipe the other side clean. Put the brush about two millimeters from the base of your nail, then push it back to the cuticle. From there stroke the length of the nail.

Paint the nails of one hand. If you accidentally get polish on the skin by the nail, scrape it off with a nail from your other hand. If you have totally short nails—thus none to scrape up mistakes—use an orange stick to do the job. Let those nails dry for about ten minutes, then paint the other hand, and now you have a dry-enough nail to dig in there and do the rescue. Also, it's wise to stagger your hands so that you have a free hand to answer the phone, write a note, or dig through your nail polish box.

Acrylic Nails

I highly recommend trying to grow your own nails at least once. But don't be embarrassed about buying acrylic nails if growing bio ones doesn't work out. But *please* take care of them and don't let fungus grow under them. Acrylic nails are best when applied and filled by a manicurist, so hopefully you can afford that. If not, try to convince a nail-savvy friend into helping you with an at-home kit. When folks say, "Are those your nails?" reply, "Yes," wholeheartedly, thinking, *Of course they're mine. I paid for them!* When folks say, "Are your nails real?" reply sarcastically, "No, they're virtual." Or "No, they're a figment of your imagination." Or sincerely reply, "Yes."

Other Tricks for Bio Nails

My mom turned me onto hoof polish. Yes, hoof polish. It's used to shine hooves on four-legged animals and can be found in many beauty supply stores. It makes your nails rock-hard and does not chip or peel. Matter of fact, it barely comes off with remover. If you're going to the GLBT&Q Film Fest Opening ("&Q" means "and questioning." Isn't that cute?), and want to make sure your nails make it through the evening, this is the stuff for you. The only setback is that it dries your nails out, so I recommend using it every now and then, not every day.

Supplements: I highly recommend the supplements sold at health food stores to help you grow strong nails. They don't always help your nails, but there's excellent stuff in them.Conversely, one product that's very helpful isn't even marketed toward nail growing: My mom takes glucosamine for arthritis and says she's not certain if it's helping her joints, but her nails sure are growing.

Drying your nails: Use a blow dryer on your nails between coats to speed up drying time. Use the cool or warm setting.

Glitter or confetti polish: This has become popular over the past few years, and I wonder if it will ever go completely out of fashion or just keep hovering like miniskirts. Glitter looks great and makes your nails hard while it's on. If your job duties keep chipping your nails, try glitter polish for reinforcement.

Removing glitter polish, however, can weaken your nails. Rubbing your nails with a cotton ball and remover can push the glitter into your nails and scrape them, making them weaker. The remover cannot permeate the glitter flakes, so the polish underneath stays dry and still adheres to your nails. Applying layers of nonglitter polish under the glitter helps a little, but not much. Just be gentle, go slow, and saturate your nails with remover for a few seconds before swiping with a cotton ball.

Winter and nails: My nails inevitably break with the first cold weather they encounter. Luckily, I now live in California, so the bitter cold night is rare. I learned, however, to *always* cover my nails with gloves before exiting a warm home. Not only do your nails become more brittle in the winter due to the dry air, but going from warm to freezing sets them up for a severe break, then the slightest touch delivers it. I promise you that the one time you don't wear gloves will be the time your nail breaks, and winter breaks are harsh: low, below the quick, bloody.

The Femme Fingernail

So you know how to grow your nails. Now you have to decide how you want them done. Do you want to do the traditional, still-so-practical, one long-nailed hand revealing your wicked diva nature and one short-nailed hand showing you care for your lover's needs? This is a quick way to easily distinguish the femmes from the straight girls. After a while people will notice this odd habit about you. It's a subtle yet powerful way to come out at a workplace.

Perhaps you'll choose to have all long nails, except the pointer and middle fingers of both hands.

Maybe you'll decide to keep them all long. You're a witch. Period. No apologies.

How to Fuck With Fingernails

First of all, you can do as I've suggested. Cut all of the nails of one hand so that there is no ledge, meaning no nail at all comes past your skin. When you're pressing or pounding into vaginal walls with your fingertips, even a millimeter-long nail can hurt. Of course, many of us think that if you have someone really writhing in ecstasy, she won't notice a nail or two. Cover your nails with latex gloves. "Active-length" nails will be just fine when covered with latex. Gloves help long nails, but you also have to work on your technique. If you have long nails, follow these exercises.

Finger-Fucking to the Oldies: The Workout

Step One: Stretch. All good workouts begin with stretching. Pull the tips of your fingers back with your other hand to stretch out your hand muscles. Bend those fingers backward.

Step Two: Warm up. Practice touching by using the pads of your fingers instead of your fingertips. You can practice on push-button telephones. Or you can push the pads down on a flat surface such as your desk. Practice that until you can go up and down on the table quickly without a nail clicking that surface.

Step Three: Form. When you've got Step Two down, practice fucking the palm of your hand. Make a fist with one hand. Your folded thumb is her perineum, your first knuckle her clit. Right under your third knuckle is her G-spot. Practice putting your finger in so that you don't feel your nail at all. Try going in and out.

Step Four: Rotating your sets. Try pushing the "G-spot" and work up a rhythm. Real sex isn't as calm, so move your fist around, go fast, go slow. Try different maneuvers.

Step Five: Pushing your limits. The next time you have a pussy in front of you begging for a finger, try out these new techniques. Wear a glove, use lots of lube, and go in slow. Once in, use the pads of your fingers to stroke her G-spot. If you don't go too deep, you may be able to go in and out while building up to a good rhythm.

Hair, There, and Everywhere

Throughout the ages hair has reflected status, power, and beauty. Oh, poor Samson, if only he had been a dyke instead of a John, I'm sure that harlot Delilah wouldn't have betrayed him. Figuring out what to *do* with your hair can be one of the most painful experiences in a woman's life. Cut it, shave it, laser it, bleach it, curl it, straighten it??? It's enough to make you throw yourself onto pair of ten-inch scissors screaming, "End the torture now!"

From razor burn to bikini bumps, bleach blisters to mustache-removal mishaps, there is always *something* going on with our hair. Not just the tresses but hair everywhere. You know, down there. Now that I sound like Dr. Seuss, why don't you lay down the scissors, grab a martini, and take some notes.

To Shave or Not to Shave? There's Absolutely No Question About It

After much debate, the word is in: Femmes shave…something. Yes, *something*. Some don't shave below the knees, above the knees, under the arms, around the nipple, chin, bikini line, pussy, butt hole, but it seems that part of the femme aesthetic is to have your own ritual around shaving. I rarely shave my legs but always shave under my arms. I do shave my legs for my birthday. I know several femmes who wouldn't stick a razor under their arms if you paid them, yet meticulously shape their love triangle, often into any shape *but* a triangle! So, my conclusion is: Pick something to shave, then shave it.

Shaving Without the Bumps

The whole point of shaving is to have smooth, beautiful skin. But then you shave, and suddenly your legs look like the chigger family reunion. If you read women's magazines, you know that shaving without getting bumps seems to be a great mystery of the universe. Well, now it's solved.

First you'll want to soften your hair. Baths are good, or plan to shower for a few minutes before you shave. Then you'll want whatever you're using as shaving lotion to soak for two to three minutes. For shaving, I use hair conditioner or Zia facial cleanser. Have you ever read the ingredient list on a can of shaving cream? Hello! And we wonder how ten-year-olds can make bombs at home.

Next, pull out a pile of razors. Your goal is to get the most hairs by using the least amount of strokes. Most women I know (for years myself included) do one good stroke and then a few more surrounding strokes before rinsing the razor. WRONG. NO big stroke, little stroke, little stroke, little stroke, rinse. NO, NO, NO. Do *one* good, effective stroke, then *rinse*. Big stroke, rinse. Big stroke, rinse. Your goal is to minimize the scraping of your skin to only what's necessary to get the hair. Use plenty of conditioner or whatever lotion you're using.

Regarding those bikini-line bumps: Well, the only thing that keeps those bumps away is to not wear any panties or thongs with aggravating elastic. Wear boxers or no undies at all, and you'll see an amazing reduction in bumps. And, if you keep shaving, perhaps every other day, you'll also reduce bump potential. I've read magazines that recommend scrubbing bumps with a loofah to "keep your pores open so you won't get ingrown hairs." This is a fast way to get an infected pore! If you do get an ingrown hair, you may choose to help release it by gently coaxing out the tip with a sanitized needle and lots of hydrogen peroxide then plucking it with tweezers. Never vigorously rub an inflamed pore on any part of your body. That's just asking for trouble. You may, however, wash the bikini area with a washcloth, which provides plenty of dead-cell sloughing.

Do not use skin lotion right after you shave. Splash lots of cool water on your skin to soothe it, then wait a while before applying anything. If possible, sit on the edge of a tub and apply cool, *clean* washcloths to the shaven skin.

For women with coarse or extra-curly hair: Apply a delicate, clean astringent to the area with cotton balls. (I say "clean astringent" because if you're a double dipper, you're playing with bacteria.) Do this everyday at least once. Using a mild astringent (one with a small percentage of alcohol, glycerin and water) keeps your pores tight, which helps you hair grow straighter. Hair curling into your skin irritates the area and creates ingrown hairs. By using an astringent, you can prevent this from happening.

Some people swear by waxing. I have to say that waxing has many pluses, but being bump-free isn't one of them. In fact, many people get tiny pimples from waxing, usually because the wax isn't brand new and carries bacteria that enters the pores, or the heat of the wax stimulates the oil gland.

Maintain your smoothness by shaving daily. Women with coarser hair should shave with olive oil. Women with thinner hair should use conditioner.

Permanent Hair Removal

Hair removal research today is more advanced than a sci-fi rocket ride straight to Venus. Today's women, men, and men-becoming-women have it better than ever. Everyday we see advances in laser technology. Electrolysis, with all its pain and time consumption, used to be the only long-term choice. Not anymore. Now a shiny new alternative appears in the war against unwanted hair: laser hair removal. Over the past two years, more than ten different laser systems have become available to remove unwanted body hair. Most of them work on the principle of heating the pigment in the hair follicle to a high enough temperature to kill the part that tells the hair to grow. Miraculously, the laser heat goes only to the pigment in the follicle, leaving the surrounding skin unaffected. Clinical studies on this laser estimate about 20% permanent removal with each treatment, making multiple treatments necessary for completely hair-free skin. But that means only three or four laser treatments versus the 100 or more electrolysis treatments required to permanently remove hair from large body areas. If you want permanent hair removal, get on the Web and find out the latest in laser removal. The procedures are advancing even as I write this. Since they do not have the history that electrolysis does, I recommend talking to people who've done the procedure you are interested in and researching the possibilities thoroughly.

Get several hard-core references for any clinics you may choose to go to. They're poppin' up like oil changers, so make certain you pick a reputable one.

Eyebrows

To tweeze brows, wash the area, then swipe it with hydrogen peroxide. Apply Extra-Strength Orajel on the part of the eyebrow you want to tweeze. (Apply the Orajel to a cotton swab from the tip of the container to prevent contamination). Warning: *Do not* get Orajel anywhere near your actual eyeball. Leave it on for five minutes or so. Wipe off the excess Orajel, then tweeze. Using cotton balls and hydrogen peroxide, wipe eyebrows after tweezing. Dampen the cotton balls in cool water, then apply to eyebrow to reduce swelling.

I recommend professionals for eyebrow waxing. They do it fast.

> **"The higher the hair, the closer to God."**
> —Old Nashville saying

Hairdos and Don'ts

If you've been around for even a millisecond you know that dykes do our hair a million ways. Unfortunately, we're known for that awful bi-level 'do that my angel friend/late hairdresser, Gerry Glasgow, used to call the UDC: Universal Dyke Cut. It does universally say "dyke," but it doesn't universally say "femme."

The ways to wear your hair are endless. As a former preschool teacher, I simply hate to say, "Don't do this," being taught to focus on the positive and all. But hair, oh girl, hair. We have really got to lay down the law about a few things. For example, banana clips. You're a woman, not a pretty pony. Banana clips shoulda never been a trend in the first place, but let me tell those of you who think they *still are*—honey, put those things in the kitchen drawer and use 'em for a chip clip. They do not belong in your hair!

Go for variety: Change your hairstyle at least once a decade. OK, if you have curly hair that you wear naturally, you are

SHLONG: ShLawng, noun: derivative of short-long. A hairstyle that is short at the front and sides of head and long in back, particularly popular among a certain sect of lesbians and redneck guys. Also: *bi-level, UDC, mullet-head, sho-lo, Camaro cut, mud flap, neck warmer, butt-rocker hair, hockey hair, SFLB (short front, long back)*. Go to www.mulletsgalore.com to see what *not* to do.

Gag me with a roller! (That's how I feel after being in the chair for hours.)

PHYLIS CHRISTOPHER

exempt. Everyone else, please try a little variety. Especially if you latched onto a big, trendy style that *everyone* had, and now, sweetstuff, look around! No one else has it anymore. Going back to the banana clip. I've gone to my hometown to find the prom queen, who was the highest stylin' gal her senior year, ten years later still fluffin' her hair up like a poodle. (For the record, Kim, I am not talking about you; this prom queen wasn't in our class.) What is that? Don't go blaming small towns or country music. All you gotta do is turn on the television and open your eyes. Reba (McIntyre) changes her hair. And you city people do it too. Hello! Jennifer Aniston herself hasn't had the Jennifer cut in years!

Embrace the curl. If you have naturally curly hair, embrace it. Don't fight it. First of all, anyone who doesn't have curly hair *loves* curly hair. All that straightening and ironing gets you nowhere in the long run. People don't look at you and go, "Oh, look at the gal with gleaming straight hair." They think, "Oh, that poor thing. Why won't she just leave her hair alone?" Now, I'm not talking about high-quality relaxers. Hell, I'm a blond: Chemicals 'R' Us. I understand. But if you're just frizzing out your hair, give it up. Go to www.naturallycurly.com and get some support.

Examine the straight road. If you have hair as straight as a toothpick, check out the shape of your face with a friend and your hairdresser. Many women with straight hair try to make their hair big or curly because they think they need more frame around the face. Often it's not true. Many women look elegant, sophisticated, or chic with simple manes draping down so shiny and soft. Straight hair is naturally shiny. Also, speaking of Jennifer's hair, trendy hairstyles often speak to the straight-haired gal. You may need to add some body with product and hot rollers. I don't suggest a lifetime of perms. I know most of us have been down that road and we get stuck with no turnoff. It's hard to grow out perms without wanting to get another one. But try it. Let your face have its beauty. You don't want the frame to overshadow the picture!

Take advantage of technology. If you have a computer, you can buy *Cosmopolitan* magazine's software program that lets you see what you would look like with different hairstyles. There are also places on the Web that can do this for you. You scan in your picture then click on different hairstyles, and the software shows what you'd look like with the latest style. If you don't have a computer, check out your Yellow Pages and find a salon near you that offers this service. The downside to doing it in a salon is that they charge too much for it.

Listen to your friends. They know you inside and out. They know if the outside is not

PHYLLIS CHRISTOPHER

Before: Steph as carnal seductress.

After: Steph as lus-cious, carefree babe. The trans-formation takes mere seconds!

reflecting the beauty that's inside. Just watch Oprah's makeover shows to find out what I'm talking about.

Be every woman: Wear wigs! Do you fret over selecting a permanent color or style? Do you love short hair but fear having no tresses to wildly toss about? Forget making such big decisions—just wear wigs. Be forewarned, though. There are two problems with wigs: They'll empty your Miss Piggy Bank, and they are hot (hot as in "body-temperature rising") as hell. Other than that, they give you ultimate versatility without commitment. What could be better?

When wearing a wig, use a hundred bobby pins to hold it down. You don't want to be constantly fretting about whether your hair's gonna land in the champagne fountain at your next soiree. And you don't want to miss any fun because you're standing stiff as board like you've got an exotic parrot on your head. You see how strippers toss their heads around? Well, they wear wigs and so can you. It's no big secret—just pin that puppy on. If you're bald, use spirit gum to stick it on. Don't slather your whole head! Just apply a border of glue. Remember to buy spirit-gum remover or else you'll come home exhilarated and exhausted from a wicked glam night, wrench off your wig, collapse on your bed, then wake up with a crown of bed lint framing your head. And can you imagine if you're not alone when you wake up? Yikes!

One final warning: Most affordable wigs are made of synthetic fibers, as in plastic. Stay away from anything superhot—hot tubs, candelabras, Sterno cans—or your hair will melt into one big blob.

When you want a big updo or just a new color, there's no easier answer than slipping into a wig.

Find a trustworthy hairdresser. S/he should walk the fine line between listening to you and going with his own expert knowledge. S/he should not completely ignore your wishes and cut whatever s/he feels like. S/he should not give everyone the same hairstyle. S/he should be aware of new trends and suggest ones that would look good on you. S/he should be able to vary dos according to the shape of your face, the level of your commitment to maintenance, the texture of your hair, etc. S/he should encourage you and listen to you and give you brilliant advice about everything. I found Gerry by stopping a complete stranger on the street and asking her who did her hair. That encounter not only gave me the best hairdresser of my life but also a cherished friend. I found my current hairdresser—who is now the best—through a reference as well.

Hair challenges can vary dramatically depending on race, geography, age, and what you drank last night. White women who bleach their hair (ahem, I wonder who that could be) will get a horribly dry scalp from washing their hair too often. The idea of washing your hair every day anyway is bogus hype brought on by watching too many shampoo commercials. Only a generation ago women washed their hair once a week or even less often than that. Now most white women wash their hair every day, and some more than once! If you have fine, unprocessed hair and an oily scalp, then everyday washing will not hurt your hair. If you're anyone else, remember that oils from your skin will condition your hair and keep it healthy. My hairdresser, Tony, and the staff at Bladerunners on Haight Street in San Francisco are well-known for their color expertise. Tony and his partner David are always telling their clients to stop washing! (It's one of my secrets for having 16 inches of healthy, bleached hair.)

Black women, on the other hand, can get overly dry scalp from not washing and conditioning their hair enough. For years black women have heard "Don't wash your hair too often." Yet, experts say you must reach a fine balance. Don't overwash, but don't neglect your hair either. Wash your hair with a gentle shampoo made especially for your hair type. This removes dry scalp and dead skin cells. Then condition your scalp with a high-quality conditioner (especially important in harsh-weather months).

No matter your hair type, do your research and don't settle for a condition you don't like.

For dry scalp or dandruff, try tea tree oil, which can be found at most health food and herbal stores. Massage it into your scalp before your shower. Ideally, apply it a little while before you shower, so it can sit awhile on your scalp. It also makes a wonderful antiseptic.

Want shinier hair? Rinse your hair with cool water at the end of your shower, after you've finished shampooing and conditioning. Many of us hate the thought of cool water in a shower, but try it. Depending on your hair type, you'll see results in as little as two weeks.

❀ ❀ ❀

Because books last forever and Web sites don't, I hesitate to recommend a lot of them. Names change, companies come and go. There is some really cool stuff out there, though. If you need to know anything about hair, you can find it on the Web.

In the end, you can at least sharpen your lingo, even if you can't straighten your hair. Simply rehearse what Gerry used to drill me on:

•Chickens are plucked—eyebrows are *tweezed*.

•Socks are dyed—hair is *colored*.

•Grass is cut—nails are *clipped*.

Making Visible: The Art of Applying Your Face

Getting Ready

Indulge yourself when getting ready. Always take your time grooming before going out with a chickie, but be willing to finish your makeup in the car after you've been dating a while.

The ensemble you wear while getting ready is almost as important as what you wear on a date. I always choose a robe that would tell good stories if it could talk.

I remember looking in awe at my friend Leah's big moon vanity. It was covered with bottles of polish, lipstick, perfume, and cosmetics of every sort, and scarves hung from the mirror, along with beads and jewelry. I wanted a vanity. I wanted "girlness" in a bottle. I wanted my girlness to spill over so much it had to be draped. Now, in California, where I and so many of my friends have altars, I realize this is what Leah had. It wasn't a sloppy catchall of necessity—what a lot women feel about their makeup bin or shelf—but a tribute to Leah's transformative nature, a place of honor and testament to her ability to reveal an alluring and seductive creature. It was a place for anyone looking to pause and marvel at her womanly know-how, at her strengths. I've always found it interesting that, in the first *Batman* TV series, Batgirl's hideway, her place of transformation, lies behind her vanity.

When getting ready for dates, makeup always goes on first because she can see you without your clothes but never without your face, unless, of course, it's been sweated off with good sex, which means she's earned a peek.

I, like many drag queens, love the art of makeup, the theater of transformation, the beauty of the colors. I could sit and smooth on rich colors of eye shadow until the cows come home. You are the canvas; your stroke is an art. As Patti Smith said in Mapplethorpe's "X" exhibit, "Art doesn't reproduce the visible. Rather, it makes visible." Later in this book you will read my assertions that you must advertise on the outside what's on the inside, just as a store creates enticing displays to lure you inside. How you wear your makeup is just one of your advertisements. Are you a natural girl or naturally dramatic? Do you want the world to know you're a Queen today, or do you want to go incognito? Makeup application is one of the pure, pure privileges of being high femme. Your choices are many and can often be overwhelming. The trick is simply to have fun with it.

The gateway to Batgirl's cave was through her vanity.

First Things First

I begin with a white cover-up to hide those party circles. White has been the key to gender transformation for decades now. Traditional drag-queen makeup works for me, so I create white half-moons under my eyes and highlight my cheekbones and temples with a little white while I have the cover-up out. You can use white cover-up for pimples too. Or apply a tinted blemish cream or a tinted cover-up. Never cover a blemish with a dark cover stick.

Foundation gives you just that, a foundation on which to build, hiding flaws and inconsistencies. After white, I apply base. Those liquid powder items so popular right now can cover your whole face or just lightly smooth over small areas. You can also stick with liquid foundation for oily, dry, or combination skin. Finding a color that matches your skin is like finding a taxi in San Francisco. It should be easy, but it's not. You need one that works with your skin type and tone. For years, anybody not in the rosy to beige shades of Caucasian skin was shit outta luck. Nowadays we have more choices. Notice I said "we." No, I'm not "black," and I ain't "white." I'm some weird shade of yellow. MAC was the first makeup to really liberate the yellow gal, but many other makers have caught on. In recent years there's been an incredible revolution in makeup for the rainbow of skin colors that are not Caucasian.

Apply your foundation and—duh—don't stop right at your jawline. Blend it into your neck, ears, and hairline. A trick I learned from a mortician—believe it or not—is to gently brush your hairline to create a natural blend of makeup into the hairline.

Cheeks

Use blush sparingly to bring out your cheekbones and brighten your eyes. Remember, it should be a shade that goes with your skin. If you're a pale and rosy gal, don't wear burnt orange. If you're dark, don't wear frosted bubble-gum pink unless you're headed for the nearest disco or roller rink. The shape of your face dictates where your blush will do its job best. Experiment by adding a slight touch of blush to areas to which you'd like to draw the eye (which also keeps the eye *away* from other areas). For example, a dash of color to your chin and a spot along your hairline, just off center, elongates the face; and a dust across the bridge of the nose (no thicker than a dime) replaces the natural color you usually receive from the sun.

Eyes

I love love love eye shadows. I could be a streetwalker just for the eye shadow. The '80s were an eye shadow orgasm. Lucky for me, eye shadow trends continue to morph, and designers continue to develop luscious colors.

Eyeliner goes on first. Oh, the choices! Self-sharpening pencils, thick pencils, thin pencils, happy-to-be-me pencils, eye pens, eye markers, liquid liners, and more. Waterproof, water resistant, water opposed, budgeproof, smudgeproof, fudgeproof. Why isn't there loveproof? Now that would be a breakthrough.

First off, invoke Endora. Remember Samantha's mom in *Bewitched*? She's the Matron Saint of Eyeliner. So say, "Endora, Endora, come to me. Streak my eyes with perfection. So mote it be." Then do a wrist twirl à la television magic. Now imagine her sitting on your windowsill. There, now you're in business. Using a pen or pencil liner is pretty straightforward (even if your lines aren't). Remember that your eyes aren't symmetrical. If you want cat eyes or anything other than liner that strictly follows the edge of your eye, then apply one eye as you wish it to be. Then, looking at your eyes, put a tiny dot of liner where you want it to end and set any other parameters. Then close your eye and fill in the job. This is especially difficult with liquid liner. Have a freshly licked 'n' twirled cotton swab ready to keep the liner where you want it. Also, let liquid liner dry completely before you open your eyes. Blow-drying your eyelid (on a low setting!) works best.

LICKED 'N' TWIRLED SWAB, noun: a cotton swab that has been stuck onto the edge of one's tongue and twirled until the cotton is smoothed down and barely damp. A high-tech, precision, makeup-tweaking tool used by makeup artists or at least Mavis.

When I agreed to shower-dance (go-go dancing in shower outfitted with a red strobe and special waterproof tip drawer at the bottom) at the famous women's weekend in Guerneville, Calif., I ran out and bought waterproof eyeliner to add to my waterproof mascara. It was fab! I danced and danced under that strobe light in my psychedelic bikini with water pouring down, and nary a smudge ensued! Warning: H2O-proof liner goes on like a liquid lawn-and-leaf bag. When it mixes with false-eyelash glue, watch out. The result is more extreme than a Lesbian Avenger with a bucket of wheat paste. If you try to pull the eyelash off, your entire strip of liner will come off with it, along with a layer or two of skin. Instead, saturate a cotton ball in baby oil, then patiently dab it on the liner. Usually the liner will break down enough to prevent this from happening. Some "eye-makeup removers" work on this combo, but some are really only meant for eye shadow and tamer mascaras. So try to not use H2O-proof unless you really have to.

Apply eye color as you wish. Eye shadow trends come and go so fast, plus eyeryone's face is unique. Look for women with eyes similar to yours whose makeup you like, and try to emulate them. Buy inexpensive cases of ten or 20 shadow colors to play with. Most of these shadows won't even stick to your eyelids for an hour, but they're perfect for trying out colors in your bathroom mirror. Then buy good creams, powders, or pencils in the colors in which you look best.

Pencil or powder a natural color into your eyebrows if you need it—or an unnatural color if you want it.

If you're going to apply fake eyelashes, now is the time to do so. Follow the directions on the package. Use eyelash glue, not spirit gum. Unfortunately, I learned this the hard, hard, ripping-skin-off way. You may need to touch up your liner after applying your lashes.

We've all heard the saying "The eyes are the windows to the soul." Well, I go by what my Aunt Connie always said: "Girl, the difference between love and lust is the look in your eye, so get mascara that's waterproof!" For years I took that to heart and only wore waterproof mascara, but now I use both regular and waterproof. Move over black, brown, and black-brown. Mascara colors now range from "invisible" and seafoam green to rouge noir and earthpot. Apply mascara only after you've powdered your face.

Powder

I remember when going from a dense-with-pigment powder to "translucent" powder was the big thing. Nowadays there are a hundred versions of liquid-to-powder foundations and all-in-one quick bases. Those products work for an everyday look, but for photo shoots, openings—any *bon soirée* where you need to be picture perfect—you need powder. A dusting of loose powder over the whole face with a big fat brush does the trick just right. Don't worry about getting powder on your lips, as you are about to read; that's going to help your lipstick stay put.

Lipstick

Like dessert, lipstick is saved for last—my favorite part. I wear lipstick constantly. Watching women cream on lipstick could be a national pastime if we'd only indulge our spectators. Never ever leave home without lipstick and a compact. And if you forget them while you're out on the town, then drag your date to Walgreen's and buy a $2 lipstick just for the night. Apply lip liner if you need it, but don't follow trends that put your liner way out of your natural lip line, and don't use drastic liner colors. First of all, that exaggerated outside line is for photo shoots and professionals. In real life your date will think you don't have a mirror at home. Plus you will be nonkissable. Smudging through the color on your lips is challenging enough without you putting an oil-slick moat around your mouth.

Back to your actual lips. To create a pouty lip: In the center of your bottom lip, put on a dab of liner a shade darker than the lipstick or gloss you're using, then apply lip color to your whole lip. At home, apply your lipstick with a brush, but when you're out, straight from the stick is just fine and gives a more sensual show.

Please, darling, I beg you, don't make the mistake I made for years. I thought I could only wear a few shades of lipstick. But my perspective changed one day when Susie demanded I try on red. I told her I didn't look good in red, and she balked. (Since then Susie has gotten me to try many things I'd assumed would look horrible on me, and many times I'm right, but sometimes I'm wrong. She recently changed my whole idea of yellow, but that's another story.) We figured out that I look good in "blue" reds, and from there I just kept trying new colors.

> **"A good lipstick should have lasting color, go on smoothly, feel comfortable on the lips, be smear-proof, moisturize and soften, maintain its shade, and give a clear, nonfeathering outline."**
> —Meg Cohen Ragas and Karen Kozlowski in *Read My Lips: A Cultural History of Lipstick*
>
> I couldn't have said it better myself. This book is a marvelous, informative read that you'll enjoy referencing again and again.

I learned from my experience in photography that many colors look the same in black-and-white photos, provided they're the same density. So a dark red will look the same as a deep brown.

A pink gloss will look the same as an orange one. See if this applies to you in real life. If you look good with dramatic lips, then you may look good in a whole spectrum of strong colors. Likewise with softer colors. If you don't like your lips to stand out too much, then buy different pale colors or glosses. Of course, some will be better than others, but as long as you look good, wear a variety. Not only will you not get bored, but also it will keep you vibrant to those around you.

How to Apply Smoochable Lipstick

Lipstick, like dessert, is saved for last.

We're lucky that we live in a time with all those kissable, budgeproof, smudgeproof lipsticks on the market. But some work and some don't. It's best to buy those with a coupon or rebate because some aren't up to Shar-par. I've only found two brands that really stick. Some are so drying that of course they don't move; they saturate five layers down and leave the top layers peeling.

Before I tell you the secret to kiss-resistant lips, you'll need to remove any old color and any old *lip*. I'm referring to dead pieces of skin. My lips have been chapped since I first latched them onto Mama Mavis's breasts. I have only one suggestion for preventing chapped lips: Chapped lips mean dry lips; therefore, work from the inside out by drinking a helluva lot of water. If you'd rather treat the symptom, apply petroleum jelly on your lips a few minutes before you shower or bathe. Wash your face. Then gently scrub your lips with a wash-cloth while they're wet. The petroleum jelly will soften dead skin on your lips, and the washrag will slough it off. You'll be back to baby-soft lips that are just waiting for a new adventure.

So now you're prepared for a kissable mouth. The traditional, tried-and-true method of makeup artists worldwide is to apply all of your makeup as you normally would, without fretting if it gets on your lips. Powder your lips when you powder your face, apply your lipstick, blot, powder your lips again, lipstick, blot, blot, lipstick once more, blot. When applying your lipstick, don't forget your moos (the two peaks of the lips).

Take Back "High-Maintenance"

It's come to my attention that many butches use the phrase "high-maintenance" as a femme-bashing weapon. They wield it in different ways but usually refer to the amount of emotional energy a femme takes or how much time she takes grooming and preparing her worldly armor. The term is no longer used to realistically describe a car, animal, or hobby that requires a certain level of time and energy (i.e., maintenance). I am, however, a highly maintained creature. I have to be. I have a delicate constitution, but if I take care of myself, I can be as strong as a Frederick's heel on Sunset Boulevard. When you hear a butch tossing around the line, "Femmes are too high-maintenance," don't take it.

You can fight with fire, by retorting, "Weeds grow in junkyards and roses grow in gardens." Or quip, "And how many pounds of hair gel are you weighing in tonight?"

There are high femmes and butch divas. There are tomboy femmes and filthy school "boys." Maintenance has nothing to do with how "easy" it is to be around someone or how much time her morning grooming ritual consumes. When I was on tour, privy to the grooming rituals of 12 dykes, I quickly saw that the butches took, by far, the longest to get ready.

To the butches reading this: Do you *really* want a war on this one? Do you really want those of us in the know to start dictating all the time and energy you're allowed to suck up? Do you want us to list the number of hours we lose in emotional vortexes with you? Do you want us to itemize the pounds of Aveda and gallons of Fahrenheit? Oh, was that blow too low? I mean, *high*-class Queens like us shouldn't go there, but don't push it. Don't take advantage of our *highly* governed manners. Every Queen is known to take off her crown and take it outside when necessary. We reap the rewards of giving time and energy so you can do your thing, so I don't wanna hear about it when we need our time. We support you in maintaining your social mask, so do the same for us.

To femmes: Obviously, a lot of the butches who scold us are not going to read this book, so advocate for yourself, babycakes.

If you know ahead of time that you're going to be *really* making out, don't even go through all that. Just pick a nice, light gloss. Apply it with your finger, rubbing your lips briskly so that they turn red with natural color. Once you start making out, your lips won't need any help getting red, and you can just shine on more gloss after you both separate.

Some brands do not smear as badly as others. Lipsticks that promise rejuvenation, vitamin E, moisture, etc., will stay everywhere except your lips. If you wear oily foundation, your lipstick is more likely to bleed.

If your lipstick won't clash with hers, kiss a lipsticked friend exactly on the lips. If it will clash, do air kisses cheek-to-cheek on both sides.

Touch-ups

The powder compact and mirror have traveled through centuries, so don't think they'll become obsolete, even when babes are checking makeup at warp speed. The powder compact provides you with powder to retouch your look or to salvage it altogether if you haven't applied it in the first place. Liquid-to-powder foundations cover blemishes easily, and traditional powder works fine alone. You can also put a dot of water on the powder, then apply just a spot to cover an eager pimple. I always take it with me for a quick freshen-up in the evening.

Makeup for the Morning After

Never leave home without lipstick, powder, and sunglasses. If you find yourself in a strange home without your toothbrush, put a little toothpaste on a washcloth and wash your teeth with it. It'll be good enough for a good-bye smooch.

Removing Makeup

Well, my big "secret" is out and is now being marketed to the masses. Baby wipes. Yes, now they're being marketed for makeup removal under the name "makeup-removal wipes" (so original). Years ago, my friend Babette and I would come home just a wee bit intoxicated with a box of KFC in tow. I, of course, didn't eat chicken, so he'd always get extra biscuits and fries for me. Then he'd pull out that moist towelette and start carving off his two-inch-thick "face." Guys' faces can handle the harshness of a KFC towelette, but women need a smidge more babying, so to speak. With today's budgeproof makeup, soap and water doesn't cut it, no matter what the ads claim. I highly recommend either mild baby wipes or the specifically made-for-makeup wipes to remove that coating from your delicate skin.

REFLECTIVE SURFACE DISOR-DER: re·flek·tiv sir·fis dis·or·dur (a.k.a. RSD), noun: disorder in which sufferer is compelled to look for her/his reflection in reflective surfaces such as mirrors or less obvious surfaces such as butter knives, pay phones, coin-return slots, toasters, etc. Most often, reflection is desired to check teeth for basil or lips for smudging. Term popularized by presidential candidate Joan Jett Blakk.

Quitting Synthetic Beauty

There are many reasons why we might want to quit store-bought beauty for a period of time. My friend Marcy recently quit coloring her graying hair. Many of her friends did not support her decision and adamantly demanded that she stop growing out her gray. But she pulled strength from remembering why she had stopped coloring: The smells made her sick. She relied on the support of those of us who believed in her judgment. Many of her friends (and a lover or two) think gray hair is ultrasexy. It purrs indulgence like a Persian kitty and roars passion like a mountain lioness. Traditionally, it symbolizes the wise woman, a woman who's been around the block and knows what she wants. That's sexy. Her body warms up and responds with a sensuality that has no match.

PHYLLIS CHRISTOPHER

In our youth-yearning world of colored hair, this "wise woman" is not "matronly." She's an out-law. Gray hair, however, shows a woman experienced yet unbridled. What's better than that?

I haven't had to battle gray hair yet, but I had my own store-bought beauty demon that had to go. Foundation makeup. I needed to quit because my acne worsened with base makeup (yes, oil-free make up still clogs your pores). The worse my skin got, the more I felt I needed cover-up. The more I covered up, the worse my skin got. I literally cried because I was so afraid of my bad skin showing. My friend Jennifer, a colleague at the preschool where I worked, urged me to stop using it. She told me she had seen me without base and that I was pretty without it, which of course made me cry again. After days of her supportive words, I went into work with just eye makeup and lipstick, and, yes, my coworkers did see how bad my skin was, but they were so loving and sweet. I realized then that I just looked like a pretty girl with acne—something I couldn't help. Eventually my skin improved.

Another friend, Memer, went through a similar process to abandon acrylic nails, which she had worn nonstop for years. She had awful fungus growing under them, and her real nails were extremely short and ragged. She worked in the corporate world and felt strong in a tailored power suit, with her tastefully long, hard nails. She could point to a graph, quickly punch up figures on a calculator, and loved clicking those things under a sales figure on the board. Her nails said, "I'm here, I'm a woman, I'm outselling all of you, and I could scratch your eyes out too." (OK, I'm exaggerating. Knowing Memer, it simply meant she was still feminine and could excel in a man's world without so much as breaking a nail.) But she needed to stop wearing them, and, once again, if it hadn't been for urging from friends and her supportive boyfriend, she wouldn't have been able to quit cold turkey. He constantly had to remind her of how killer she is. Now she has tasteful natural nails.

So, whatever kind of store-bought beauty you're trying to quit, you'll need the support of friends, even if it takes some searching to find friends to support you. Change can be hard not only on you but also those around you. Remember that when you shock your loved ones by denouncing your bottle-blond hair.

Lastly, for some reason, drinking lots of water, going on 40-minute walks, and eating garlic soup seem to help people quit everything from cigarettes to fake eyelashes.

Creating the Youtopian Collection: Fashion

Dress to Impress Yourself

Only recently have femmes had the freedom to dress as we please. And, in many ways, we still don't. I've answered the door for a date all dolled up and have been asked by the so-called date if I couldn't "just wear jeans." How many of us have been told we "try too hard"? Try too hard to what? Oh, then there's, "You're all dressed up," said like you're committing a crime. Some folks assume you're trying so hard to impress them and therefore, you like them "too much." They don't realize you're just being your glittering, shiny—indeed, overwhelming—royal self. Our egos can get severely bent out of whack by negative reactions such as these. There are numerous reasons someone might feel uncomfortable with a high-femme babe. I really don't care. Sure, if a femme is no fun because she'll never let loose or go casual, then maybe a friend has the right to try to talk to her about that *in the same way a friend would talk to a butch or anyone else about being a stick-in-the-mud.* But for the most part, those "jeans" people need to keep their bad, judgmental attitudes to themselves. I will dress how I want to. You appreciate it, or you don't get it. If you don't get it, you don't get me.

Many dykebabes do not feel good in jeans, so stop asking us, "Why can't you just wear jeans?"

Many women do not feel comfortable, erotic, or appropriate wearing jeans. Jeans simply do not fit most female bodies. They were made for cowboys in the 19th century, so you figure it out. I wear huge hand-me-down jeans from my 6-foot-2 friend Brian, but jeans that supposedly "fit" me hurt my stomach and cut off my circulation. Women with curvy butts or bellies and small legs have a real hard time finding jeans that fit. Then they often think they don't look good anyway, so why bother? Stop the terrorism of the casual dresser! We can wear skirts if we want!

Have a Look and Work It

Know your glamour history. Go to the nearest library and ask for a couple of issues of *Vogue* from each decade. In my high school drama class, we had to draw up costume plans for a play. Delving through costume book after costume book made my head swim with brilliant outfit ideas. After all, fashion always goes in cycles. The '90s had a '70s retro feel, and the '70s were spin-offs of the early '40s, etc. Also, keep an eye out for old pattern books at used bookstores. Seeing trends from days gone by gives you perspective and a good base to draw on as you direct your own style. And when you find yourself stuck without an outfit for a party, you can always go vintage. This basis will also help you to spiff up old clothes around the house and make them look new. Add a trim of marabou around an old sweater collar and cuffs and you've got a whole new outfit. Rip off boring buttons and replace them with gemstones.

**For butches we like boxes.
For femmes we like curves.**

Have two looks: one obviously prepared (your dolled-up look), the other a look that is also prepared but no one knows (your *just-so* disheveled or windblown look). Always say "Thank you" and smile when told you look good when you're dolled up. When disheveled, brighten your eyes, smile real big, as if a little surprised, touch your hair, then go, "Oh, gosh…thanks," or the equivalent.

Learn how to put your own styles together. Don't wear outfits straight off the mannequin. Pay attention to magazine spreads you like, women you see about town, and movie stars—new and old. Make sure, though, as you thumb through the fashion rags, that you pick women who look something like you or are shaped like you. Many a hairdresser laments the straight-thin-haired blond woman who thinks she can have thick and curly black hair. Unfortunately, magazines don't always include pictures of people who look like us, but you can at least find similar features: round face, wide eyes, big nose, curly hair, long limbs, etc. And although you might not see models who look like you, actresses and public figures do come in all shapes and sizes. It's just harder to find as many pictures of them. So go through that magazine rack page by page. Watch the fashion shows on TV. Mix and match your wardrobe at home in front of the mirror. Experiment. You're not obligated to wear it out of the house; just see what looks good together and what looks hideous. Also, note pieces that are almost-but-not-quite, so you'll know what to shop for. Does

It's Sew Easy

The idea that a femme knows how to sew is so antiquated that it's not even a myth to debunk anymore.

To replace a button you must get the right size, so bring an old one from the item or the garment itself and try buttons at the shop.

To sew a hem you use the basting stitch. Or fold it and iron it, then glue it down with Tacky Glue, a special glue you buy in the sewing section of department stores.

Use a basting stitch to add feathers, lace, or marabou to necklines, shoulders, or hems. Tie a big knot in the end of your thread. Do not double the thread. Start from the underside of your item, then just do loose loops to attach your frills.

a big skirt or a narrow one look good with that shirt?

You might become known for a particular style you do well—your signature style. Maybe you're a Lana Turner or an Audrey Hepburn. Maybe you always wear uniquely designed hats or dramatic earrings or toe rings. Friends seem to love this, possibly because they always know what to buy for your birthday. Hopefully, you sincerely love your signature style and don't feel a slave to it. For example, if you wear hats because you think you look bad without one, then keep trying new hair styles until you find one you like. That way you'll have the choice of looking fabulous with or without a hat.

Don't be afraid to try outrageous outfits. You're a Queen. You are larger than life, so you can get away with outrageous accessories, outfits, or shoes that would look silly on anyone else. Try crowns, feathers, boas, jewels, fake fur, trains, veils, gloves, beads, and anything else that isn't nailed down. Need ideas? Go to Mardi Gras or your local drag bar.

The Joys of Black Clothing

Ah, basic black, what a comforting thought to some of us. Even in this age of color, black is still the staple against which other hues are measured. One year trendsetters were claiming, "Navy is this year's black," and the next season, "If navy was last year's black, brown is this year's navy," and on like that. I'm not going to toot black's horn from the latest trendsetter perspective. Black is dramatic, looks good on most people, and no matter the "latest," it is always in. It is always classic. Furthermore, if you don't have a wad of cash to drop on your wardrobe, remember that a monochromatic closet is the cheapest way to go. Everything matches. You can make one black dress into several by changing your brilliant jewelry, and everyone will think you've got five dresses.

Your Lingerie ~~Drawer~~ Dresser

You don't have a lingerie drawer, you have a whole dresser…or closet. If you're young or broke, then start collecting now, take care of your garments, and your collection will eventually evolve. Lingerie is like the fabulous gift wrapping between the birthday girl and a precious treasure, and baby, that treasure is *you*. Wearing sexy undergarments makes you sexy. It means you're ready to be sexful at the drop of a skirt. Wearing sensual next-to-you things can also remind you that you are a Queen no matter what you have to be wearing on the outside. I used to wear camisoles and lacy slips underneath these ghastly uniforms required by the hostess job I had at the Ramada Inn. Try wearing a velvet or embroidered bra under your McDonald's uniform. Or a PVC G-string under a power suit. No matter what costume we have to don to face the world, our lingerie is our armor protecting our inner Queen and keeping us sane with reminders of our true nature.

The Brassiere

Oh, Mr. Frederick, of Frederick's of Hollywood fame—you know the one. Mr. Frederick is dead now, but his ability to create cleavage out of the tiniest of tits lives on—on chests like mine, that is. His purple store still stands on Hollywood Boulevard in Los Angeles. When the Wonderbra came out, I just about threw up. There were ads for it everywhere. At the BART train I would stare at the oversize ad consuming every descending escalator rider's vision. The media acted not only as if these bras were doing miracles, but also as if they were the first bras to perform these miracles. Every one of Mr. Frederick's bras has been doing wonders for decades. Yet here comes this new bra marketed so cleanly to the "average" woman. Not to sluts or easy women. Not to women who can't afford to shop in the downtown department stores where the Wonderbra is sold. How classist.

In the '80s, shopping at Frederick's implied you were a streetwalker (literally—most in-call gals had more money to spend), tranny-queen, or a slut (a blue-collar slut at that). People forget that Natalie Wood's cleavage in *West Side Story* was not formed by her size B breasts but achieved through a design by Mr. Frederick. Madonna, Cher, and Mae West have all donned Frederick's designs. Do you really think all those actresses of the 1950s and '60s really had big pointy breasts? There was many a tiny tit in Tinseltown, and we never even knew it because of the silent deeds of Mr. Frederick. No one, absolutely no one, makes affordable undergarments that push, pull, support, and display—as in *on a shelf*—natural assets (or store-bought ones) better than Frederick's. I'm glad they're making a comeback. Regarding the rest of Frederick's clothes, if you want a dress that doesn't show every curve and doesn't stop about a foot too high, try shopping somewhere else. I'm just talking lingerie.

Back to bras. Big or small, boobs are where it's at. If you're naturally endowed, then your only problem is finding good support and clothes that aren't too small in the chest. This *one* problem is bigger than Jane Russell! Finding a good bra has become a lifelong obsession for most big-breasted women. Oprah even did a whole show on it! When you do find a suitable bra, they usually cost $50 or more, so most women can only afford one or two. And when you return for another, you find that style is no longer being made! I've asked around, and the only advice I hear is obvious: Save your pennies, and when you find that special bra buy five at a time.

My friend Christina has an ample bosom. She recommends the Cradle Bra by Frederick's. She, like everyone else I know, says just forget buying bras at Victoria's Secret.

> **"You can do any-thing with some duct tape and a clothes pin."**
> —Mavis

Don't hide your chest. Be proud of it. Except for those times you want to downplay your curves, celebrate them. Breasts remind the world of woman power.

If your breasts aren't large, you can show off your natural shape by not wearing a bra. Tight "baby tees" have recently made a comeback. This is one trend that looks spectacular on straight-aways or curves.

I have smaller breasts, and I didn't even own a bra until I realized that a bra can be like bracelets. It's an accessory I can use to dress up an outfit at my choosing. I say, "I'm wearing my tits," if I'm wearing my push-up, padded bra, because the change in my shape is so obvious. Donning tits creates a dynamic silhouette. When I wear one of my bras with an outfit, I get more compliments on it than when I go bare-chested under the same outfit (um, unless it's a really, really tight shirt, tee-hee). I can hardly keep up with the latest in padded bras like the ones with silicone pads or the "H2O" bra, which has water built right into the bra. I confess—I felt up a friend wearing the H2O, and she felt all squishy and natural. Hand candy!

Krafty Korner: The Masochist Strapless Bra

If you don't have a strapless bra, if you do have size C breasts or smaller, and if you don't mind pain, then you can create a strapless bra with duct tape. Lift each breast where you want it to be, then put strips of tape diagonally underneath the outside curves. I suggest that you have a really good time at whatever event you do this for, throw back a cocktail or four, then bring home a good babefriend or slightly kinky date to rip the strips off you. You'll be red for days, but think of it as a thorough chest exfoliation.

Whether your breasts are large or small (but not tiny), you can also use duct tape to create major cleavage. Christina figured this out when she was on tour with singer Pussy Tourette. Stick the end of a piece of tape firmly to the top of your nipple. Lift your breast, pushing your flesh up under the top, so that your breast is almost folded over, making your nipple touch your chest under your breast. Then tape your nipple down. Now slink into your favorite bustier!

Panties, Thongs, and G-strings

Oh, the vulva shelters abound. What should a babe wear? I think nothing at all is always good, but let's explore the other possibilities.

The importance of being panties. Earlier we talked about your having a signature style. Well, how you cover your hoo-hoo says more about you than your latest pantsuit, that's for sure. Are you a "hipster" or a "brief"? Always the trendsetter, Mavis was the first in line to buy bikini-style panties, even before the bikini itself was on the market. (She was the first in that as well. A pink checkered one from Frederick's, no less.) She said she would buy one or two pairs of bikini underwear a week, until the day she actually counted her plentitude and found out she owned 45 pairs. Mommy.

Panties can cause panty lines, bikini-line bumps, feelings of restriction, and a rise in your body temperature. They can also save the crotch of your clothes from stains, give you a secure feeling, keep you warm in the winter, and allow you to undress without having to commit to going "all the way."

Panties can be such a delicacy. I mean, they are not required (unless a nun is watching you dress in Catholic school). Panties are often an item that's for your eyes only. I know many women who must match their undies to the bra they are wearing whether anyone else is going to see it or not. We choose panties for ourselves. Yes, we may meticulously plan our undergarments for a particular date, but even that is our domain. What am I going to show you about myself? My style? How I value myself? What do I allow to touch me *there*?

Before deciding, you'll have to consider not only many styles but also many fabrics. Do you choose satin or cotton or, better yet, silk or velvet? I have a lavender crushed velvet G-string that's as soft as a puppy's belly.

No matter what style or fabric you choose, select thoughtfully. Honor the precious position your panties hold. Consider their commanding location. On the inside panties touch you in the most intimate way. On the outside they're a privacy stronghold! Ask yourself, "What does it take to get me out of my panties?" Military strategists have nothing on the lustful dyke scheming to get her hand into a babe's pants.

Panties versus G-strings. Oh, a debate so raging, it even hit Washington. Forget the cigar— we all now know Monica wears thong underwear. That's my girl. I admit it. I'm a thong gal myself. Panties are too bulky for me and rub my pubic hair all the wrong way. I have other friends, though, who wouldn't be caught dead in a G-string. Steph, a leopard-panty gal all the way, can't stand them. She bought a thong at my insistence and now wears it as a headband. My friend Susie, a nudist at heart, thinks if she is going to wear something down there, it at least better be big enough to do something, like guard her tampon string. Somebody once tried to tell me, "Only you skinny girls like G-strings." Au contraire, ye narrow-minded. My babefriends of all sizes—and Monica herself—worship the thong.

But wait, is it a thong or a G-string? To a certain degree, the difference is much like that of "pornography" versus "erotica." Nothing but class and whether you're trying to scare your grand-ma. Then again, I do think of a G-string as much smaller in the front with only a strip of elastic going up the back, and more decorative than thongs, which I think of as larger in the front, with a matching inch-wide strip of lace, fabric, etc. going up the back. Thongs usually lie flat so there are no lines, even on your hips or belly. Thongs can be V-shaped in the front, go straight across the hip line, or come up as high as your belly button. Christina says the hip-line kind looks best on full-figured gals. I like the V-shape, and I can't imagine who the belly-covering type looks good on. I feel like all belly in those. If you haven't tried a thong, then do. You may be a convert like many of us. We can barely even remember the panty years.

Boxers. Many femmes eschew panties and thongs for the comfortable and genderbending boxer. They don't cause panty lines or chafe your bikini area (unless they fit wrong and bunch up). My friend Denise remembers the day she exchanged her practical yet tasteful Jockeys for Her for boxer shorts. She'd seen a woman in boxers in an ad and immediately ran to her nearest men's section. Talk about personal style—she felt so sexy and so "Denise" when she'd strip off layers to reveal her underthings: the ultimate in black-lace bras and boxers. Her dates would cream; they'd never seen anything like this before. She's so femme she can rebel against her own image all in one outfit. She doesn't genderbend; she gendercurves. Besides feeling bold and arousing, her boxers were comfortable. Nowadays, a woman in boxer shorts or briefs is no rebel—she's just smart. Of course, Denise also owns some lacy, dainty thongs to use with dramatic evening wear.

Try boxers under pants and jeans, or even flowing skirts. Some swear by boxer briefs made popular by Calvin Klein. They are the snug, stretchy cotton style. Others prefer classic boxers or boxer shorts like you'd imagine Steve Martin wearing. Believe me, you'll look nothing like Steve Martin. Most women wear their boxers down on their hips like men do. The brief type are usually cut short in the crotch so that you can wear them low on the hip and still have the crotch near your hoo-hoo and not mid-thigh. Wearing classic boxers low may occasionally cause too much fabric to bunch up in the crotch. Try rolling the waistband down one or two rolls so that the crotch is where it's supposed to be, yet you'll still have your belly exposed with the elastic across the hips.

The Mystery of the Garter Belt

My first stockings were silk, from Italy, given to me by my first lover's mother. For some reason she knew her daughter wouldn't want them and presented the black thigh-highs to me as the exotic gift they were. I blushed, not wanting to tell her I didn't own a garter belt (like she expected an 18-year-old to have one). I hit the streets of Chicago in search of help, winding up at a Frederick's. At that time, the mid '80s, thigh-high stockings had not yet made their comeback and garter belts were hard to find, which made the experience even more of a challenge. The clerk who sold it to me also told me I would want a G-string/thong as well.

Garters are the fabric-covered elastic bands that go around the thigh to hold up stockings. They conjure up images of high-kicking saloon wenches in can-can skirts. A garter belt is just that, a belt to garter your stockings. It has fasteners on the end as well as an adjustable waistband. These days, most garter belts are more for show, with plastic or rubber fasteners that can support only the thinnest of hosiery. Vintage garter belts are the best, so shop for them any chance you get. They have metal fasteners and thick rubber tabs that hold stocking tops securely. When shopping for a new one, check the thickness of the rubber tab. If it's too thin, it'll never hold the stocking and you won't even be able to wear the belt. If you lose a tab on your garter belt, guess what? You can go to your nearest fabric store and buy a package of them.

Thigh-high stockings come in two types: stay-ups and regular. Stay-up thigh-highs have rubber or elastic or both at the top, so they stay up without a garter belt. Regular stockings have the nylon or silk doubled over at the top or a stronger lace there so they won't snag on the tabs. The rubber ones have a lace band at the top of the stocking. Look inside and you'll see zigzagging lines of rubber grippers along that band. People always ask if stay-ups really stay up. The answer is yes and no. The ones with elastic at the top stay put on almost everyone. Most of the ones with rubber-reinforced lace tops stay put, but be sure they have at least a little elastic, since rubber alone won't hold. I wear these kind with a garter belt. Finally, many stay-ups fall down on women who have very thin or straight legs. When choosing stay-ups, buy opera length or a half-size up so that they reach all the way to the top of your thigh—that little corner where your pussy and thigh touch. Many women's legs go in just a bit there, giving a little ledge above the flesh for the elastic to securely grip. If that doesn't work, stick with the garter belt.

Some of the nicer stockings with seams up the back look inviting in the package, but beware of stockings that are so old-fashioned that they have no stretch. These will wrinkle around your ankles and knees, plus they don't stay up at all, and I am talking with a garter belt (these types never come as stay-ups).

So you have your new or vintage garter belt and your stockings. Put on your belt and tighten it until it's very snug. Your stockings will be pulling down on it, so snugness is imperative. Loosen the garter straps until they hang to the middle of your thigh in front and even farther down in the back. Between your thumb and fingers, gather up your stocking until you reach the toe. Sitting on the edge of a chair, pull it on and put your foot immediately into whatever shoe you are planning to wear (you don't have to buckle or fasten your shoes yet). Now do the second leg. Stand up in your shoes and adjust the stockings if you need to do so. Fasten the front garter onto the stocking, then tighten the strap until there's no slack. Now, reach behind and grab *just outside* the back center of the stocking in one hand, then fasten the back garter with the other. By grabbing your target before you try to fasten, you're ensuring that you won't twist your stockings around when *you* are twisting around to fasten them. Do your other leg the same way. When both legs are done, tighten the back straps until they're straight and snug against your buttocks but not too tight. Even though they're elastic, if you make them too tight you'll put undue stress on your belt when you sit down. You'll notice that back straps do not go down the center of each buttock; they go down just outside of the center. That way, when you sit they'll go to each side of your butt, which leaves your ass framed and not striped.

If you're going to wear a G-string, panties, or dildo harness, put them on *after* you put your garters on, so that you can pull down your underwear without taking off the belt. How convenient.

Panty Hose

What about panty hose? They aren't alluring to many of us. Some people find them uncomfortable. I cannot stand anything tight at all on my stomach, so those horrible elastic waistbands drive me nuts. But panty hose are useful for when you want hoo-hoo covering with no lines under a tight dress.

Years ago I engaged in a heated argument with my old friend Robin about whether panty hose are sexy. Robin was one of the first women I ever kissed. She introduced me to Chicago and seemed to know everything about anything "city." She was bi and loved scaring her boyfriends with exaggerated stories about her lesbian-feminist roommate.

The fight started with my adamantly stating that tan lines were not sexy. (In retrospect, I realize that I hated tan lines on principle: I hated that the government and fear of sleazy men could mandate clothing on beaches.) We never fought—especially about anything trivial—but I had completely offended her with my generalization. I still don't remember how this debate turned to panty hose, but we were really going at it when she wagged her finger at me like a schoolteacher, standing there wearing no panties, her tan lines glowing under her nude-beige, sheer-to-the-waist hose. She said, "You're wrong. A lot of *men* find panty hose sexy!" She knew that would shut me up.

"Really?" I asked innocently, imagining a world of men getting an erotic charge from a dressing ritual I still connected with getting ready for church.

I guess I should send her an Elmer Batters[1] book in apology because she sure was right.

When buying panty hose, read the box carefully or you'll end up with all the wrong thing. There's sheer-to-the-waist, panty-built-in, reinforced-toe, sheer-toe, and multiple versions of control-top. If you're going to be wearing a miniskirt, then you won't want control-top because the "top" goes down to mid thigh.

If you want to cover up leg hair or varicose veins, take a tip from cross-dressing men who don't want to shave: layers. Buy opaque lycra tights in a natural color that will somewhat go with your skin tone. Get ones with a slight sheen to them. They reflect light, which makes your legs look fabulous. (Some people put on a few layers of natural hose for assured opacity.) Next, put on your stockings. Black lacy thigh-highs will complete the illusion. The average eye will see no faults, just seductive legs.

Finally, what about all those tips for preventing runs in your stockings, putting them in the freezer 'n' such? I do carry a bottle of nail polish with me at all times for a variety of reasons. It helps stop a run before it spreads. But I always say, "A run in your stocking is better than one in your heart." A few unexplained bruises and some ripped stockings usually means a good time in my book.

The Smooth Line

Having a smooth line under your clothes is what lingerie and foundation garments are all about. Curves are fabulous, and we want curves, not lumps. Want that hourglass figure? Try waist nippers. You used to have to go to a specialty boutique for the precious items but now they can found at Macy's and most department stores. Is the waist nipper squishing you out down below? Wear foundation bicycle pants (sold in the lingerie department), then put your waist nipper on over it. You'll have a fabulous Marilyn Monroe figure after that. Corsets are fabulous for some and simply dull on others. Oh, stop arguing with me. I know that 80% of women look great in them, but Christina and I don't. So there. And we are two completely differently shaped women.

Of course, then there's the indispensable power slip (a girdle and slip in one, made of lycra blend to hold you in) which leads me to…

A Femme Named Desire: The Slip

Courtney Love. Elizabeth Taylor.

I wanted that to be the whole section, but the powers that be just begged for more.

A slip is one of the most practical, inexpensive, and seductive items a woman can own. First the practical stuff: Slips keep your skirts and dresses from riding up or gathering in places they shouldn't. Slips make transparent skirts opaque (remember the Princess Diana faux pas?). They also keep your skirts and dresses cleaner from the inside out because your body doesn't touch the fabric. Which also means that your can wear a slip to protect you from irritating fabrics such as wool.

Now, the fun stuff: The mighty slip has finally been empowered; she stands alone, no longer needing the dress or skirt for validation as a garment. Just as miniskirts have stuck around despite projections that they would retreat back into the cedar chest every year since 1985, I predict that the slip as dress will hang on for quite some time in one form or another. After all, no matter how many issues of *Vogue* have proclaimed the solo slip to be "in," they're still not seen as outerwear by many people. Only a few days ago a guy yelled out his car window to me, "Hey, I can see your slip! Ha, ha!" The male mind never ceases to amaze, does it?

I've seen $300 dresses that are made to look like slips. Why didn't the designer just make a $300 slip? Because, this way, teenagers can tell their moms, "It's a *dress*. Get off my case"? Or so grown women will feel their $300 purchase is somehow justifiable?

A secondhand slip will always be a sexy summer dress for poor girls who won't or can't drop bucks on something that covers the same amount of skin yet gets the big title of "dress." The entire Sister Spit[2] 1998 group (OK, not Linnie, Sini, Sash, or Ida), which was subtitled "The Femme Spit Tour," wore slips the whole trip except in Provincetown (it's a little breezy there). Many of us wore the *same* slip the entire time. I wore a very light slip, and the desert air sucked up moisture like a starving baby, so, I just swished my slip in rest-stop sinks and it dried in minutes. During the day I wore my silver thong Birkenstocks, and during the night I slipped on my high glitter wedgies and rhinestone necklace. The look of my slip transformed in seconds.

You can wear foundation garments right under your slip.

When worn as underwear, a slip is one more girly item you get to striptease out of. You can go through the motions of undressing, yet you'll still have on the same armor as Elizabeth Taylor in *Cat on a Hot Tin Roof.*

Lingerie for the Boudoir

The fun stuff! Just pick up a Frederick's catalog and go crazy. If you're strapped for cash, buy vintage lingerie at secondhand stores. Also check out Ross Dress for Less, Marshall's, and Kmart. My mom bought me a red, disco-ball sequined bra for $2.99 at Kmart just the other day.

Do you fret over a lover seeing you in your birthday suit? Lingerie is the perfect way to feel sexy and be naked all at the same time. Most naturalist communities (nudist colonies) often pick a night or event where they suggest you wear clothes. To them, total nudity is not the ultimate erotic body. Instead, dressing yourself up, deciding exactly what you will reveal and what you want to keep hidden for a while is much more charged. I buy that.

It also gives you control. You can focus your love thang's eyes wherever you want them to be. Want her staring at your ass? Frame it in lace. Christina wants her loves to focus on her chest, so she chooses full-length, silky, or see-through robes with long, fitted sleeves that frame her cleavage and tie just under her breasts. The front opens up just a bit to show her belly button, then falls away from the rest of her body, not touching her hips. The perfect figure.

It doesn't have to be the standard teddy either. My friend Marcy has the sexiest legs in town and plenty of bosom to throw around, but then she frets over her belly hiding under those tits. She feels sexy wearing her black lacy bra and a low-cut T-shirt. It's "rock and roll babe" mixed with "Diva romantic."

Lingerie transforms you into the bewitching sex goddess you wanna be or, in Marcy's case, the slutty teenager. You can never, ever have too much lingerie.

Latex (that rubber stuff like Batgirl wears)

The first time I saw a latex dress was on a model in the magazine *Skin Two*. She gleamed like a superhero. Latex shows all of your curves yet perfects your surface into that of a shiny Maserati. I think it merges the best of the female body with the best of the automobile: beauteous, slick, shiny curves wrapping unbelievable power. Latex is much like a second skin. When you wear it, you stay warm where it is warm and cool where it is cool. You can feel every breath and the lightest touch. That's deceiving because to your audience you look like you're hand-dipped in candy steel, but little do they know that through it you can feel the separate plumes of a feather. That's what makes it so erotic. You're naked, but no one knows it.

If you've never worn latex, then you must, must, must try it sometime. Preferably, come to a fetish store in San Francisco for the full cornstarched, hand-polished experience. They'll push you up and tuck you in. Do not be dismayed if it doesn't scream *you*. The one for-sure downside to latex is that your skin does not breathe in it, so you perspire *a lot*. A second downside is that some people are allergic to latex. They cannot use condoms or latex gloves, or wear latex garments. If you have never touched anything latex before, then test it out first. Buy some latex gloves at your local drugstore and wear them a while. If you're allergic, you'll find out soon. Some women feel claustrophobic in latex, too revealed, too something, but many others just melt, in a good way. At Stormy Leather, a fetish store in San Francisco, the staff reports that their favorite thing to hear is a customer sighing, "I didn't know I could look like this!"

To put on a latex garment, gather it in your hands like stockings, and indeed, treat it as delicately as stockings—no fingernails or rings to snag it. Then gently but firmly pull it on, unrolling your gathers as you go. To move it around once on, put your hand inside your clothes, between you and the latex, palm out toward the garment, and, using the flat of your hand, move it to where you want it to be. Never pinch and pull; you'll snap it right in two. There's no way to repair latex once it's ripped.

To polish latex for wear: Polish as explained in the following section until you remove all the outside cornstarch, then put on the garment and continue to polish or be polished until desired gleam is achieved. Try this: Have someone spray Black Beauty (a latex cleaner sold at fetish stores) on you while you're wearing the latex, then ask her to polish you with her bare hand. She'll get the hang of it. Bare-hand polishing makes latex as reflective as a mirror.

You might want to wear, as I often do, a latex dress to a fetish ball or event. At these events, spankers congregate, spying the best bottoms for a whack. Oh, how dangerous. Fetish folks need to educate themselves with cross-fetish training, so they'll know you can't spank latex. It can immediately rip like a taxed rubber band, and then you're left standing there naked. It's not funny. You may also wish to buy latex to strut your stuff at a parade. Wrong. Latex cannot be worn in the sun. Don't be fooled by the uneducated folks whom you may have seen wearing latex in the dead of August. Believe me, it was probably the first and last time they did. Not only will you have a coronary from the heat, but also your latex will get sunspots and will warp in places. Some latex simply rips.

Be careful where you sit because you'll lose the gleam on your ass. If possible, keep a bottle of polish in your purse for touch-up jobs. Or do my trick. I dampen a soft cloth with polish before I go out, seal it in a Ziploc bag, and put that in my purse. It's not as good as saturating your outfit, but it'll work just fine for touch-ups.

At the end of the night, you'll have to get out of your latex (unless you love it so much you plan to wear it *forever*). Once worn, it will stick to you like Super Glue. Don't fret. Just start at the top and roll it down. It's the reverse of putting on a condom—just roll down that rubber. Then step out of it. If it's a shirt, roll it up. A long gown will end up a three-inch-wide rubber band at your feet. That's OK. Once you're free, unroll it and follow the instructions below.

Cleaning and Storing Latex Garments

Buy a cleaner specified for that use such as Black Beauty. Or buy STP. Do not use any other rubber cleaner since improper chemicals may damage the garment. Rinse the item in cold water if you have left sweat stains or have otherwise juiced it. Do not use soap, including Woolite, which has chemicals that could harm your latex. Let it dry. Heavily spray the article with Black Beauty. Using one-directional strokes, polish the garment with a soft rag. An old T-shirt is best. You don't want to use a cloth that will bleed its own color onto the latex, and nothing that carries lint. You may reapply the polish as much as you want. Then let the polish dry completely (just a couple of minutes). Dust the latex with cornstarch, inside and out. Loosely store it, ideally in a closed container to keep out air and sun. I hang my latex on padded hangers so that the wire or plastic does not "bite" into the garment and leave marks. My friend Carol stores hers in a large hatbox. Do not fold your pieces nicely. Let them loosely fall into your container, then close the lid. Latex is a natural product that is harvested. It needs to be fed to stay supple, so you'll need to polish your latex every six months, if not more often.

PVC (that shiny stuff like Catwoman wears)

PVC is very shiny and looks like patent leather. It has a fabric matte side and a shiny outer side. PVC is as shiny as latex without having to be shined. PVC is much cheaper than latex. Remember in *Batman* when Michelle Pfeiffer ripped up an outfit to make her Catwoman disguise? That was PVC. She wouldn't have been able to do that with latex. PVC doesn't allow the skin to breathe, so you'll perspire in it. Unlike latex, which is glued and therefore seamless, PVC has sewn seams that do let a teensy bit of air in.

PVC is definitely the slutty superhero attire. Choose a size that will be tight; there should be no wrinkles or creases. It stretches a little, so make like melted butter and pour yourself into it. Hopefully, you'll be able to sit down, but umm, not comfortably. That's how tight it should be.

Unfortunately, PVC is made out of all kinds of yucky things that aren't only bad for you but also dreadful for the environment. Because of that, it was almost invisible at this year's fetish-wear trade shows. Latex may cost three times more, but it is a natural, and higher-quality, product.

OK, that said, I love PVC pants. You can dress them up or down. Throw a college sweatshirt on with PVC pants, and you're a perverted coed. Wear them with a leather corset, and you're a millennium maven. PVC halter tops are equally versatile. Don't let your dog jump on you while you're donning your shiny stuff—snags can't be fixed, and neither can most rips. Maybe you can find used PVC, so you'll be recycling.

To polish PVC for wearing, spray lightly with window cleaner, then polish it, or spray a rag with cleaner, then polish the garment until all obvious streaks are gone. Now put the PVC on and have someone else polish you. If your polisher can check her teeth by gazing into your thigh, then you're shiny enough.

Cleaning PVC

To clean it: Turn it inside out, then dunk the garment in cold, semisoapy water. Just dunk and lift, dunk and lift a few times. Do not scrub hard. If there's a particular smudgy to which you want to attend, just rub it a little with the pads of your fingers until it loosens or disappears. Then fill your sink with cold rinse water. Dunk and lift, dunk and lift. Repeat until you're certain you have rinsed out all the soap. Hang up to dry. It's best if no parts are touching when you hang it. For example, I hang my PVC pants upside down on a skirt hanger with each clip only holding one side of each leg. The legs gap open, allowing for full air circulation. If you're going to just throw your PVC over the shower rod, then take it down, separate the stuck parts and re-throw now and then so different areas will get a chance to dry. After the garment is completely dry (hours later or the next day), you can store it hanging up or in a drawer. PVC, especially unpolished PVC, won't stick to itself too much, so you can fold it. Do not smash it tightly together. If you're going to pack it in a small box or suitcase for a long time, lay another garment on top and roll them together so that the PVC is not on itself.

1. Elmer Batters was a low-end fetish photographer who took hundreds of pictures of women's feet and legs in panty hose. His work is now available in several books published by Taschen.
2. Sister Spit is a touring San Francisco–based clan of freewheeling, loudmouthed girls who hold all-girl spoken word and open mic events.

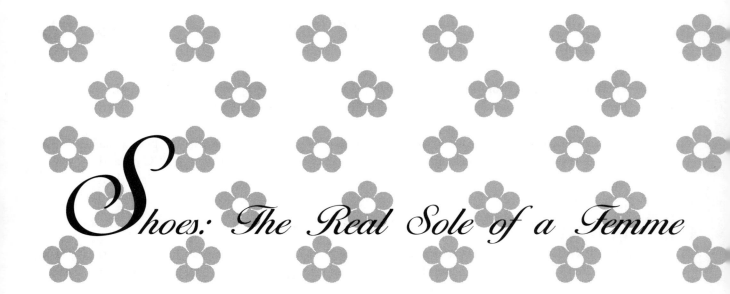

Shoes: The Real Sole of a Femme

Extending Your Reach...Climbing Up Those Six Inches to Divadom

Remember, *you* are the Queen, and shoes are the throne upon which you are perched, so choose that throne wisely; you wouldn't want any trash in the palace.

Or, if you prefer, you are the goddess, and your shoes are the altar and are therefore to be approached only on bended knee. If your gal doesn't have religion, she will, because honey, it's worship time. The shoes you choose to don make a strong statement to the world about who you are. I have fastidious rules about shoes that guide the novices and remind the experts of the femme's exalted position of sex and beauty in society.

Rule 1: Move over, Imelda! Own as many shoes as possible. Every moment transforms into something new and unique. Express yourself with the appropriate shoe change. Nothing makes or breaks an outfit more than shoes. I've seen women put together entire outfits and not concern themselves with the shoes. Check your doorbell, sweetie, 'cuz I'm saying, HELLO! I base entire outfits around the shoes or boots I wear.

Rule 2: Pack 'em up. Don't listen to anyone who tells you to travel with fewer than three pairs of shoes, even if you're just taking a 24-hour trip. Of course, you'll need much more than that if you're taking a long trip.

Rule 3: Buy in bulk. If you ever buy a pair of shoes on sale for $12 and, from the look of the rack, no one else is buying them and you wear them for three days and just love them so-o-o much—go back to the store and buy two more pairs. Put one pair way back in the closet so that you forget about them and find them in ten years…at which point you'll thank me. Put the other pair just somewhere kind of far back, but not too far out of reach, so when you rip off a heel you'll have backup pair.

Rule 4: Pull a "Nancy." Own a few pairs of boots. Boots vary with the terrain of your environment. But they are always handy for accepting a motorcycle ride. A single femme like you doesn't want to refuse that invitation! If you own a bike, then you probably have tips of your own to offer.

Rule 5: Don't bitch. Train yourself to wear heels without wobbling or complaining. If your feet hurt, all you need is a perch and a pose. Find a suitable ledge and drape yourself across it. Or even better, locate an appealing lap and nestle down on it. Depending on the event, you might take

The pope says kiss the ring. I say kiss the shoe.

MELINDA GEBBIE

your shoes off and dance barefoot. After all, breaking the rules is sexy. Doing this is OK if you're partying into the wee hours, but if it's only 10 o'clock and the opening was at 8 o'clock, you're not breaking the rules, you're just being a wimp. Sit and look fab or lean oh-so-casually. Always have a Band-Aid or two hidden in with your IDs to take care of blisters.

Rule 6: Employ Cinderella's secret. Have you found a pair of shoes you absolutely must, must have, but they're a size too small? Go to the store in the morning and bring some powder. Wear stockings, powder your feet, and you should be able to get your foot into the shoe if it is a half size or one size too small. Once in you'll be able to stay in for probably two hours before you just can't take it anymore. This won't work for strappy heels, only open toe or closed toe pumps. **Warning:** If you try to squeeze your size 9 feet into 7s or wide-ass feet into narrows, you'll end up with curly fries for toes, so use this information wisely!

Your Shoe Checklist

Unfortunately, a gal can't live in high heels alone. You'll need a spectrum of shoes and boots to be ready for any occasion.

Heels:	**Miscellaneous**	**Boots:**
Slingbacks	Sandals	Cowboy
Pumps	Thongs, flip-flops	Black: GBX, Skechers,
Mules	Flat dress shoe: a chunky loafer or	Docs
	saddle oxford works for many outfits	Hiking
	Athletic shoes	Go-go
		Dressy, lace-up

Shoes to Avoid:

Topsiders, black high-top Reeboks, Earth shoes, Wallabees, moon boots, jellies. Only wear Birkenstocks that come in metallic colors (they exist). **Warning:** While wearing Birkenstocks I tripped and fell down a San Francisco hill. I broke my elbow and heavily damaged my knees and wrist. I'd refused to ever own a pair, but Susie and I were in Key West and she insisted on buying us matching metallic ones in the thong style (going between the toes). She got copper; I chose silver. To be honest, they are very comfortable and we both loved wearing them. I just tripped all the time. When I'd tell my friends I fell and broke my elbow, they'd ask, "Oh, Shar, were you skipping in your platform acrylic mules again?" I said, "No. I was wearing Birkenstocks. Need I say more?" During all the years that I've stumbled out of bars, cars, and boudoirs, I'd never been so injured!

Other Tips

Patent leather shoes can simply be wiped down with some petroleum jelly, then buffed to a high shine.

Do not wear used shoes. Any orthopedic surgeon will tell you the dangers of this. But for infrequently worn vintage high heels, you certainly must break this rule.

Want to be comfortable, street-tough, yet sexy and sky-high? Take your favorite pair of boots to a cobbler and ask them to add a thick rubber sole. You'll have extra inches of rubber cushioning, you'll look kick-ass, and you'll be *able* to kick ass. Teach this trick to any butches you know who want to be taller, but who certainly won't don stilettos.

Alas, there is also the reality of protecting ourselves and our backs. If you have a bad back, you won't be able to wear heels for long. If you're worried about walking home safely, you may choose some other foot covering. If your back problems are acute, then you can't wear heels at all. Below I offer some stylish options. Your choice will be affected, of course, by your weather, terrain, and urbanometer.

URBANOMETER: ur·ban·om·eh·tur, noun: (1) internal tool for measuring one's degree of urbanization by adding up signals from biological sensory (eyes, ears, etc.); (2) the degree to which a place is urban.

High-heel alternatives: I like Chinese satin slippers. They give a unique, chic look to pants or full skirts. Or even the Chinese dress, the cheongsam. Let trends work for you instead of against you. When I had a car accident and needed more cushioning for my spine, I found psychedelic platform tennis shoes. I planned my outfits from my feet up and wore baggy pants with baby tees. I seemed to be vanguarding the latest trend, but really I was just giving my back two inches of rubber.

A must-have for bad-backed femmes is low-heeled, lace-up, Victorian-style boots. If you start looking now, you'll be able to find a pair sooner or later. These can be worn with almost any style of full skirt and most slim skirts. They're especially helpful for women who require Mistress (as in "May I serve you, Mistress?") attire.

Missing your sashay around the house in mules? Flat sandals in silver or gold look great with nightshirts, silk pajamas, and nothing at all.

with fun man-made uppers such as fur and flashy vinyl or patent leather have been popular the past couple of years. And they're extremely practical. You can wear them with anything.

Good, sporty walking shoes are a must.

Most doctors agree that by simply wearing a variety of shoes you'll alleviate many uncomfortable physical problems. Change your shoes two or three times daily, if need be.

Aerosole sandals, which come in alluring styles and wedgies, coddle your feet like a masseur's hands.

And remember, if you really want to wear five-inch stilettos, you can, even if you're in a wheelchair. Just pose pretty and make everyone come to you, princess!

Walking in Heels 101

What You'll Need: High heels, masking tape, good music, runway.

Observation Exercises: Watch runway models as much as possible. Notice their arms, fingers, asses, shoulders, feet, hips. Take time and study each body part individually.

The Heels: The key to walking successfully in high heels is to wear shoes that fit snugly. High heels need to be stuck to your foot. They can be from Thrift Town or Neiman Marcus, but the heels that are dangerous are ones that wobble on your feet. Whether they are six inches or two, make sure that they're strapped down and snug around your foot.

Some shoes wobble no matter how snug they are. This will be hard for a novice to detect—is it you or the shoe? On a pro like me, if a shoe wobbles, it is improperly made. The shoe heel needs to feel solid under your heel. Make your legs rods of steel and try to feel if the shoe is supporting you adequately. If you really can't tell, then start out with thick heels or closed-toe pumps. Those are usually the most solid.

Walking: Choose some excellent walking music and clear a path for your runway. Using tape, create a line down the center of your path. Do not wear your shoes yet, but do wear a great femme outfit, lingerie and all. A flowing robe is also divine.

The Position: Thrust your hips forward, shoulders back, arms loose at your sides yet elegant (fingers extended gracefully like a ballerina). Stretch your neck to the sky, chin slightly up. Your body should feel light, like air. Your arms should feel like they want to float up. Your neck, hair, breasts (if you have them), and kneecaps should all feel light.

Exercise 1, The Flop: Walk using mostly your hips to move your legs forward. Your hip will go up and forward, and the momentum will flop your leg forward. Don't do this clunkily. You are light. But it is floppy. The ball of your foot will most likely not leave the floor. Your toes may curl under at the beginning of each flop forward. Keep your shoulders way back. Flop those legs forward. Undulate your body in almost a vertical S shape. Now try to aim your legs so that your foot lands on the tape each time. Do this over and over until you're giggling and really doing it. This move will prepare you for "slinking" in the future.

Exercise 2, Runaway Runway: Once again, practice this without shoes. You are a runway model on speed. You are cranked up. You are having an acid dream and have to model without shoes. Assume "The Position" from above. Now walk as fast as possible down the runway, staying on your toes. Don't let your heels touch the ground! Walk on the tape, each leg crossing over the other to hit the tape with each step. Inevitably, you will feel unbalanced. (If you don't, then you're doing something wrong.) Swing your arms to the beat until they begin to balance you. Your arms and legs will begin to move opposite each other until they are in harmony. Move fast. Your movements should be exaggerated. Stay on those toes! Don't walk like a German solder. Your knees can bend, but your foot can't. Practice this exercise until you can do it for a half hour straight or longer. Have fun with it!

Exercise 3, Crossing the Line: Assume "The Position." Walk on your toes and cross the line with each step. In kindergarten we called this the "scissors step." Cross your right leg way over to the left of the tape, then cross your left leg way over to the right.

Exercise 4A, The Zen of High Heels: It's finally time to put on your heels. Feel them holding your feet. Your foot is a treasure, and your shoe is the chest holding the precious jewels. Instead of feeling it as a whole, feel each part. Close your eyes. What can your toes feel? What does the inside of the shoe feel like? What about your arch, ball, heel? Don't judge the feelings as good or bad; just feel.

Breathe in; then, as you breathe out, let your shoe become your foot. Your shoe is an extension of your foot. Stand up. Your weight should be balanced between the ball of your foot and your heel,

Walk your tape, ladies. Slink, slink, slink!

sort of flaring out from your outside anklebone, so that you are neither falling forward nor leaning backward. As a beginner, you'll need to stay mostly on your toes. The earlier exercises should have helped with that. Being on your toes needs to feel natural. After you become a pro, you'll feel weightless, and the toe/heel distribution will be moot.

Exercise 4B, Gracing the Line: Once again, start the music. Do not assume "The Position." This time pretend there's a string going from your spine to the ceiling as well as one pulling your sternum forward ever so slightly. You're still light, but this time your head feels light and pulls the rest of you up with it. Your head is the balloon and your body the ribbon following it. Now walk forward as gracefully as possible while your toes hit the line. "Graceful" is not "stiff."

The Mistake: Many people try to control every muscle in their body when doing this. You may feel out of control or like you're going to fall over, so you may try to control every muscle. This is the big mistake. Pull yourself up, uP, UP. Let your arms sway in response to your legs; they'll balance you. If you have to, put them out airplane style, as if you're on a tightrope. Let them move slightly forward and backward in that pose until they feel lighter and lighter and move on their own. Your body knows how to balance itself. You just have to let it.

Final Exercise, Clear the Runway!: You're the top model on the runway. You glide like a cat. You are air. Put on your heels and your most fabulous outfit. Assume "The Position." Now walk, baby. Remember that your toes should always hit the tape, but don't be mindful of it. If your outfit allows, take big strides. Your feet and hips should lead the way. Swing your arms.

Extra Credit, The Slink: The slink is the end-all and be-all of walks, in my opinion, because its subtlety ensnares the essence of its beguiling nature. Your steps are small, only a couple of inches between the heel of one foot and the toe of the other. Your thighs brush together with every step, never parting (this is particularly challenging for boy-femmes). You move slowly. Everything from your waist down sinuates forward, your shoulders wave slightly, and the rest of you glides.

How to Fuck in High Heels

(If you have a bad back, I am very sorry—been there. Anyway, use this as a visualization.)

Oh, please. I do *not* mean leaving your shoes on in bed while you roll around like a Playboy Bunny. I mean you fucking someone else with your feet stilettoed firmly to the floor—or five-inch-wedgied to the floor.

I have to admit it. I love that I can fuck a girl into complete ecstasy while wearing six-inch platforms. When my butch sisters are plowing into a babe, look to the floor. They root themselves in clunky boots that could hug a Harley, if not a mountainside. Feelings of control and power snake through me as I go at it—no slipping as she pushes back into me, saying, "harder, harder." Yes, we all may feel that way when we have sex wearing our old jammies. But this is showing off yet another level of "mistressy." Sexing her in heels takes incredible balance, grace, and determination, not to mention a strong back.

Fucking successfully in heels also requires quality heels. What is quality? Just something that is snug and not wobbly.

I would love to see one of those Easy Spirit commercials featuring a woman fucking instead of playing basketball.

There are a couple of ways to strap it on while strapped in heels. First off, you can kneel or lie on the bed, keeping your shoes on. But when you're on your knees, what's on your feet doesn't matter that much, so why bother? You could also end up poking holes into the comforter and sending feathers flying everywhere. Or you could rip holes into the flesh of your lust-one. (That could be a plus or minus, depending on your style.) Overall, the fun and point of your actually *fucking* in your heels (as opposed to the fetish charge of your simply *being* in them) is lost in lying-down positions.

Another technique is for you both to be standing up, leaning against a wall. This position's success depends on your height being complementary. She needs to be two to four inches taller than you in shoes. If she's small enough, you can just pick her up. But please be sure you *can* pick her up (or wear a weight belt). Anywhere with a sturdy bar overhead makes for a great standing-up fuck arena. You both can really get some leverage and utilize your upper-body strength. A third position is for her to sit on a counter top while you pull up to the bumper. Then there's the forgotten ladder. Cats love ladders. I love ladders. Really, unless your living space is too small, I highly recommend owning a five-foot or taller sturdy wooden ladder. I'll let you figure out those positions on your own.

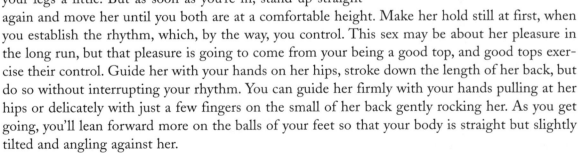

My favorite position is for a beautiful babe to be bent over a piece of furniture while I'm doing her from behind. I get the full benefit of seeing her ass cheeks, sweet butt hole, and pussy as I fuck her.

On to technique! Don't be afraid to move her around to where you want her. Bend her over, spread her legs until she's at the right height, where your legs are slightly spread but *not bent* more than just the tiniest bit in your knees. Most likely you'll have both legs between hers, but not always.

As you guide in your dick, you'll probably need to bend your legs a little. But as soon as you're in, stand up straight again and move her until you both are at a comfortable height. Make her hold still at first, when you establish the rhythm, which, by the way, you control. This sex may be about her pleasure in the long run, but that pleasure is going to come from your being a good top, and good tops exercise their control. Guide her with your hands on her hips, stroke down the length of her back, but do so without interrupting your rhythm. You can guide her firmly with your hands pulling at her hips or delicately with just a few fingers on the small of her back gently rocking her. As you get going, you'll lean forward more on the balls of your feet so that your body is straight but slightly tilted and angling against her.

If you want to do a very teasing fuck, get your dick in the right position, then have her close her legs together while you push in and out slightly.

When you really get going she will most likely be pushing back into you, which could throw your balance. You can simply slap her bottom and say, "Stop fucking me back." Or you can let her succumb to her desire and simply brace yourself by putting one foot between her legs and the other back just a bit. This will keep you at an angle leaning into her.

Varying your position not only spices up the sex, but also helps you fuck longer. Even the slightest position change will draw on a different set of muscles.

Every now and then you might want to put your legs together and bend your knees a bit and fuck that way for a minute or so. This gives your back and legs some variety, which will waylay a spasm. Bending over her back to kiss her neck, bite her shoulder, or kiss her back if you can't reach her neck is not only a sweet and intimate thing to do, but it will also give your back a cat stretch. Also, have her stand up and lean back into you for a minute. Kiss. Stroke her stomach, pussy, and chest. Call her your baby, stud, princess, or dog. Then push her back down and fuck some more.

For the most part, different positions and rhythm changes tease your partner. When she has really started rising into that preorgasm high, try to fuck as long as you can at that pace. Find a rhythm and stick with it. So you're going at it at a pace that works. Does she need to touch herself? You could do that yourself, depending on how your bodies are shaped. Your touch sends electricity through her body, but chances are if she really wants a good fucking, you're best served with occasional touches to her clit. For the most part, though, keep your hands on her back, shoulders, or neck. Suggest that she help herself if she wants more friction between her legs. Pump 'til you drop or until she lets you know she's had enough.

She might tire of this position after a while—not necessarily her pussy, but perhaps her elbows, back, or mind. Let her roll over onto her back where you can lie on top of her and indeed rip those heels into the bedsheets. Or, if it's your turn to be devoured, lie on your back, hook those heels behind her ears, and go for it.

Part V

Being Sexy...Body and Mind

Only good girls keep diaries. Bad girls don't have time.

—Tallulah Bankhead

Conjuring Up Some Sexy

The Power of Delightful

Girl, you don't need a *gris gris* to get your mojo going. That's boys' play. We're heading into the world of enchantment, self-assured allure. Of course there are many important battles to fight in our world, but if you aren't on the front lines (and I mean literally, as in a war, and even then, the gals wear lipstick to remind themselves of better days, to give themselves a glimmer of hope and a feeling of respectability), then do something for your corner of the world by being delightful. That's right, *delightful.* You may have to pull out a dictionary for this one because that word is archaic in some regions. Full of delight, enchanting, delectable, pleasurable, captivating, happy, enjoyable, charming. It's kind of that chicken-and-egg thing. I'm going to tell you how to be sexy, and feeling sexy makes you delightful, yet you need to brew up some delightfulness to be sexy.

Delighting in one's assets, and letting your peacefulness from that overflow into your neighbor's world, doesn't mean you're a pushover. It means you're living in the moment. And most moments you are sexy, delightful, compelling, powerful, and peaceful. This makes you that much more commanding overall. When you do need to blow your top, folks will know you're serious and not just being reactionary. They'll respect your power because they'll know you carry it with you every day and know how to wield it.

How to Be Sexy Against All Odds

OK, I lied, not against *all* odds. If you're a bitch, there's no help.

My friend Stephanie says we never outgrow what we looked like when we were 13. Sure, on the outside you look different, and when you're being rational you feel like "the shit" and you work it, but on those low days, here comes 13-year-old Shanila, with pimples, too-small tits, too-big feet, and not fitting into any pair of jeans the way Popular Polly does. I think Steph is right: Your weaknesses in puberty rear their cancerous heads during your low moments.

Growing up, I was considered an ugly duckling. My family always referred to my cousins as the attractive ones. Natalie had naturally blond hair, blue eyes, and dimples. Renee was simply pretty. Me? I was called "funny" or "unusual" or "unique," lots of *U* words, which I felt were used in place of the big *U* word: *ugly*. I would stare for hours at this one picture of my mom as a child where she didn't look so cute. It gave me hope, because my mom grew up to be one hot *mamacita*. Was she ever sexy! But that sexiness didn't hit until she was in her mid 20s. By the time she was in her early 30s, she could knock you over with one sidelong glance.

I felt the essence inside me. I knew I would grow up to be like her. By the time I was a teenager, I'd try on suggestive clothes in front of the bathroom mirror with my high heels and think I was certainly way off the 10 scale, although I acknowledged that the rest of the world probably thought I was a 5. I remember seeing Bette Midler being interviewed by Barbara Walters along with Bo Derek and some other popular models. This was during the "perfect 10" mania. Barbara asked each woman to rate themselves on a scale from 1 to 10. Bo and the models each said, "a 7 or 8." Bette, who is funny, creative, and very *un*usual, said, "Hell, honey, I'm a 55!" My eyes widened, and I saw light at the end of the tunnel.

That light was elusive, flickering on and off again, but I knew it had something to do with being grown up, something to do with owning your own body—and only just a little to do with the pages of *Vogue*. When other teenage girls in my hometown were reading *Teen* and *Seventeen* magazine, I was reading *Vogue* and *Bazaar*. I desperately wanted the clothes in their pages and often tried to make them at home. The thought of the sleekly shot, glossy pages of sling-backs made me gooey. Those shoes belonged on my feet. Nikes and Calvin Klein jeans (the rage at the time) didn't do it for me. I wanted glamour. High heels and slim-fitting skirts.

Then, in my freshman year of college, it happened. Some folks saw what I had seen in the mir-

PHYLLIS CHRISTOPHER

As the age-old adage goes, if you've got it, flaunt it!

ror. They appreciated my offbeat style and funny soft face. My sophomore year, I even had my first photo session. Me, Sharlene, who had ripped my picture out of group photos all through high school.

One of my dorm mates was a budding photographer and begged my friend Brian and me to pose for her. Looking at the pictures of us, I fawned over his hard features, his sharp jaw and cheekbones, but the photographer pointed out it was the contrast between my softness and his sharp angles that she liked.

After moving to San Francisco, I modeled for many pictures that ended up in photo books and magazines, on anthology covers, and more. Those lucky enough to know my cousins get to witness their beauty firsthand, but I'm the only one on the covers of nationally published books. Being "ugly"—meaning physically unattractive to the mainstream, *not* being ugly at heart—gives you soul, makes you think twice about your fellow human beings, makes your story a little more interesting in the telling. In the way a pearl emerges from a smelly, icky ol' oyster, the most sublime of beauties emerges from the *un*likely, from the ugly.

That's my story. Now let's talk about you, you, and you. Much of this section covers polishing up your sexiness, but for those of you starting at ground zero, let me just tell you that in reality there is no ground zero. No one is *not sexy*, period. But there are women who don't know that and who might think there is a "not sexy" category that they fall into. Sorry, um, you'll just have to step over into the "she doesn't know she's sexy" category or the "she hasn't harnessed her sexy potential yet" category. Great. Hope you're comfortable there.

The greatest obstacle to being sexy is not feeling sexy, so let's address some of the more common myths that blind us to our sexiness.

Wait a Minute! Why Should I Be Sexy?

This is one of those times when I assure the class that no question is a dumb question. Some women *do* ask this. They think sexiness is a product of male this or that. Mmm, OK, let's see. I'm a woman, I make myself sexy, and what does that have to do with any man? I'm the boss. Let's start with what we know in our toes and build from there: Being sexy is ours, our scent, our bodies, our thoughts, our desires, our images, our essence.

Some women wonder, *Why should I have to change to get a girlfriend? People should like me for me.* Yes, they should. But ask yourself this: Are you advertising what's on the inside? I have one femme friend, Sammy, who inevitably wears muted brown shirts and jeans then wonders why "her type" never approaches her. Her type, by the way, is a big, studly leather daddy who will bend Sammy over her knee and give her a good what-for after a long ride on her Hog. When I finally wrangled Sammy into a miniskirt and leather halter top, she started getting noticed by the right gals. You wouldn't sell lollipops by advertising wineglasses, would you?

Dating is shopping. You've got to advertise the wares that are inside the store! Not only that, you must keep in mind that looks do make a strong first impression. If you owned a store that carried top-notch linens, would you make a window display with your old period-stained sheets? No, you'd put your most inviting display in the window. Again, dating is shopping. Make sure your goods are displayed nicely, so chickies will know if you're on their shopping list. Have you ever bought a box of instant potatoes, only to open it up at home and find a smoked salmon? Well.

Make your window display count!

Getting Over the Negative Stuff

The greatest inhibitor when it comes to being sexy is not feeling sexy. Ask yourself, "What stands in the way of my feeling sexy?" If we were all in the same room, we'd hear lots of answers. Feeling tired or fat; being too worried about work, zits, or yeast infections; feeling unwanted. But all these things aren't what prevents you from *being* sexy; they're just not helping you to *feel* sexy. To feel sexy, you must face your demons head on, dismiss what you consider "frivolous" or unnecessary concerns, and tackle the things you *can* change about yourself.

Frettin' Over Body Size

I always hear talk about "the messages the media give women about body size." Magazines, folks who want to make money off unhappy people, and television do *send* lots of messages that women need to lose weight or look different. But communication is a two-way street. If no one *receives* these messages, then what messages are there? Yes, a lot of people think women look better if they're smaller. And you know what? A lot of people think women look good if they look good. The demon that a woman bigger than a size 9 has to face is *not* a potential date or the cover of the latest fashion rag—it's herself. Your eyes are the most critical eyes that will ever fall on you. You may have been called names in the past or may even now hear snickers here and there, but these criticisms come from shallow people who do receive empty messages from society and the media. They're weaklings who are too immature to take control of their brains. They are the sheep. You, my dear, want a wolf. You are yummy, and you want to be eaten alive!

I crawled out of my sickbed to interview Dr. Ruth. (Don't I look l ike a giant next to her?) She wouldn't tell me her sign or favorite fantasy or anything personal. Strictly bizness.

If your weight bothers *you* physically or mentally, do something about it. For good health, you should be able to move with ease (basically being able to go up and down stairs without getting out of breath. Ask your doctor if you're at risk for heart attack if you're unsure whether you're at a healthy weight.) If you're doing something about your weight but still don't like your body, look in the mirror and tell yourself, "Girl, this is why the Goddess made different strokes for different folks. I may not like what I see, but I'm damn sure glad others do." We shouldn't get our ego from others, but this isn't therapy, honey, this is the real world, so don't disbelieve a lusting face or wagging tongue. Frankly, in Shartopia it's a sin against the Goddess to not like your body no matter its limitations. It can do *something;* you figure out what that is and like it. Your body needs to be able to laugh, cry, receive affection, and give affection.

Some of the sexiest women I know also happen to be the curviest women I know. I'm not saying that to be politically correct, mindful of diversity, "inclusive," nice, or even to get more voluptuous women into my fan club (although that could have some advantages, tee-hee). I say it because IT'S TRUE! A lot of the women I am referring to really show their curves and know how to do it up. And, as you'll read later, that *is* what I recommend (because I advise all readers to show off their assets no matter their waist size). But, my earnest chickadees, I have to tell you that one of the first women I knew who could/can just ooze sexiness was my Aunt Connie (and she certainly isn't some skinny stick). Aunt Connie never pulled an Anna Nicole Smith, donning satin corsets or revealing bustiers, yet she's definitely sexy. What's that all about? Here's the short answer: She's sexy because she *knows* she sexy. (The long answer is the whole next section! Patience, *ma cherie,* patience.)

There are a lot of skinny girls who are very sexy. Why are they sexy? Because they *feel* very fucking sexy in their skinny bodies. They got a booster shot from our culture.

You need to figure out how and where you can get this booster shot. Give yourself whatever it takes to help you feel good about yourself. Read *Mode* (a fashion magazine that features the more curvaceous models). Look at images of sexy women who also happen to be big. Check out *Nothing But the Girl: The Blatant Lesbian Image* by Susie Bright and Jill Posener.

Finally, I not only want you to get over your negative stuff about size, but also I'm going to take this moment in the spotlight to make a plea for you to help others get over theirs as well. When I worked at *On Our Backs*, I went through what every editor and photo editor there has experienced: being criticized for the majority of our models being skinny, us constantly begging all women to model, yet few big women stepping up to the lens. If you're bigger than a size 9 and you want to change the world, submit your spectacular self to the camera. It takes courage and a little chutzpah to change the status quo, but you can do it!

Out, Out Damned Spot: Bad Skin

Acne reigns as one of the worst fugly-causing monsters around. It make us worry over our look more than anything. We'll get a pimple, then slather our face with makeup to hide it. I've had acne for more than ten years. I've tried every product on the market and have partaken of many different lifestyles during the last decade. I've lived in town houses and vans, been married and single, eaten buckets of chocolate and lived without any sugar at all. I've used $50 cleanser and just a bar of Ivory. I've lived with hard water, soft water, and no water. I've been a club girl and a couch potato. Nothing, nothing, *nothing* changed the fact that once a month my face broke out with scarring pimples that would then take at least a month to go away! Now, years later, for reasons that have nothing to do with skin, my doctor told me to stay away from dairy products. Guess what? My skin is now totally clear. Unbelievable. Turns out that your skin is your biggest elimination organ, and for some reason dairy is toxic to me. If you want to try this, here's how: You have to be completely dairy free (completely, no little bites, no cheese, no yogurt, no dairy at all. No milk chocolate!) for about three weeks before you'll know if dairy is your problem. If this doesn't help, please try to go to a dermatologist. I know it's pricey, but it'll make you feel so much better. And no matter what, buy or have your library order *Natural Skin Care* by Joni Loughran.

Also, if you really want to clear up your skin or your system in general, try a safe, fasting diet such as the one listed in the *Nutritional Health Book*.

The Date Pimple

So what's the deal with the date pimple? You know, the mountainous, perfectly synchronized-with-a-new-date, red beacon that shines from your forehead, chin, or nose. I've got a recipe for you. Don't skip a step.

Supplies:

benzol peroxide blemish cream
peppermint tea (noncaffeinated kind such as Celestial Seasonings)

Instructions:

Brew a cup of peppermint tea with two tea bags. Take one tea bag out and let it cool a bit.

Glob blemish cream onto the mountain. Let it dry a little. You don't have to wait for it to dry completely, though.

Put the slightly warm tea bag onto the blemish. You're essentially using it as a compress. Let it sit on the mountain for ten to 20 minutes. Then turn it over and redip it into the tea. Finally, add ice to the tea and remaining tea bag. Glob more cream onto the mound. Put the new, cold tea bag on it now. Let it sit for five minutes or so.

This procedure usually diminishes the mountain, leaving only a red spot that you can cover with foundation.

Draggin' Disco Legs: Energy for the Femme on the Go

How can you feel anything— much less, sexy—if you're exhausted? Lack of sleep can contribute to bad skin, poor color, lifeless hair, anemia, concentration problems, depression, anxiety, poor diges- tion, not to mention puffy, cir- cled eyes.

There's no easy answer to this one, except to get plenty of sleep and rest. Prioritize your rest the way you prioritize projects.

A disco nap keeps you pretty and witty and gay!

Power Nap: Nap taken during the day to reenergize. Don't sleep more than 15–20 minutes or you'll feel more tired than ever.

Disco Nap: Nap taken after dinner to re-energize so you can party all night. Disco naps are often about two hours long. If you can't sleep for two hours, do it for only 20 minutes.

Chronic Fatigue Syndrome and Other Energy-Sucking Conditions, Including Mononucleosis and Hepatitis

"My sweet tired angel, she waits for me at the bar.
She wears a rhinestone tiara, left her dirty wings in the back of the car."
                    —from "Cheap Ass Wine" by The Hail Marys, lyrics by Jackie Strano.

I had a mystery disease for one and a half years. At first they thought it was mononucleosis, then my doctor kept bringing up chronic fatigue syndrome (CFS) and I'd say, "I don't think it's that since I'm getting better," even though my "getting better" was as slow as a snail. It was more like I refused to think I had CFS.

As it turned out, I suffered from a combination of disorders that sucked up my adrenal and energy reserves. I won't bore you with the details, but I do want to share some ideas and tidbits for the large percent of folks living with the CFS *that is from not environmental illness.* First of all, eat some salt. Recently, research has shown that about one third—a considerable amount—of CFS sufferers have a condition in which their blood pressure bottoms out when they stand up. This causes a few adverse effects, one of which is a period of fatigue each time it happens. (That's the new breakthrough information.) Doctors involved with these studies prescribe salt pills as well as low blood pressure medication to their patients. The point is keeping your heart all plumped up with blood and your blood pressure even. Some of the people suffered for five years and were better within *one month* after simply increasing their salt intake. Ask your doctor.

Often, health-conscious people don't eat enough salt. In recent years, studies have confirmed that all this antisalt propaganda isn't based on actual facts. Yes, *some* overweight individuals with high blood pressure shouldn't eat much salt. But many people show no changes in blood pressure when they increase or decrease their salt consumption. A *few* other conditions mandate salt-free diets. But in general, this antisalt sentiment has gotten way out of hand. Most people who try to be healthy restrict their salt intake, which actually could be worsening their fatigue-related conditions.

But before you go harnessing up to a salt lick, try eating three pickles a day. When friends choose not to salt their fries, you go for it. Soy sauce, which is high in sodium, can be added to many foods, such as soup, potatoes, and noodles. You might be in the two-thirds group that won't be affected by increasing your salt intake, but one third is a huge portion, so maybe it will help. It helped me, and I'm forever grateful this research came out when it did. A pickle a day keeps the bed away.

Energy-sucking conditions not only debilitate you physically, but also inhibit your ego, sex life, and passion. One of the first things that goes is your social skills, which can include passion, patience, and concentration. You suddenly know the real meaning behind the saying, "Save your breath," since you really do have to save it for when really you need it.

Your ego and social persona may be invested in your outwardly femme attributes, but not only do you not have the strength to put on makeup, but after a while you don't even care about being without it. Your friends are shocked, and a part of you remembers you used to care, but you can't even ponder why that was.

Take care of yourself as best you can, and certainly, certainly don't spend a second fretting if you don't take all of my advice. Remember that your energy is like gasoline. If you drive 35 mph, you'll have gas longer than if you drive 90 mph. Use this knowledge. Much of the time you'll probably want to go 35 and save as much energy as possible. Maybe you'll be able to go to the bank *and* do your own dishes. Wow, what a feat. But sometimes we want to drive 90 mph. Maybe you can blow off the bank, leave the dishes in the sink, and go to a party for an hour instead. An hour of fun and seeing your friends is, at times, well worth the consequences.

Don't live by "shoulds." Call a friend to do the dishes and use that saved energy to get out of the house. Also, I recommend using megadoses of vitamin C and herbal remedies. At the same time, I advise, if you want a glass of wine (even though you know it'll put you to sleep for the rest of the night), go ahead and have one occasionally. Chances are you're going to be fatigued anyway. Have a cup of coffee. Constantly policing yourself will only depress you and make you feel like a victim. Don't lock yourself in a homeopathic stockade.

Put on some makeup. Leave a lipstick, mascara, and mirror by the bed. Just sit up and put some lipstick on. It will ease your friends' worries and make you feel like the old you, even if only for a few minutes.

Speaking of sitting up in bed—do *sit up* in bed. Even a healthy person can't lie down horizontally for weeks on end without feeling dizzy when standing up. Your heart becomes accustomed to not having to work hard to keep your blood pressure even-steven. To keep your body assuming it *should be* vertical, you need to keep vertical as much as possible. Prop yourself up with lots and lots of pillows. Sit in chairs so that your legs are lower than your heart. Sit up and stand up very slowly so your heart has time to regulate your blood pressure.

Finally, even though it seems hard to believe at times, hold on to the fact that you will get better. You must accept where you are now in your struggle, *and* you must not accept any notions that you will stay at that level forever. Luckily (not for them), I had friends who had suffered from fatiguing and chronic diseases. They, and their families, told me stories of how tired they were, how their lives fell apart from not being able to work or go to school. For example, two of my friends had mononucleosis. Did you know it takes five years to fully recover from mono? I swear, if I hadn't had these people around to reassure me, I'd have gone to the bridge (I would have been too tired to actually jump, of course). They bestowed hope every time they said, "You'll get better." I could look at them and see them moving, breathing, and alive with energy. The years you suffer might seem like a long time, but you *will* get better and they *will* shrink into memory.

Repetitive Stress Injury (RSI)

I mentioned this epidemic earlier in the "Working Girl" section. I am compelled to write about it further because I love dyke hands. RSI (an ailment that includes carpal tunnel syndrome, tendinitis, and thoraxitis) disables more and more woman-lovin' fingers every day.

I have a fabulous femme friend, Ann Widden, who *is* the reason Manic Panic invented red. Ann not only looks brilliant in vintage bustiers, but she also inventively lives with RSI.

Just because RSI can limit the motor ability in one's hands doesn't mean it should also limit one's sexuality. Ann has worked as a sex educator for years, so she's quite articulate on the topic of giving sexual pleasure (i.e., fucking, licking, etc.) without frustration and pain—not to mention receiving pleasure as well.

The Importance of Discussion

First and foremost, according to Ann, is for you to talk about your limitations honestly with your sexual partner. Hiding it won't work and will end in frustration for both of you. It might be difficult for you to talk candidly with one-night stands, but it's still important. We want to be sexy, and discussing our limitations can seem unsexy, but what's really unsexy is being in pain, hurting ourselves, or getting ourselves into situations we don't like.

Take responsibility for your limitations and for communicating them. Tell your partner you'll speak up loud and clear when you can't do more or when you're in pain. Otherwise, your partner won't be able to relax while receiving pleasure because she'll be wondering at what sacrifice you are fucking her/licking her, etc.

If your partner suffers from RSI, trust that she'll tell you her boundaries. Reassure her that you're fine with limits, that all you need is communication. Also, be willing to try new kinds of sexual positions. Be flexible. Finally, find out what you can do for her nonsexually. Cut her vegetables and bagels for her. Loosen the lids to all her jars. Carry her grocery bags. Make her fruit salad. Save her hands for the really special task of whipping up a passion-lust smoothie for you!

Remember, the faster you recognize and respect your (or her) limitations, the faster you (or she) will heal.

The Act Itself

Vary what you do.
  • Go down on your partner some, finger-fuck her some, use a dildo some. No matter what physical challenges you might have, variation seems to be the key word I hear most often.
  • Become more ambidextrous. Jack that clit of hers with your left *and* right hand. Move around.
Be aware of your positions and hers.
  •Sit comfortably between her legs while finger-fucking, and use your whole arm, shoulder muscles, and back to power your fuck—not just your wrist and fingers.
  • Lie on your back and have her sit on your face, as opposed to you bending over her pussy.
Use vibrators wisely, if at all.
  • For most hand-, wrist-, arm-, and chest-related repetitive stress injuries, you should not use vibrators at all. But having your partner hold a vibrator on herself while you put your fingers inside her may work for a little while.
  • Have her use a vibrator in place of your lovely fingers on her clit if you can't use your fingers that way.
  • For *your* pleasure, try lying facedown on a vibrator instead of holding it. You can combine this with a partner by having her fuck your ass or pussy while in that position. Or you can lie face-to-face with the vibrator between the two of you. Have your partner hold the vibrator on you any way you like.
Use dildos and straps.
  • Remember the saying "Look Ma, no hands!"? Well, YEAH! No fancy hand work needed for these instruments of love. Use them as much as you like! Strapped-on vibrating dildos are fabulous. Call your local women-owned sex toy store and ask about the Bobbi Sue by Vixen.

The time of day when you make love can also be important. Morning is often a bad time for some, and the end of the day can be bad for others. Pay attention and change your love schedule accordingly. Finally, consider your favorite ways to enjoy lust. If your partner really likes an activity that's hard for you, try doing different things to work up to it and save the favorite things for dessert or special moments.

❧   ❧   ❧

Getting over the negative stuff is the key to both feeling and being sexy. This chapter has covered only a handful of things that may be keeping you from reaching your sensual apex. Remember, we're our own worst critics, and whatever pitfalls we feel may be in our way, with ingenuity and the appreciation of all we have to offer, once we *feel* sexy, we will *be* sexy.

How to Be Sexy...For Real

> *"The real secret to loveliness is being lovely."*
>
> —*Girl Scout Handbook*

We've gone over all our obstacles to feeling sexy, so now let's explore how to be sexy. Do you want to just ooze sex? Be one of those gals who walks through a room, and people—men and women alike, straight or gay—melt into her?

Sexy women have sex. Sexy women think about sex. A sexy woman's sexuality winds around her essence like ivy, always a part of her.

You may say, "Oh, I like gals who seem to be sex nerds. It's their innocence that turns me on." That, my dear, is about you, not them. You may find any "type" desirable or attractive, but haven't you ever found yourself drawn to someone who isn't your type at all? Someone whose sexiness pulls you in and you don't even know why? That's about *her*, not you. That woman is a sexy woman, and that's what I'm talking about.

Funny, so often "sexy" is what much of our culture says is undesirable. For example, eating makes you undesirable. Fat is undesirable. Messy clothes make you undesirable (if you're over 25). You're supposed to be thin, sitting neatly, in perfectly feminine clothes. Then why is it so sexy when a feminine woman wears men's clothing?

Because *breaking the rules* is sexy.

To me, eating is sexy because it shows hunger and desire. Eating reveals that you're in touch with your raw needs, that you know they need to be met.

Wearing lingerie or carrying a sex toy or safer-sex items is also sexy because once again it means we have thought about sex, we're ready for sex. Wear sexy underwear even when you know no one else is going to see it. Let the knowledge of how hot you are underneath your work clothes give you a secret thrill. A lot of women think a butch gal packing a dildo is sexy. Is it because we think the actual physical bulge is attractive or hot? A few women will say yes, but the majority of us think that packing is sexy because of what it says about that butch. *She's ready for sex.* As she prepared for her evening, she thought about her desires and passion. On whom was she imagining unleashing that desire?

MELINDA GEBBIE

You know what they say: The eyes have it.

Where Were You When I Needed You?!

Have you ever noticed that sex begets sex? Have you ever had a dry spell, then when you start to date someone, you suddenly have plenty of offers? You think, *Where were you when I needed you?* People can read that you're having sex. Maybe they don't say it to themselves that way, but there's something about you that just smells sexy. Their little noses start to twitch with your getting-some scent. You don't have to wait for outside irrigation, baby, you can do your own rain dance and stop that dry spell right now.

Try this: Either in the morning or early evening, light candles, play your favorite music loudly, wear something scant and titillating, grab some massage oil, and pull out your toy box. Apply oil to your feet, knees, and elbows. Massage some into your chest, then head south. Rub it into your pubic hair. Massage your outer lips and pubic bone. Rub and rub and tease yourself for a long time. Get out your toys, but don't just do what it takes to get off. Instead, tease yourself as long as you can. Do new things with your toys that you haven't tried. Talk dirty to yourself. Say those key words you think are really nasty, the ones that make your clit stand on end. Then go for it. Do yourself in every direction possible, then end in as many orgasms as you can stand. Roll around in the afterglow. Drift in and out of sleep if you need to. Go pee, wash yourself up a little if you want, but do not wash completely. If you ravaged yourself in the morning, then go out to your favorite café where there might be a dyke or two. If you did it in the early evening, go to a nighttime event or local bar where there will be some lesbians. Do not tell the world you just jacked off. No, no, no. You're acting desperate again. Just go. Do whatever you usually do at these events. The only difference is now you are transmitting sex. Your walk, scent, and attitude all send out the message, "This gal is having fun. Hook up with her and maybe you'll have fun too."

What Isn't Sexy

Actually, I'm sure the following descriptions will be sexy to someone—they can fend for themselves. As for the rest of us, vaginal infections aren't sexy, so take care of your pussy. Nose hairs aren't sexy, so clip 'em. Emotional baggage is about as unsexy as you can get, so please check it at the brain station if sexy is your destination. An unwashed anus doesn't hit high on the sexy scale either. Be nook-and-cranny prepared; that's sexy. Finally, chicks with snotty attitudes definitely

Thinking About Sex: Your Assignment

Don't:

- Pine away wishing for it
- Convince yourself that you don't deserve it
- Indulge thoughts that you're never gonna get any
- Tell yourself you suck at it
- Think no one wants to have sex with you

Do:

- Picture yourself having sex with someone. Imagine it in detail and masturbate while you do this. Give yourself a great big orgasm while this is going on. Writhe around in the afterglow.
- Play a positive past experience over in your head like a movie. If you don't have one, make one up. Don't get sad that it isn't happening. Pretend it *is* happening.
- Look at other people and imagine what they would look like having different kinds of sex. (You may or may not want to have sex with them. It doesn't matter.)
- Imagine your body moving in different ways with someone you like.
- Imagine yourself in Shartopia, getting whatever you want, a very indulgent sexual fantasy, whether it's having your entire body rubbed down by ten different women or getting gang-banged at a truck stop.
- Carry these thoughts with you in your day-to-day existence. Be married to your sexuality.
- Get human touch the best ways you can. Get massages if you can afford them or trade massages with a friend. Why should our lovers have the corner on touching us? As children, we hug, kiss, hold hands, and walk arm in arm with our friends. Just because we're grown-ups doesn't mean we don't need touch. Invite friends over for movie night and pile up on the couch together.
- Wear clothes that make you feel enchanting, provocative, or sensual. I've met women covered head to toe in tie-dyed skirts and turtlenecks who just oozed sexiness. And I've met chicks in miniskirts who would leave you cold. Sure, if you feel comfortable in your body clad only in a thong, you might get a higher boner response than someone in a muumuu. But it's not just about parts showing, it's about *you* showing, you actively showcasing your parts. Your confidence must come through physically, even if it isn't there mentally.
- Fake it 'til you make it, sweetheart.

don't score well on the sexy-o-meter. Sure, they turn a few heads, but those heads turn right back around in boredom at a gal that shallow and insecure. (Remember, those who seem the most conceited are the most insecure, a universal truth to which I've never encountered an exception.)

Part VI

Gathering From the Galaxy: Creating Your Court

So now you're a living, breathing queen. You've lotioned your elbows, stocked your toy drawer, bedecked your palace…now who do you want to invite to share your throne? Onto whom do you want to wield your sexiness? I've told you my theories about us all being objects of desire, but how do we manifest our femme sexuality in real situations? We may flirt with everyone, but who do we groove with and curve around? Follow me, chickadees….

What's in a Name?

Femmes have loved butches for eons, and at one time this was the only acceptable way to be among lesbians. If you weren't into the femme/butch dynamic, you were shunned like eggnog at a hot summer picnic. Then, during the women's movement of the '70s, femininity was eschewed among lesbians, so, like the baby with the bathwater, femmes were thrown out with their lipsticks. During those years, you didn't really use the word *butch*, but let me tell you, the outfits worn by dykes were nothing but bulldagger. Supposedly, the point was that men didn't own the corner on overalls. Now they became "women's clothes."

Then androgyny progressed into the '80s mainstream pop culture. Boy George and Annie Lennox became idols. In those years the androgynous ideal reached its peak—boys and girls dressed and looked alike. In my crowd, eyeliner and shoulder pads were communal property. Boys were girls and girls were boys.

Next, the early '90s: The fashionable-lesbian years hit. In many communities trends dictated a more femme appearance, although the word *femme* was rarely used. (Outside San Francisco and New York gay ghettos, the most you could hope for was *lipstick lesbian.*) To be butch meant you were trying to be a man. Egad, not that! That's being like the enemy!

These days, in gay communities, being a femme and calling yourself one is pretty OK, and being butch and calling yourself that is also OK. Note: I say "pretty OK" because, depending on your age and your community or lack of one, you might still have folks around you who judge gender presentation. Show them this chapter so they'll know how many decades *late* they are.

All this is called "identity politics." Some people are startled by the idea of using what they call "labels." "I don't want to be labeled," they say (or whine). Often it's these very people who take labels far too seriously or stick to them rigidly. Choosing to name your sexuality and/or your gender helps to put you on the map. To name yourself is one of the most empowering things you can do. You can change what that name means, allow for wide definitions, let the name itself fluctuate, keep it for yourself, let others take it over, walk away from it, or stick to it the rest of your life. Most of us wear a social mask to move through the world. Its purpose is to make our lives easier, but nothing's written in stone (even if you *are* stone femme).

I bring all this up because how we see ourselves affects who or how we desire.

Last year I was temping at Good Vibrations, and a coworker, Ray, was making a run to the café next door. I wanted a bagel, and he naturally asked, "What kind?" I said, "Oh, my favorite is 'everything,' but if they don't have that, get 'plain.'" Everyone laughed at my extremes: Give me all or nothing.

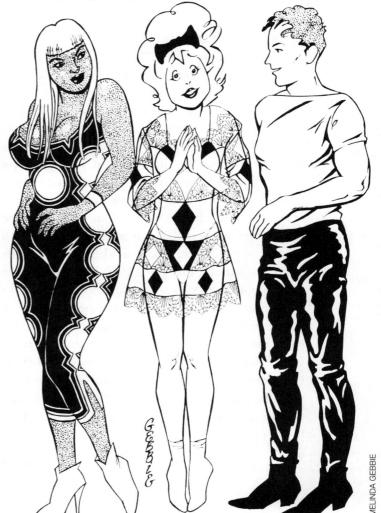

Life is filled with delightful choices.

MELINDA GEBBIE

My bagel preference provides a perfect analogy for my love of the extreme, of butch or femme women. I'm not attracted to anything in between, although I am attracted to people who embody dramatic elements of both. I like staginess. I like drag and pageantry. I like the bewitching theater of self-creation. Something about that dramatic flair beguiles me, draws me in.

A lot of femme dykes are bisexual. The types of men that bi femmes hunger after run the gamut from high queen to macho stud. My delightfully royal colleague Carol Queen warns newly out bi femmes that they might be limiting their choices without even knowing it: "You may think that if you like guys, you must like straight guys," she says. "Or if you like women, you must like feminine women. You broke out of society's boundaries by discovering that you're bi. Don't let them tell you who to like. Let your hormones do the sniffing and see what you come up with."

Queers are frequently more articulate about our desires than are straight people because most of us had to analyze ourselves like a science experiment before we told a soul we were queer. Straight people don't have to go through that. In the same way, experienced bi femmes are often acutely aware of their proclivities because their self-analysis went even further. Carol says that her self-examinations, instigated from being a bi femme, left her with a secure understanding of her attraction to both masculinity and femininity, and the various creatures that trigger her desire.

Because of my personal perspective, I'm focusing mainly on femme-on-femme and femme/butch desire. My tastes aside, these are the folks that most femmes date. Maybe you can show me a few examples of high femmes loving plain Janes in the middle, but "few" is the key word. You may not have too many choices where you live, so maybe you've spit-shined up a local. (I've done that in the past.) If you're high femme and climbing, then you're dramatic. Most likely, you'll be attracted to those who, like you, push the envelope (whether they push it on purpose or, as with me, their very existence pushes against boundaries).

Mirror, Mirror on the Wall: The Magnetism of Femme²

Femme², fem•skwared, noun, adj. (a.k.a. femme on femme or lipstick lesbians): (1) two femme women romantically involved with each other; (2) a femme woman sexually attracted primarily to other femmes.

If you've read any of my fiction, you know I'm quite prolific on the topic of the dynamic of femme/butch romance. Yet, for all my talk of hot butches, I have to tell you, I really have a penchant for the taloned side of the gender wheel. Hello? I was raised in modern-day America like the rest of y'all. For centuries feminine women have been the inspiration for artists, writers, and musicians. We're curvy; we create life itself. We not only embody pleasure, but also our strength has inspired men and women alike throughout the ages.

When two femmes get together romantically, watch out. They aren't doing what the Playboy Channel says they're doing. No walking through sheer, flowy curtains, no tongue flicking! When you put two femmes together, you're doubling all our fire for life, our overwhelming creativity, our unadulterated femaleness. I know it sounds hokey, but it's all woman. Sisters doin' it for themselves.

In the whirl of this enrapturing passion lies our own version of drama. Our feelings can get

Unadulterated femaleness.

PHYLLIS CHRISTOPHER

hurt in the blink of an eye, and our empathy is instant. Who else can wound you so fast, then instantly understand (when she wants to) and be very sorry (which of course leads to making up)?

I can just hear the butches saying, "I understand and I'm sorry." No, I'm afraid they don't. The key word here is *instantly*. Of course, these are generalizations; each person is different, and many circumstances can come into play, but overall, much of femme/butch arguing/processing/fighting is about understanding *what the problem really is* because butches and femmes do not communicate the same way and often don't even use the same language. Once a femme and butch figure out what the other is saying, there might not even *be* a problem. With femme[2], it's about *the problem itself,* whether or not some infraction is intended or "deserved." Then it's over. She may have been so busy with her project that she stepped on your feelings; as soon as she takes a breather and you point it out, she instantly gets it. Or maybe she knew it would piss you off for her to go out with the girls for cocktails when you thought you were having dinner together, but frankly, she just doesn't care.

She's gonna do it and will deal with the consequences later.

I've seen many arguments between femme/butch couples come down to someone feeling that she's being owned by the other and worrying over whether that's right. The resentment surrounding this is usually at the core of the argument.

But two femmes don't touch that one with a ten-foot cigarette holder. It's in the Out-Diva Clause. You *will not* disrespect a femme. No one understands this more thoroughly than another femme, so if an infraction is made, it most often knowingly done. Oh, sister, this is a fight among equals. Remember, the nail that scratches the itch can take out an eyeball as well. Take cover. Turn over that vanity and wait for the smoke to clear. No stone will be overlooked; one may remain unthrown, but she's just saving it for a bad hair day and you both know it. See, that knowledge is the difference. Equal and same are two different states. Butches and femmes can find equals in each other; many of us actually like finding an equal who can call us on our shit. But femmes speak the same language, and when you mix that with passion and love, no amount of lipstick can stand in the way.

Femme^2 couples also face a unique set of challenges. I've been to different leezzzbian events where I was ostracized for showing up with another femme (i.e., prejudice^2). Femme^2 couples have no dyke passing card in certain "wimmin" areas. In other words, having a butch (i.e., visible lesbian) with you can arm you with a passport into the dyke community. Actually, depending on how butch a butch is, she might not be welcome either. She has to look "andro" to the wimmin who haven't copped a clue that "andro" to them is butch to everyone else. True androgyny is embodied in the lovely transgendered folks that make you go, "It's a beautiful fag."

"No, it's a handsome woman."

"No! It's a beautiful fag."

"No, it's a…" You get the drift. Anyhoo, femme^2 couples don't look andro, which can cause problems in certain situations.

I'm not one to assume clichés are true or that people don't change. (Hence, I wouldn't have been in Texas last year—different story.) I point this out because I've been dwelling in Shartopia, assuming things are better than in the olden days, which they are—for the most part. For example, I know all kinds of gals who go to women's music festivals who would never have been welcome ten years ago. But I have to point out that I still get negative femme shit to this day, usually from clichéd sources such as those wimmmmmmmin people at wimmmmmmmmin weekends. Hello? You are a stereotype. Like, break it. If you're going to be clichéd, at least pick a good one like sending roses on Valentine's Day. Onward.

I've also heard that just regular ol' dykes (not the "wimmin" kind) often won't see a femme^2 as just that. They try to make one of the gals butch. The bigger one, the darker one, the one with short hair, one of those two must be butch! I'm sure this is what Xena goes through. Folks can't face that she can be that tough *and* femme at the same time. She's a big-boned femme with a delicate femme sidekick. I realize these are only TV characters, but I'll take any role models I can get. Folks just can't believe that we're here, we're in Bebe, and we're fucking each other. Of course, not every town is that way. I still hear reports that Los Angeles doesn't allow butches into the county, so all couples there must comprise two girlygirls.

As far as the rest of the world is concerned, if a femme dyke or lipstick lesbian is invisible, then femme on femme is doubly invisible. People don't consider you a couple at all; you must just be touchy straight girls. The few who do get that you're a couple think your sexuality is the latest *Penthouse* soft porn, existing merely for them to fantasize about.

Sometimes, though, it's not just outside-world influences. Two lipstick lesbians can also feel competitive with each other. For example, if I put on lipstick, then you have to. And once we start really putting on makeup, then I want to do my liquid eyeliner. Or I thought we weren't dressing up; now I have to wear a little black dress too. Pretty soon it's a whole fashion show, and we're just going to the grocery store! (Or if you're like me, the fashion show leads to a whole 'nother show and we never even get out of the house!)

There's such a wide range of femmeness out there that there's still plenty of room to appreciate the Other. I'm fair and slender, so naturally those dark, sultry, curvaceous girls trip my trigger. There are tough femmes, faint femmes, punk femmes, classic femmes, tomboy femmes, high femmes, and low femmes. Or then there are femmes who, for real, look like sisters, women who look and dress alike. In San Francisco we call it fagging, liking the same type as yourself. (Butch-on-butch is also called fagging, and some butches call themselves "fags" or say they're into fags, which is being very specific.) *Fagging* or *cloning* as verbs mean "liking the same" or "imitating each other."

If you're not a relationship-with-another-femme kind of gal, don't rule out sexual flirtation with femmes who can fill your stocking when a girl needs some lovin'. You might see her pointed talons and assume she won't fuck you as good as a short-nailed stud—don't jump to conclusions. Remember what I always say: "If her nails are long, she might just be lookin' for a scratchin' post."

Femmes often get the more ritualistic side of sensuality. Just the other night, my luscious femme friend Bella and I pressed our foreheads together and breathily exchanged "What if we did" talk. I promised her a full spa treatment. What's so sexy about that? You can read it here, but remember, I *purred* it to her: "I'll pick olive branches with my own hands and beat you with them until your skin is as rosy as a plump cherry. I'll knead you with sea salt, then sponge you gently with icy champagne before I rub vanilla oil into every muscle, working and kneading my fingers in between each and every muscle. I'll find all your nasty knots and...." She licked up each word as if it were chocolate ice cream and returned them to me with frothy meringue. We both got so worked up that our chests were rising and falling with restrained yearnings. Just over the thought of a spa treatment.

Femme fuck friends can also combine girly understanding with their passion. There are times when we're down and think we've got the fuglies, 'cuz we do. We're just not fitting right; we don't fit in our bodies, or our bodies don't fit into our clothes, or our minds don't fit into society. During these times we need some easy affection, easy in that we don't need to figure out the big problems to take care of our little problem. Sometimes I've phoned a friend and just said, "I need some loving," and then it's over to her house for a video, manicures, and a little scratch-scratch behind the ears.

Ever hear that saying, "You know how the plumbing works"? It's usually used to explain why gay sex rocks, specifically why fags can suck dick like nobody's business! Femme on femme is a little like that. Not that we all want the same thing in bed—believe me, we don't—but when you're both OoDs, you're organically empathetic. You've felt what she's feeling, so you can manipulate your lovemaking with insider experience.

Her X-rated knowledge of babeness also means she has femme X-ray vision and can see right through your every move. I realized this once when I was finger-fucking a femme friend. I was so sexy kneeling between her legs, my small titties outlined in a men's undershirt, throwing my hair around. I had practiced and practiced looking really hot while fucking, because it's a nifty trick to get between a reluctant butch's knees. Then I brought my sultry eyes up from our hand-pussy action to her eyes and there she was with her eyes closed, writhing and moaning like she was in a porno, paying no mind to me. I joked about it later, saying that with two femmes it's "Look at me," "Oh, no, look at me." You don't realize how much you get and need that object-of-desire attention until there's a mirror lying there at the end of your fist.

Finally, since we know there's an art—a high art, at that—to being femme, there's really nothing like another femme to deeply appreciate that art. It's like sports, like knowing a game: "She batted those eyelashes right on cue. The crowd goes wild!"

Jumping the Gender Fence
Try a Femme and Call Me in the Morning:
For Butch-Loving Femmes

Reasons to try a good femme:

(1) There aren't any good butches in your town. I hate starting with a butch negative instead of a femme positive, but I have to include this because it happens to an overwhelmingly large number of women. Depending on what town you're in and what phase of butch evolution your community is in, there may not be a *good* butch around for a couple of light-years.

(2) Femmes are hot and sexy. Even a kitten femme oozes power, which can be a rush just to be around.

(3) Femmes on the whole are more in tune with our bodies, even if we grumble about them. Being with someone in tune with her body means you don't have to do guesswork because her sexuality is close to the surface.

To jump the fence:

You know how to flirt, or at least you will after reading this book. Just flirt with a femme. She may assume you're not shopping; if so, don't laugh away your flirting. Say, "I'm not kidding," with actions or even words. Buy her drinks and stay by her side all night. Do you want to kiss her? Two of my favorite lines: (1) "Wanna see if our lipsticks clash?"; (2) Hand her a cocktail napkin, to which she'll say "What's this for?" You say, "To blot your lipstick. The more you get on the napkin right now, the less there'll be on my face in five seconds."

You can woo her with "top" protocol, such as making sure she gets home safely, flagging her a cab, letting her sit down before you, or opening the door for her. Or if *she* shows "top" energy, you can answer up for any tasks she needs done.

For the Love of Opposites: Seeking Butch Affection

"The Butch is the ultimate romantic lesbian figure, androgynous to-die-for, an icon of outsider status and forbidden desire."
—Susie Bright, *Nothing But the Girl: The Blatant Lesbian Image.*

The Organically Bigendered Creature: The Butch Woman

Why do we love butches? Let me count the ways…. They're strong and soft at the same time. They ooze masculinity but don't smell like men. There's nothing like a seasoned butch's fingers. Most likely those fingers have ached for a woman's flesh for as long as she can remember, and no matter how many women she's been with, the ache of longing still fuels her passionate touch. Butches can make you feel safe, even if you're the one with a black belt. When you're with a butch you can be more femme than ever. Femme-loving butches know you embody strength, that you're not weak and exploitable. She won't use your femininity against you, and that knowledge allows you to freely relax into your femme persona. What a relief!

Women wear butch as many ways as RuPaul wears hair. They're punk, vintage, leather, conservative, rock and roll, and country. They're daddies and little boys. They're shy ones and show-offs.

They straddle Harleys and hot femmes. They strap on dildos and tool belts. Just try putting a butch into a box and she'll muscle her way out of it. Sexually speaking, butches are bottoms and tops and everything in between.

Butch-and-femme lovelust burns uniquely. The femme embodies the ultimate, ancient, female archetype—not any modern-day stereotypes where the feminine is weak. (Maybe not in the greater metropolis of life, but at least in her own little femme/butch world, the femme gets to have her cupcake and eat it too.) She personifies the femme divine—potency intact! The butch embodies everything studly, honorable, and charming in masculinity, yet she understands cramps and second-class citizenship firsthand. What a combo!

The Femme/Butch Dynamic

Femme/butch love is a complementary love that fits together like yin and yang; each component has just a touch of the other at its center. F/B passion matches up like a cosmic puzzle cut with lustful precision. The tension of polar opposites pulls stronger than any planet in orbit. F/B love is a space safari where both partners explore the unknown—going where no man has gone before—in each other. I'm not sure how much one person can ever know another, but that unknown is nowhere more pronounced than in the F/B relationship. F/B relationships are for adventurous, curious spirits who thrive on the dynamic pull of polar tension. These partnerships are compelling, and the magnetism can become obsessive, like you're drinking and drinking this magical potion that's quenching an overwhelming thirst you didn't even know you had until the potion touched your lips.

If straight people think lipstick lesbians fuck like the women in *Playboy* videos, then I really don't know what they imagine F/Bs do. Nowadays, there's plenty of erotica written from the mare's mouth, so there's no reason for guesswork. Editors Susie Bright, Carol Queen, Marcy Sheiner, Tristan Taormino, and I usually include explicit F/B romances in our erotica anthologies.

Luststuds and OoDs

I'm always spouting off about femmes being OoDs, but many butches embody the masculine version of that. I call them "luststuds." They can be great to date, or they can be your biggest nightmare. If a luststud is *insecure,* then grab your ego, kick off your mules, and run like crazy! If a luststud is experienced and *secure* in her ego, then she can take everything you dish out and throw it back for more. Once I made Jackie pose for me in one of her dapper outfits—snappy shoes, suspenders 'n' all. She stood right on the bed looking down at me while I lay on my back jacking off to her image. Lovers of butches don't have many butch images, two-dimensional or three-dimensional, to fantasize about in our culture. An occasional calendar or film at a once-a-year festival and that's it. So turn your butch into your luststud. Have her pose for you. She might feel uncomfortable at first, but keep reassuring her by showing your lust and telling her how much she turns you on.

There's nothing like a butch to appreciate the OoD in you. Her power comes from a different source than yours, so you're much more than a Queen to her. Since the source of your potency is so mysterious, you become a *Goddess.* This is similar to the awe I feel toward people who can sing. If I had to sing for my supper, I would surely starve. Jackie has a remarkable voice with which she leads her band, The Hail Marys. When she likes a singer, she likes them. But when I like a singer, I am utterly amazed and am convinced that angels are present here on Earth. When Jackie sings, I sit in awe of her talent, but I'm also overwhelmed by the mystery of it. I will stare at her mouth, wondering, *How in the hell did that come out of there?* She just opens her mouth and these wonderful sounds pour out—truly miraculous. As complementary forces, we not only get to marvel at one another's talents, charms, and personality, but also we get the added luxury of being enigmatic to one another. It's like being in Disneyland and never finding out there's an 18-year-old in the Mickey Mouse outfit. Live the miracle. Savor each difference. Join the Mutual Appreciation Club. *Enjoy* each other.

Working Out the Kinks

F/B relationships, however, are not always strawberries, sugar, and cream. Femmes and butches speak different languages, which can sometimes be problematic. I have polled many, many F/B–relating chicks and they all agree that most of the arguments in F/B relationships wouldn't happen if we simply understood each other. Of course, there are deeper issues, but oftentimes it's about miscommunication. The femme thinks she's addressing one issue, and the butch thinks they're talking about something completely different. I can't tell you how many F/B arguments ended when the couple simply realized *what* they were arguing about and that it was nothing worth arguing over! If you're in an F/B relationship, remember that y'all speak two different languages. Try to work on how you argue instead of the issues you think you might be discussing. Learn to vocalize exactly what you're feeling: Are you angry or embarrassed? Don't be afraid of prompting her as well. Ask her, "Are you angry or hurt?" And give out your own emotional barometer reading when necessary. If you're in a bad mood but it has nothing to do with your stallion, say, "I know I look pissed, but it has nothing to do with you. I need to cool off alone, then I'll be yours." Don't make her guess. One sentence is all it takes. (If, by the way, it takes more than that, she's either a worrywart or a "process king," so tell her to check it. There's enough real drama in the world without her making double Ds out of A cups.)

An added problem is the concept of "busting her balls." Her balls may be silicone, but, sister, are they delicate! You think you were just stating your mind and she thinks you were trying to make a fool of her. "What?!" you cry in disbelief. The next thing you know, it's World War III.

Fighting with butches drains both partners. The butch already feels vulnerable inside. That's why she acts so scary and tough on the outside. You forgot for a minute that we don't live in a perfect world, that everyone isn't equal, and you didn't give her the extra props she needs in public.

This challenge takes compromise. You *do* need to give her props in public because the rest of the world doesn't. She's a stud because you enable her to be one. That bit of information is *not* me having delusions of grandeur; it comes queer from the stud's mouth. It's kind of like that eternal question, "If a tree falls in the woods and no one's there to hear it, does it make a sound?" If a butch walks down the street, she's just a bull dyke walking down the street. If she has a femme on her arm, then she becomes a stud. She fucks pretty women, even if she's the bottom. She's not a eunuch. And if she's a freak, then she's a freak who's freakin' a hot babe. She's telling the world, "Yeah, stare at us, asshole. We're having fun here in the circus. How 'bout you?" Even if the femme she's with is just a friend. I never said any of this is *real;* our whole culture is an illusion, so let's just control the paintbrush when we can. What if that butch is in a dyke space? It's still true. If she wants a femme to be yearning for her and there are no lustful femmes to be had, then the hottest butch is going to be an asexual lump on the nearest barstool. Oh, sure, she may laugh with friends or lead games of pool, but get real—she's not feeling like a stud.

So, knowing all this, you can see that when you walk across the room and she acts like you have her ego tucked into your garter belt, it's often because you do. Both of you need to be aware of how real this feels and at the same time what a fake piece of societal bullshit it is. How do you do that? Compromise.

You: Give her props in public. Be nice. Watch the tone of your voice when you *ask* for things or she'll think you're *telling*. Butches don't like to be bossed around in public, but they do love to make you happy—if you're kind and appreciative.

Her: She needs to calm down and listen to you, and to realize you're not questioning her power when you ask her to do something or to listen to you for a moment. It's simply you giving input, and that's not a crime. She needs to give you a few minutes of attention and take your input. Then you won't become a nag.

You: Accept that things won't get done your way each and every time. And who would want that anyway? I often do know the best way to do things, but isn't it great to let somebody else be in charge at times? It's just hard for us to remember to let go because we've had to do it ourselves for so long.

Your butch doesn't pass in the straight world the way you do. Even if you're a flaming Queen like me, femmes get better treatment on the streets than butches. She has to wear a different kind of armor than we do. Once she's off the streets and in your arms, it may take a moment for her shields to come down. She can't just wave a sword and be human instantly. She may need extra love and attention when coming in from the world. Your arms, her favorite drink, and a few minutes to chill is usually all it takes.

Out and About

When a femme and butch come together romantically, the world stands still, literally, to stare at us. If two femmes are walking down the street together, they could be just two girlsistergirl-friends, even if they're holding hands. If two butches are walking down the street, they could be two buddies. But if a butch and femme are together, they stand for queer sex. The butch queers the femme and the femme sexualizes the butch. Unlike the femme-on-femme couple whose challenges often have to do with invisibility, the femme and butch couple face their own set of challenges because of their blatantly queer sexuality.

> "But I did get some [sex] once or twice. From some of the most beautiful girls in the world. Strippers, poets, photographers. Rockstars. OH, yeah. I would think, ha they want these girls so bad it hurts and WHO ARE THEY FUCKIN', PAL? HUH? THEY'RE FUCKIN' THIS DIRTY LITTLE GUTTER DYKE, not your tired fancy car drivin', business-suit-wearin', hang glidin', golfin', world travelin', handsome self! HAHAHAHA."
>
> —from a work in progress by Lynn Breedlove

On the street a feminine woman with a "dyke" might incite violence in some men. They think the butch is stealing one of "theirs." Right, whatever. Your butch, if she's at all old-fashioned, will feel obligated to defend your honor. It doesn't matter if she is 5 foot 2 and he's a gorilla. They both know she's the protector. It's up to you to be aware of the balance between your butch's ego and y'all's safety. She may be wise to the world herself and know when to fight and when to run. That's a part of getting to know each other: seeing how you both react in adverse situations.

Even as I write this, though, I can list many butches who don't step up to fight. I also know couples in which the femme is the hothead. Individual tempers can, of course, vary. But because many men (not all) will listen to a femme or instinctively not want to hit her, the femme often (not always) wields a particular kind of power on the street. Use it to avoid ugly situations. Humor, a chill attitude, and showing your smarts can often head off a collision. Or, use your power to confuse them long enough for you two to make an escape. By all means, if you think you can't win, then get out alive. That's the ultimate victory.

There are also times when you know you have a fighting chance. Your femme force will throw off the typical ways guys provoke fights. Butches can do that old-fashioned kind of macho fighting, but when a femme's in the picture, you're a winning combo (unless they have numbers or guns, so watch your back, sister). You can fight dirty, "girly," or just plain go crazy on their ass. Walking with steaming hot drinks in your hand helps. My friend Denise has thrown many a hot latte in self-defense. I've talked my way out of most tight situations, but then there were times when I just went psycho. Like the Incredible Hulk, I've been filled with an unknown strength and have thrown over tables, drinks and all, not to mention tossed men across whole rooms. My friend Michelle has knocked guys out with everything from her huge rhinestoned Grandma bag to a Dijon mustard jar.

Even in the gay and lesbian community, femme/butch romance can get shit. Assimilationists don't like us because they think the femmes look like bimbo sellouts and the butches look like bulldaggers or men. How are we going to placate the heterosexuals if we don't play nice and try to blend in? They, the assimilationists, are always trying to convince the greater population that we're "just like them." Well, we *are* all human beings. We do all love and shit and drink and eat and joy over our babies and cry over our mamas. But, no, we are *not* "just like them." Drag queens and butches are screaming realities of our queerness. Assimilationist gays and lesbians would rather see a Subaru banner at a gay pride parade than a topless butch dyke. Hello?

Then there are those who somehow think we're aping heterosexuals. That is so old, child. Get a *herstory* book and educate yourself.

Oh, and how about the trendoids? Right now in SF the fashion à la mode is to be a "working-class butch," even if you were raised in a mansion. Trends come and go. I'm sure that in some cliques butch and femme romance isn't "in." Hopefully, F/B love won't ever have to retreat into the closet like it did in the '70s. The outside world is harsh enough without homosexuals coming down on F/B amour.

I think that with soft butches like Ellen and k.d. Lang coming out, with straight celebrities gender-bending on stage, and transgendered people making themselves more visible, the world is starting to accept butches. The easier the bulldagger has it, then the easier the F/B lovers have it.

Femmes' supercharged attraction to butches has stood the test of time. Masculinity harnessed in the female body serves as the only drag high enough to balance us. The magnetic allure between a femme and her butch is so strong, it will always flourish despite dark or ignorant forces.

Jumping the Gender Fence
Stud-Love Therapy for the Femme-Chasing Femme

Reasons to try a good butch:

(1) There aren't any good or available femmes in your town.

(2) Butches help you to relax into your femmeness, instead of having to be on guard in our rough 'n' tumble world.

(3) *Good* butches will treat you like a lady, which always helps to make you feel like a Queen.

(4) They smell nice.

(5) They radiate queerness.

(6) Butch sexuality is like an avocado: From the outside you'd never guess there's such silkiness underneath.

To jump the fence:

If you're known as a femme lover or your community ostracizes femme/butch romance, you'll need to show her you're willing to go both ways. She may have you written off as someone who wouldn't go for her. I've already shown you the ropes of flirting, so flirt.

If you want to kiss her, tell her to hold out her hand, then kiss her palm, curl her fingers around your kiss print until her fist is closed, and say, "That's a kiss to save for later. This one's for now." Then kiss her.

In bed, you're gonna be the only girl, so go for it. Revel in your differences. Pull tight against her. Allow your oppositeness its natural tension.

Butch Boot Camp or, If You Can't Find One, Train One

Maybe you have a fabulous butch who stands out in terms of knowing how to treat you, so you think this chapter doesn't apply to you. *Au contraire!* Read on. Some of my methods can be applied to eliminate bad habits that otherwise great butches have picked up from past girlfriends who perhaps didn't appreciate them or bring out their best. For example, my ultrasuave wife had this annoying habit of handing me my ticket at the theater. Finally, I just let her drop it into thin air. She had to scramble around for the fallen ticket, and we backed up the line, thus embarrassing her, but she definitely got it that it was not for me to hold the tickets. I smile politely at the ticket ripper as she hands them over. That's my job. If this chapter doesn't help you directly, then you can pass along the info to a sister in need (there are more than enough of them). Onward.

Oh, bother! You've looked up and down and sideways and you can't find a good butch, or not even *a* butch, to save your life, much less ego and libido. What's a girl to do? Well, fret no more. It's simple! If you can't find a good butch woman, then you'll have to train one. Yes, it's more work than you'd ordinarily take on, and it can be quite an

investment of time and energy, but a gal's gotta do what a gal's gotta do. If your needs aren't being met, it's high time you tackled the world in front of you and changed it. Many of today's hot butches once seemed anything but butch, so take heart. The potential is out there; it's just up to you to nurture it.

Findin' Some Rough in the Diamonds: Spotting Potential

First you have to find a creature with potential. Potential butches come in all types of packaging. We've already discussed flirting with the whole solar system as a matter of habit, so as you do this, note any woman with whom you've had interesting encounters. Don't worry about how she's dressed or what kind of boots she's wearing (or not wearing). Just ask yourself the following questions:

(1) Does she appreciate the femme in me?

Example: Has she complimented my outer femmeness (hair, nails, dress)? Or my *inner* femmeness (comments, thoughts, perspective)?

Note: She might not respond to the actual word "femme," but just to your Princess/Diva/Goddess/Kitten/Bitch self.

(2) Do you catch her staring at your ass? I have found *the* most andro, yuppie, "I'm just a woman" types staring at my ass like they were seeing Mary in the sky, mouths open, eyes glazed, transfixed at first then overwhelmed with thoughts running through their andro minds such as, "I'm seeing something that looks like hope, but I'm not sure, and how does it even apply to me…and who is it for? But who cares, really, because, look at it! It gives me this feeling in my body like *ooh*." Then they sigh and become transfixed again.

(3) Does she get kind of flustered when she sees you in full drag?

Examples: Feelings of nausea, tripping a lot, stuttering. Note: If she stutters saying, "I, I, I…" smile and say, "Oh, I'm sure you would." That'll boost her ego and make her think like the Little Brando Who Could.

(4) Subtly ask what kind of toys she played with as a child. If she didn't play with dolls but liked playing with G.I. Joe, guns, trains, or anything involving a lot of dirt, that's good. Many girls

played with these toys, but femmes also played with dolls.

(5) Where's her center of gravity? Many women wear makeup and throw around their long hair, yet stomp around with their pelvis tilted forward (like there's a weight going from the end of their spines to the floor). Soon enough, they wipe off that makeup and end up being butch. Note: Keep in mind, there are many femme gals who are tomboy femmes and walk better in boots than heels and also many femmes are sex workers and prefer to stomp around flat footed when they're not working.

(6) Does she smell butch? Do you find yourself relating to her like she's butch (leaning on her, asking her to fetch your drink, etc.), then you catch a long glance at her again and realize that on the outside or from her talk you have no reason to think she's butch? Maybe your subconscious sniffer is catching something that your conscious self passes by.

Hopefully you'll find someone who meets at least a couple of the above criteria. With some luck, she'll be younger than you. This helps establish authority in your training. But don't worry if she's older than

PHYLLIS CHRISTOPHER

Does your butch-in-training get kind of flustered when she sees you in full drag? That's a sure sign of potential.

you. Just tell her you're an old soul and that she's a young one.

Some women realize immediately that they long to be trained. Maybe they're simply longing to be in your grip. Don't trip on it, just take advantage of it. With these women you can do a hard

> "I merely glance at her crotch / Knowing a good-butch is always / prepared for those critical moments of sudden urgency."
> —from "The Latin-Angel & the Gangster Butch-Gentleman" by Tina D'Elia

course of training. With others you might have to take a softer approach. You'll notice they'll start to adapt in a way that's complementary to you.

Overt or Hard Training

You may be into S/M role playing and decide to re-create *Exit to Eden* for your training. That's certainly overt. It's also overt to just be conscious that you're giving your time and energy to help this woman try on a social persona, to mold herself, to embody a masculine persona. If you've chosen the right woman for schoolin', this will feel natural to her, like going home, like the way some of us felt when we realized we *did* have a sexuality. Homosexuality and that moment of realization didn't actually feel wrong, but rather, right—no more trying to squeeze a square peg into a round hole. Well, many women feel that way as they ease into allowing themselves to be butch. They most often don't *become* butch, rather they *allow* themselves to *be* butch. You can play a vital role in helping them to create a space—mentally, emotionally, or sexually—that lets them relax into their true nature.

By "overt," I also mean she knows she's trying on this persona. Maybe it goes unsaid, but you both know this is the dressing room and you're the one handing over the tailored slacks.

During training, don't walk the middle of the road. You're the older, wiser woman, and she's your beast. You'll both be happier this way. Think "pack-animal" mentality. Teach her the ropes gently but firmly. Patience, persistence, and praise. Praise helps a lot.

You don't have to be a dominatrix top. You can be the biggest pillow queen in town. How do we call puppies? Sometimes we coax and sweet-talk them, and sometimes we stomp our feet and yell.

Soft Training Or, Covert Facilitation of Her Awareness

Perhaps she doesn't want to be your puppy, and maybe she doesn't even buy that she's a young soul. You need to believe what she says and act accordingly. Be aware that whether you're training covertly or overtly, you'll encounter kinks and roadblocks. One way is not necessarily more effective than the other. But this method provides that delicate "nudge" that might not make your teachings so obvious to butches-in-training (thus saving them possible embarrassment and/or preserving their dignity).

Covert Training Tips (adjust according to how obvious you aim to be)

•Have her read the "On the Date" section of this book.
•Be simple and suggestive.
•Go shopping with her and ask her to try on the tailored suit in the men's section. Or do the opposite: Encourage her to not dress up. Say, "Honey, I like you in Levi's." When she complains about putting on makeup say, "You're gorgeous without it. Why bother?" Say it even if she doesn't complain.
•If you both financially contribute to dates or outings, say, "I can spend $20 tonight. I don't care how or where we spend it, but I don't feel like holding it. Do you mind putting it in your wallet?"

•Once she has your money, she has to pick up the check, purchase the movie tickets, etc. Do *not* let her hand you your movie ticket! Simply say, "That's ridiculous. You hold both of them."

•Wait for her to open the door. If you must be sneakier than that, accidentally drop something so that you're bent over when you reach the door, then fiddle with the something so your hands are tied up. Any reasonable human being will go ahead and open the door for you under those circumstances. Next time say, "Do you mind getting that? My nails are wet." Yet another suggestion: Say, "Do you mind? I pulled my shoulder at the gym." Have an excuse for each door and she'll soon get the hang of it. If you do this often, she'll respond like Pavlov's dog. Whether she likes it or not, she gets trained to open doors when you're by her side.

•Tell her what you want either as a demand ("Fuck me now, goddamn it!") or as a compliment ("I love when you grab me like that.").

•When she admires especially femme things about you, prod her to say them aloud. This is an old sales technique in which the consumer validates the product. You can simply ask, "Do you like me in teddies?" If she's noncommittal, give her a choice: "Do you like me better in my silk gown or a teddy?" Now, here's the key: Let's say she chooses the teddy. Get her to say it. You might have to fish a while, so ask something such as, "If you could pick out any kind of teddy for me, what would it be?" Or "What do you think I should get at Frederick's?"

•Beg her to wear a men's undershirt while you jack off staring at her.

•Tell her how irresistible you think she is in boxers. (You might not want to do these two exercises back-to-back if you're trying to be subtle.)

•She knows you're strong in many ways, but find a way that you aren't strong or a time that you don't need to be strong and let her protect you. Then reward her, and yourself, with sex.

•If she gets her hair cut "too short, damn hairdresser," run your fingers through it and tell her she looks great. If it's really short, you can rub her head between your breasts. Knead it.

•If she has long hair, one day when she's wearing a ponytail suggest she wear her baseball cap backward.

•Get her to carry things such as boxes or the trash, then reward her by rubbing her muscles.

•If she's butchable, these things will become second nature to her without much effort on your part. She will revel in your feminine side and find herself standing more sturdily so you can curve around her.

Stone Butch Blues & Boogie

Set in Stone

I'm including a chapter on dating stone butches because femmes who date these women often get little support or understanding from their partner. This lack of support can lead to bad communication or mistreatment in a stone butch–femme relationship. I've cried over many a mishap with a stone butch. I've also wiped up the tears or boosted the egos of too many of my girlsister-girlfriends who have had the stone butch blues.

To most lesbians, "stone butch" refers to a butch whose gender presentation keeps with the most traditional characteristics of butch, including the one most talked about: her vulva does not get touched, and most likely her breasts don't either. (There is, however, a growing group of butch women who call themselves "stone," but do not adhere to some of these traditions.) When we ask, "Is she stone?" We know what we mean: "Do you get to fuck her?"

I've been with women who were *stone* stone. No pussy, no tits. Not only do you not touch them, you don't look *for* pussy or tits, much less *at* them. My sex with stone butches consisted of them doing me, and that's it! Some had orgasms while fucking me, but if not, they came on their own time. I've also been with what I call "relatively stone" women, women who forbade me to touch their womanly parts but let me see them and watch them jack off.

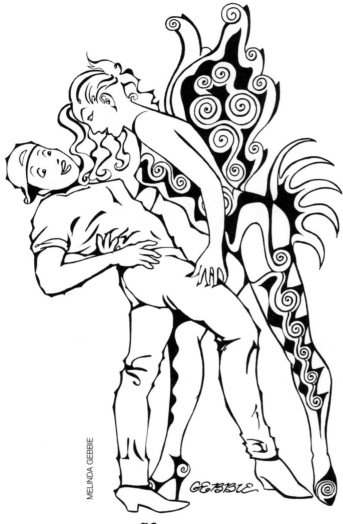

MELINDA GEBBIE

GEBBIE

Venus romancing the stone.

Femmes often feel guilty about receiving physical pleasure without giving sexual gratification. We worry they aren't getting as much pleasure as us. It's a myth that stone butches "don't receive any pleasure" when doing you. First of all, the obvious: She gets pleasure out of doing you. Pleasure is not strictly defined as sexual orgasm. Many of us find extreme pleasure in certain activities—eating particular foods, listening to music, rock climbing—that do not lead to sexual orgasm, but we still love that stuff. When it comes to sex, why do we suddenly narrow the definition of pleasure? She's loving every minute of what she's doing…period.

Secondly, many women do reach orgasm when penetrating another woman, whether they penetrate with their fingers or a dildo. If positioned correctly, the base of the dildo can provide clitoral stimulation. But, frankly, that's usually not the sinker; the shared experience is. The pure bliss of pushing *you* into bliss and feeling you rise to ecstasy can push *her* over the orgasmic edge. It's tantric. Try deep breathing during sex; this shoves oxygen into those red blood cells, which pump up your muscles and make your pussy swell up. It's divine. A butch who's never even heard the word *yoga* is breathing deeply if she's fucking you hard.

One way that butches revel in the pleasure of fucking has to do with their insanely perfect sex memories. Many butches have confided in me that they memorize their partner's every moan and move during lovemaking, then later replay it in their heads over and over while they jack off. You may think you two had sex just once, but little do you know that, sure, *you* did it once, but she's on number 150. She reruns that movie reel over and over. You had five orgasms, but she's coming for the 200th time. Every butch reading this is sinking into her seat right now because they know they've been busted! I just told their little secret to the whole world. Or maybe they're pleased that I'm confirming their stories, so you'll know she really *does* love what she's doing. The point is, stop feeling guilty or worried about her pleasure. She's having a good time and plenty of orgasms because of you.

Practical Hands-Off Advice

Now that I've given you the 411 on the "pleasure" thing, let me offer some realistic advice you can put into practice. I'm going to lead you through this one tiptoe at a time, so bear with me. When we like or love someone, we often want to share great experiences. You're thinking sunsets. Yeah, they're better when you're with someone, but in general, I've found this sharing thing to be tricky. If Jackie and I are going to a fancy party, I wear some cute dress. I don't expect her to wear a little black dress. She wouldn't feel her best in that; she'd feel like a clown. She and I each dress up in our own way, and that makes us feel good.

With sensual experiences, though, there's no clear line in the sand. If I get an ice cream cone that I love, I'll insist that Jackie take a bite, and then I'll want her to ooh and aah over it just like I do, even if it's not her favorite flavor. How come I get it about the black dress but not the ice cream? Because inner stuff is harder. No one experiences pleasure or pain the exact same way. A strong scent to one person is a mild scent to someone else. It's easy to get caught up in wanting to touch this hot butch (who happens to be stone) the way she touches you because *you want her to feel what you feel* when she touches you. But that's like me and the ice cream. Ooey gooey chocolate mocha just ain't gonna do it for everyone. Getting touched by you the way she touches you just doesn't feel good to her. Matter of fact, touching her in those ways might feel plain awful to her. If you try to push yourself on her, you'll both end up frustrated. You can't say to yourself, *Hey, I love it when she shoves her hand into me, so I'll do that to her.* Different butches desire different amounts of touching. Some stone butches enjoy having their nipples squeezed, receiving fingers in special places, or oral sex. But what she doesn't want is to strip naked and jump on her back. She would feel like an upside-down turtle; it's just not a natural position for her. Do you and she both want to sneak up on her girly parts? Many a butch lover has advised her gal to "sneak up" or "trick me." Usually the thought of exposing herself that way is worse than the action itself. She actually likes it when you get a finger in but tells you, "Don't go rushing things."

I propose you round out your love scene by mixing things up a bit. For example, if you say "nipple" to an old-fashioned butch she thinks "woman tit." Hello! Everybody's got nipples, and men love for theirs to be sucked, pinched, and teased. So here are some more ideas for keeping your butch masculine during the most intimate sex acts:

Refer to her breasts as pecs.

Call her dildo her dick or cock.

One thing your butch might love is a show. If she'll jack off in front of you, then give her the vibrator. Dance over her face, moan, pull at your nipples, pretend you're in *Hustler* and spread yourself wide open. Grunt and rock the way you do when she's bringing you to an orgasm (but don't be too good at it or she'll think you're faking it—as if!). You might feel it's a lot of work lying there showing your pussy, but it's not any harder than her pumping you for an hour.

Try a move that Fanny Fatale does in the video *Clips*. Fanny's butch, Kenny Mann, is lying on her back. Fanny is between her legs sucking her cock. Look closely at Fanny's shoulder: She's shoving it into Kenny's groin, thus making the base of the dildo rub into Kenny's clit.

Everyone, male and female, has a butt hole. Try to work your finger or tongue in that direction.

Combine acts that make her feel macho with any of these new recommendations. For example, suck her dykedick while you edge your finger past her special gates.

Tell her you know a lot of guys who love having their nipples pinched. Would she want you to do that to her while you're straddling her cock?

You'll occasionally run across a mostly stone butch who says she wants to "try" being on the receiving end of your dildo. Don't scare her away by transforming into Mack Daddy Top. As you get between her legs, be sure to let the top half of your body be as girly as ever. Look almost like you're riding her dick, even though you're the one with the dick. Above the waist is no place to be subtle. Try stripper moves. Throw your hair around. Pinch your nipples. If you two like dirty talk, then talk about *yourself*. How excited you are, how wet you are, how bad you're going to need be fucked. Pull her hands up to touch your chest and talk about how sexy her hands are. Then let your pelvis indiscreetly do its thing. I know this sounds complicated, but it usually works, as long as she's not in physical discomfort from the dildo. Do occasionally ask, "Is this OK?" referring to your penetration. Don't process or fret over it any more than that. Believe me, you'll find out loud and clear if she doesn't like it.

But let's say your desire to touch her doesn't come from your wanting her to feel what you feel. Instead, it comes from your desire to ravish her. After all, if you're with her, you're a dyke or bi, so what if you want to touch her because that's how you want a woman?

I'm sorry to tell you this, but you two are going to travel a rough road. Depending on her age and experience level, chances are she's already tried letting girls touch her and didn't like it. You don't want to make *her* feel awful, yet *you* feel awful being restricted in such a way. This may be a time for non-monogamy. If that isn't an option, then, sad to say, this incompatibility might ultimately lead to your breaking up.

Tell Me a Story

Try lying next to her while she uses a vibrator and whisper a dirty story in her ear. The key to hot erotic storytelling is to include vivid details, especially those that you know turn on your lover. Does she love short skirts? Then tell her how you slowly bent over the pool table in yours. Lips? Describe how you were putting on your lipstick, looking into a compact, when you caught her eye. Try retelling one of your real-life sexcapades— maybe the one you just had—describing how great she felt inside you, how horny you were, how much you ached for her fingers.

Some women won't want you to talk because they want to visit the fantasy inside their heads. Since you don't have a script for that fantasy, your talking would mess up the movie in her head and inhibit orgasm. You might be weaving a tale of you nude with your hair flying in the wind as you ride a stallion bareback to her castle. Meanwhile, she's imagining you hanging from the ceiling in a steel cage, with Gothic-cross pasties, as you're doing a snake dance. Your voice can be as intrusive as the blare of the alarm clock interrupting the best part of a dream. Your story has to match hers for her to get off.

So just ask, "Do you want me to tell you a story?" Get her to actually let you in on the script so that your words will match the fantasy. Otherwise, just lie beside her while she jacks off, thinking loving thoughts.

More Complications

As if the preceding roadblocks weren't enough to maneuver around, there are even further obstacles. For example, *some* butch tops, especially stone ones, claim they don't want to be touched, yet they secretly do. They think if you really, really, really wanted to touch them, you'd keep trying and break through their barriers, their internal struggle. Yet whenever you bring up the subject in words or actions, the gates come slamming down. You get the message loud and clear: "No way." Most of us have had a dose of "respecting boundaries" training. You certainly don't want to make her feel bad, so you back off. She may make you feel really bad, that you want too much from her, that she can never give it to you, and on and on. You're in tears. One minute you were turned on, trying to make someone happy, and the next you're Medusa incarnate. You retract that finger out of the latex glove and put it right back on your lap. Little did you know you were navigating an

> # "I'm not apologizing for what I did— I'm apologizing for what I didn't do."
> —Femme Violet to butch Corky in the film *Bound*

obstacle course and that you just missed a hurdle. Sorry, you flunked her head game. That's right, she actually really wanted you to fuck her/touch her. She wanted you to plead through your tears, to beg for her to give you some. This is a big one: She wanted you to *seduce* her more. You could have tried harder in the seduction department. Some butch tops want their gals to go through barrier after barrier to get to them. I wish they were articulate enough to just say that, instead of making it all skullduggery.

The problem is, they can't say it because they think they aren't supposed feel desire that way, much less think about it. For whatever reasons, they take all the potential wanting-to-be-touched-type desire and chain it up in a far, dark corner of their souls. When those chains start to rattle a bit, it scares them. Still, the clattering won't stop. One part of her wants you to read not her mind but her complete and utter subconscious. This is the root of the mind fuck. Her subconscious desire wants help breaking free, while her conscious social-mask-keeper is trying to beat the desire down, contain it, so she can pretend it's not there. Part of her is this giving, stoic stud who doesn't need "soft, girly" pleasures such as sexual touch. The other part of her wants to let down her defenses and allow herself to receive your touch. She can see the reflection of her inner struggle in you, so she strikes out at what she sees, that mirror, shattering you. You're crying, not knowing what you've done, and she turns her anger down, soon comforting you and wiping your tears. So it worked…for a while. The mirror is gone; there's no reflection to scare her.

C'mon, Venus Girl. You can get back up on that pedestal. Now that you know what's going on, there are a few moves you can try. If she responds to them, you two will have the opportunity to break through this conundrum. If she doesn't respond, you might decide to move on to someone who's already faced her demons. You don't have time to play exorcist.

I'll give you an example of a mind fuck and suggestions on how to handle it. Let's say you've got a finger going toward her special gate. She sighs, acting bored, essentially dissing your attempts. You ask her, "Is there anything I can do to make this more fun for you?" Make suggestions. "What if I put my ass in the air so you'll get a good view?" "Why don't you pretend you like it for just a *few* seconds? C'mon, like a game. For me." Ask her, "Would you like it better if you were telling me what to do?"

If she out-and-out disrespects you, then plainly say, "You just disrespected me. If you don't like what *we* are doing, just use your words and say so." Try to remain unemotional. Try to remain still. She wants to make you back up, using your emotions against you like a fiery torch. Instead, be as still as you can. If she's disrespecting you, chances are you'll have to try again another time.

These are the only techniques that have worked for me or my friends. But remember to not let yourself get too ego-slammed, because one of these times you might not recover.

If you maneuver through the turbulence with humor, kindness, and honesty in a loving, respectful way, then you could move forward on a sexual journey to the special kind of intimacy that comes only from partners being vulnerable and trying new things together.

Part VII

Sex and the Single Femme

Whether you decide to boink babes or butches, ya gotta get your ravishing royal butt out and about for you to rise to your possexibilities. Read on, and I'll help you cultivate, regulate, and circulate a meteor shower of sensuality and affection. Girl, get out there and throw your gravitational pull around!

Single, Coupled, or Married?

The Benefits of Being Single:

When you answer the phone it's always for you.

No responsibility.

You can smoke if you want to.

You don't have to inhale smoke if you don't want to.

No check-ins. Do you want to go out with the gang after work? Then go. Do you want to wander around the mall aimlessly? Go. No need to call anyone to tell them if you have plans and no need to call at all, period, even if you know you don't have plans.

You can drink if you choose.

You can decide not to hang around drinkers if you choose.

You definitely keep more of your paycheck. I know it seems weird. You were probably assuming that you mated, then stayed in eating homemade spaghetti and watching TV. Cheap, you thought. No, no, it doesn't work like that. Couples cost a lot. It's kind of like the mystery of the missing sock; no one knows exactly where it goes, but it definitely goes.

Decision making is simplified. You answer to yourself. Until you're in a couple, you don't realize how much energy it takes to constantly consider two people.

You have only one biological family to deal with. As single people we have plenty of obligations with our own family and friends; adding another person's to that is so-o-o time consuming.

You can rise and retire as you please. You like to vacuum at 4 A.M.? Who cares!

You get to meet intriguing people and, even better, date them!

You can enrich your life with the people you meet because single people are out there more.

You embarrass only yourself, or rather you don't (married people have this tendency to think their spouse's actions/comments reflect on them—blech!).

You are more gorgeous.

You get to date as many people as you like without the brain-ache a coupled person gets.

And chances are you have more time for your art/passion/hobby/politics/sport. (Some couples do that sort of thing together, but I've heard many coupled people admit they regretfully lost passion or time for their own projects after they hooked up.)

The Queen's Alliance

Now, Shar, where do you get off preaching about the joys of being single when you're not only in a couple, but married for life?! Well, I was lucky enough to meet my soul mate and true love, Jackie Strano, in the spring of 1993. But I certainly wasn't sitting around pining away, hoping for true love. Matter of fact, I had taken a vow of celibacy the week before. I hadn't dated anyone for a while because it seemed there were too many crazies out there. When I told friends I was going to "aggressively chase celibacy instead of passively accepting it," my coworker Robin pointed out, "Shar, you're working the sex club next week."

"Oh, right. Damn, a kink in my brilliant plan."

But it was a good thing I'd made those plans with the Club Cream organizers. I met Jackie because I was so hypersingle. I was being the best Shar I could be, hostessing a lesbian sex club that night where my beholden had volunteered to decorate. We had a little exchange, then kissed, at which point my knees went weak and I saw stars.

Sex is not what made us the great couple we are, although that alone would have been enough for me. I'd have been thrilled for her to be my pretty-fuckin'-great love. I can honestly

Unswervingly Slinkin' Down the Unadulterated Path of You

Imagine your life is a path. If you live your life to its fullest, being the best "you" that you can be, your path will remain true to its course. Whether you're following plans or being spontaneous, if you follow your heart, rise to your potential, and be kind to yourself, then you're being you. If, for a while, long or short, someone else's path runs parallel to yours, it's astonishing—you're really meant to be together for that time. It is a destined relationship no matter how long it lasts.

say if our love was even half of what it is, I still would've followed her anywhere. But our intense, passionate love isn't why I married her. I think marriage is a partnership. Jackie doesn't make me weaker; she makes me stronger. I'm not only the best me I can be but actually better. It's like we've made each other the Bionic Woman without surgery. If you're considering marrying someone, please first consider your compatibility. You can burn your passion high and large without getting married.

Security on Lonely Nights

"Some defend what they cannot see with a killer's pride—security."
—Bob Dylan

When I was single, I had my share of lonely nights, crying myself to sleep wishing I had a pair of strong arms to hold me, but I still felt secure in those weepy moments. I knew I was my own person, that my future was in my own hands, no compromises. Many people have down moments living with someone else, but they cling to that security in those situations. They think, *Oh, I may be compromising myself for wishing I were doing my own thing instead of going to that picnic at her friend's house, but it's worth it for the security.* As a culture, we think nothing of the negative aspects of coupledom; matter of fact, we have endless support for them—everyone *under-*

stands marriage. But we beat ourselves up with a five-pound clog if we experience the negative sides of singlehood.

If you start compromising yourself, your personality, your wants and needs to be with someone else—in other words, if you change your path for someone else—you're screwing with destiny! Not only does it take an incredible amount of energy to curve your path—and Goddess knows what else you could be doing with that energy—but you're also fucking with Fate. For example: You're choosing between scallops or shrimp for two at Safeway because it's your turn to cook, even though you hate cooking, or maybe you don't, but if you were just being you, you wouldn't be hungry at all right now, so you would have wandered, like you do, into the bookstore. You would have strolled to your favorite section, nibbling white-cheddar popcorn, and would meet this other gal who loves chicks who eat white-cheddar popcorn and has just finished reading the book you're looking at. See? Be the best "you" you can be and your path will remain true. Of course, it may seem curvy or bumpy to you, but it will still be true. A mountain pass is supposed to be a mountain pass. A straightaway cutting through the desert is a straightaway. Take away your judgments of "good" or "bad." It's all about where you're supposed to be.

Remember, though, finding dates and love partners is a numbers game. There are a lot of people

> ## "Never settle for second best, baby. If the time isn't right, then move on."
> —Madonna

on this planet, so for you to meet your destined mates, you'd really better get out to the bingo hall. The odds of that person being born next door to you are .000000004% or slimmer. Give Fate some help by just being you so that Fate can look down your road and see where you'll be next Tuesday.

Disclaimer: Now, don't get all persnickety on me and take what I'm saying to ridiculous extremes. Of course, I believe in compromise, and you do not get to be waited on 24/7. But you

True Love

How can I possibly define what I mean by true love? Here are some of the words the dictionary lists under the entry for *true*: real, genuine, faithful, loyal, sincere, unfeigned, unswerving, fundamental, essential, accurately shaped or fitted, accurately placed or delivered. I like *essential*. We often think of *essential* as meaning *necessary*, but I use the word in the sense of "of something's essence."

If you're being the best "you" you can be and someone else is being the best "her" she can be, and while you two are doing that life brings you together, and your paths run parallel without you even trying, and you smell right and love each other with endless curious passion and are compatible being the best "you"s you can be, then that's pretty damn close to true love.

know what I mean, because we've all done it. We've all wanted to say, "Make a pot pie. I'm going out."

As long as you're being the best "you" you can be, if you're meant to have true love in this lifetime true love will find you. True love is love that is destiny, meant to last forever and, not only that, but it would take Armageddon for it not to last forever. My point is that you need to live your life. If true love is meant for you, then it'll find you and you'll be knocked flat on your ass. It's not subtle. It's not like you'll blink and miss it!

Marriage—Yick!

"Marriage is insurance for the worst times of your life."

—Helen Gurley Brown

I never really believed in marriage. The concept of romantically loving only one person as long as you lived seemed fishy to me right from the start. Maybe it was my mother rushing down the hallway during fights with my father to pause at my doorway and say, "Sharlene, never, I mean *never*, get married."

I never had an example of true love in my family, and I didn't really believe what I saw on TV. At a certain age I realized true love did happen to some people, and while I think that's sweet, I still maintain that no one should wait around for it. I also think you shouldn't cut off your chances of being ready for the possibility of true love by promising your life away to Ms. Mediocre.

How many couples do you know who are far from perfect? As a matter of fact, all your friends know these people should just break up. But they stay together, not because of a desire to be together, but for fear of being apart or alone. Or what about a not-so-extreme example: a couple who is, well, OK together, but not that much fun anymore. One or both partners wants to expand her experiences (be a painter, spank a boy, whatever), but doesn't because she's just too comfortable to move. She's too busy making dinner for the in-laws or getting the VCR to work. She's too afraid of upsetting her lover. If she were single, would she be doing these things? Or would she be taking a photography class?

When I told people I didn't believe in marriage, most of the time they thought I'd been hurt before and was being a bitter Queen. Nothing could be further from the truth; I wasn't bitter in the least. I believe in the good of every moment. And I don't believe in wasting your life waiting by the phone for Ms. Perfect. I also don't believe in not getting your needs met because you've promised your life away to Ms. Will-Do. Does that sound contradictory? It's not. No promises and no waiting. That's the bottom line. Ms. Will-Do and Ms. Perfect can knock on your door as much as they please. It's sticking them and yourself into a predetermined, heterosexist, constrained relationship that sucks. You certainly can get what you want and have your needs met without buying into the whole marriage farce and myth. You deserve to have a full life with no compromises. How do you do that? Read on, *ma cherie*, read on.

Dating, or Shopping, as I Like to Call It

Q: Shar! Enough bitchin' about marriage! I'll stop looking for true love and let it find me. What do I do in the meantime?

A: Date, of course!

Dating is shopping, and when you know that and are as practiced at it as you are at shopping, you won't get confused. What does shopping involve? Let's break it down:

(1) Wanting something

(2) Knowing you want something

(3) Deciding where to start looking

(4) Getting ready:

    •logistically (*I'll need transportation, money, shopping list.*)

    •mentally (*It's going to take time and money to do this.*)

    •physically (*I'm going to wear slip-on sandals for on-and-off ease.*)

(5) Shopping. You go shopping. You stop when you find what you want or something that'll do for now.

But sometimes we don't know what we want when we go shopping. We just feel itchy even though we don't think we want anything in particular. So let's think about those steps:

(1) Wanting something

(2) Knowing you want something

(3) Guessing where you might start to look

(4) Getting ready: This may be a little involved. You may change clothes or rearrange your schedule, or you may just walk out the door. You want to be prepared for the possibility of finding something, so you grab your ATM card or Visa just in case.

(5) Shopping: You stop when you feel satisfied, whether or not you buy something.

Finally, sometimes you want to window shop; that is, shop without buying anything. It makes you happy to just go through the motions and look.

OK, Now Let's Apply the Steps: Dating as Shopping

(1) **Want something.** (This step happens without any help from us; it just happens! So, number two is the important step.)

(2) **Know you want something.** The reasons can be obvious—you haven't had any lovin' for too long, you need a date just 'cause a girl's gotta eat, you want someone to admire your new outfit, or there may be just some kind of itchin' going on. Maybe it's in the front of your brain where you can name it

NEED

NEED NEED NEED NEED
NEED NEED NEED NEED
What?
Try a corned beef on rye.
Puke.
Try a cigarette.
Cough.
Try a whole box of
chocolate chip cookies.
Blecch.
Try a man.
Frustration.
Try masturbation.
Lonely.
Try a beer.
Belch.
Try music.
Cry.
TRY TRY TRY TRY
TRY TRY TRY TRY
Still
NEED NEED NEED NEED
NEED NEED NEED NEED
What?

© 1972 Marcy Sheiner

Addendum, 1979: Need twat?

One of the single femme's tools for titillation and girlsister-girlfriend support: the babephone.

or perhaps it's in the dusty record-store lobe (the same place song titles that you can't remember but are on the tip of your tongue go) where you can't quite articulate what's going on but you know you need *something*. Now you need to make a list of what you need to shop for—as much as you know.

(3) **Decide where to start looking.** Where can you find what you want? If you need some lovin', let's be specific. Maybe you're coming off your period and need some sex ASAP. If you were a guy and needed some right now, you could pretty easily find some anonymous sex. But what we have to do as women is sow some seeds for the future.

This was a little difficult for me to grasp until I got into the habit of it. I'm a pretty impatient person, mentally and physically; I really live for the moment. For example, I have a high metabolism and need to eat almost as soon as I get hungry, or I black out and all kinds of nasty things happen. It took me years of being that way before I started to plan out meals ahead of time. Now I cook and have food ready and waiting for me. If I'm not hungry when it's ready, it sits there and I microwave it later, if necessary. And even when I screw up and am not prepared, I know to just grab a bag of chips to tide me over until the food is ready.

But what if I were hiking a mountain and had to fish for my food and build a fire and cook it *and* I had no trail mix! Can you imagine? I'd be in quite a predicament if I weren't prepared every minute. Dating women and depending on them for sex is kind of like being on the mountain. You have to plan ahead and not wait until you have those hunger pains. Many women are slow. I can even be one of the slow ones myself if I'm in a certain mood. So have a fish on the line, some berries spotted in the field, and some trail mix in your pocket. That is, have a few gals at the ready and always have a good friend or two who you have sexual energy with who'll help you in your time of need.

(4) **Get ready.** *Logistically:* Do you want to go out with a friend? Do you have a car or taxi money? *Mentally:* Do you have any limits tonight? (This also is part of the "what do you want" category.) You don't know what you want? Great, know that. You're overworked and a little cranky but still want to try? Know that. You want to be kissed, dance, etc? Know that too. *Physically:* Clean up, girl, and clean your bed and sex toys too. Also, have some safer-sex supplies ready.

(5) **Go shopping.** Now that you know your needs, you can start to get them filled. And certainly don't fret about how many people it takes to do the job! Let's go back to step two and say that you know you need to bake a chocolate cake and want to serve it with vanilla ice cream. It would be perfect if you had a car, could buy all the ingredients in one store, and drive them right up to your door. But in the real world, you might not have a car, or perhaps you don't have enough money to buy everything, so you have to borrow a cup of sugar. Or maybe you're a specialist and want chocolate from Ghirardelli, ice cream from Ben & Jerry's, and flour from Baker's Mart in the neighboring town. My point is, there are many times you can't or don't want to get everything you need at one store. But if you're determined to get that cake baked, then you'll get what you need to get the job done, no matter how many stores you have to go to to get it. Your needs and wants are the same as that cake. Follow your shopping list and take care of yourself, no matter how many stores/dates you need to go to/on.

Compiling Your Shopping List

What do you want? Do you even know?

Make a list of your needs. Don't be embarrassed; write down *everything*. Think in detail, and separate your individual needs as much as possible. You may realize that you listed two versions of the same thing (e.g., affection and love). Amend your list, taking note of the various angles of everything you need. Finally, don't be skimpy or a martyr. If you need something, say so!

Here are some examples:
• sex (Divide this up: need to make out; to receive touchy attention, such as cuddling, foot rubs, etc.; to put my fingers in someone; to have someone fill me up)
• someone to shop with
• someone to cook for me
• someone to fix the car
• someone to polish my latex before an outing
• someone to polish my boots in general

Now make a list of how you like to be treated. For example:
• Dates must be prompt.
• They should give me flowers and/or chocolates.
• They should have reliable transportation.
• They should shower me with compliments.

Now make a list of your wants. No one else is going to read it, so don't be embarrassed to list even frivolous stuff:
• I want a girlfriend who has a motorcycle.
• I want a date to take me to the Hyatt Regency.
• I want a girl to massage my shoulders for a whole hour.
• I want a foot rub every Friday.

Your Step-by-Step Dating Guide

Let's see, what's left on your checklist? You've got the palace set up with at least a beginning of sex toys and have some latex ready. You've mentally prepared by making your shopping list.

The Babephone, a Palace Necessity

A babe about town like yourself definitely needs her own phone. No need to share with roomies. If you must, then at least have an extension in your bedroom. If you don't want to pay the phone company to do that, just buy a $6 splicer at any department or drug store. Your phone is the Babephone. It cradles the

The Single Girl-Goddess Checklist:

❑ Babephone
☑ sex toys
☑ safer-sex supplies
❑ a trail
❑ a map
❑ possexibilities
☑ shopping list

Fashion Phone Sex

My friend Stephanie just loves fashion phone sex. For that matter, she likes fashion foreplay, haute couture hard-core, and accessory comedown! "What are you wearing?" isn't clichéd—it's tried and true! Ask your gal one night as your voice softens for bedtime. She might release a nervous laugh, but those nerves will head south in seconds. When she asks you the same question, forget that you're wearing a plain T-shirt; she'll never know. Go for full fantasy effect. Once again, details are the key. Don't just say "a silk nightie." Describe the color, how it feels against your skin, where it's tight and where it isn't. Maybe you've taken off your dress but are still in that vintage slip that makes you look like you just walked off a Tennessee Williams stage set. Whether it's flannel pajama bottoms or the shirt she left at your house, be specific.

Tell her what you like her to wear. If it's something she's worn before, tell her all the nasty thoughts you were thinking when you saw her. Embellish.

Be vivid and detailed and slow. Describe your movements as the clothes come on or off so she can picture it.

Meow over the phone. Make your mark. Practice your purr.

Queen's delovely ear often and hovers near her lips. The Babephone is a special, highly respected piece of equipment for these reasons. Some of your best seductions will sinuate across those wires. The Babephone delivers the woman of your choice right to your mouth. Never disrespect the Babephone.

Pay attention as you talk with possexible dates (and anyone else) on the phone. Don't include your roommates in the conversation or refer to inside jokes. You don't have to take notes, but listen to what she says so you'll have something to ask about or refer to later. Remembering details about someone is flattering and provides a link to the next time you talk.

Answering Machine

Like, duh, have one.

It seems the good gals always call just when you've left the stupidest message on your machine, so be sure to record only date-ready messages (no canned recordings of "Nobody's Home" to the tune of Beethoven's Fifth).

How many of us love to call a girl when we know she's not going to be home just to leave that special message. So rehearse before you dial. And if she has voice mail, then lucky you. Most systems allow you to push the star button to erase what you've said and let you try again. Be sure this is the appropriate method for your girl's voice-mail system before you stumble through a message only to find out you can't erase it! Make your message a spontaneous yet charming little vignette. You're always inadvertently charismatic; you can't help it. The good news is that practice on one girl transfers to your next dates. It might seem difficult at first, but you'll become skilled at sounding relaxed even if you aren't.

It's handy to call her machine first because then if she calls you back, you'll know she really wants to talk to you. It's a tease.

Call Waiting

Some people think it's rude, but I think it's a necessity. Most everyone has call waiting or a voice-mail system that instantly picks up if you're on the phone. I prefer call waiting because you can talk to a friend while nervously waiting for your possexible date to call instead of sitting there alone staring at the phone. You'll never miss a call, yet, if you choose, you can ignore call waiting if you're talking to someone who thinks it's rude. If you want to show that special gal that you want to talk only to her, ignore the beeps and say, "Oh, they'll call back." On the other hand, call waiting gives you a handy excuse to get off the phone when she's too much. You can also turn it off before a call by dialing *70, followed by the phone number.

The Single Girl-Goddess Checklist:

- ☑ Babephone
- ☑ sex toys
- ☑ safer-sex supplies
- ☐ a trail
- ☐ a map
- ☐ possexibilities
- ☑ shopping list

A Trail: Helping Her Sniff Her Way to the Red Carpet

Let's say you meet a potential date, but your meeting is not at an appropriate place or time for exchanging numbers. Maybe you're on a date with someone else or you're with your mother picking out flowers for your great uncle's funeral. Think of a way to make a safe yet easy-to-find trail to yourself. The simplest way is if you can be reached at work and your work number is listed in the phone book. You can sigh over the flowers and say, "I always want to buy flowers for my workplace, but, unfortunately, where I work, at *Sweater Shack in Richmond, California,* we can't have flowers because of people's allergies."

Maybe you volunteer somewhere and can work that into the conversation. No matter what direction the discussion takes, just stare off preoccupied for a minute, then say, "Oh, I'm sorry. I volunteer at the Food Bin at 7 A.M. every Thursday, and I just realized I promised to pick up our fliers on my way here. Anyway, what were we saying?" Of course, whatever method you choose, you have to add a secret flirt in a different place in the conversation. (I did say "secret"; it's rude to flirt if you're already on a date.)

The Single Girl-Goddess Checklist:

- ☑ Babephone
- ☑ sex toys
- ☑ safer-sex supplies
- ☑ a trail
- ☐ a map
- ☐ possexibilities
- ☑ shopping list

If you're self-employed, it might be a bit harder. That's when planning a few options in advance is crucial. Think of as many ways as possible to work your career into a short conversation. You should already be able to do this for simple business and marketing reasons. If you're at a public place, perhaps you'll say to your date, mom, whomever, including the PD (potential date), "Excuse me for a moment. I see they have a bulletin board. Maybe I should post my services." And pin up your business card. You can always go back and take it down a couple of days later. Or if you and the PD have anyone in common, especially someone who's off limits as far as dating, thrust your card into her hand and say, "You're friends with Miriam, right? I've lost her number and just *have* to catch up with her. Would you pass this on? How is she in that commune?" I say "sincere" because you have the luxury of being sincere. You don't need to know that the PD is going to copy your number down long before Miriam gets your card.

Think up a few ideas. You'll never know when you might be studstruck and left stuttering. Hopefully, you'll be able to think on your heels, but planning ahead always helps.

A Map…of the Sexiest Spots in Town

"Aren't we putting on the shoe before the stocking?" you ask. No way! This is the kind of planning that turns a plain date into a mind-blowing, memorable mosh session! Take a tour around town and jot down notes when you're out and about, scoping out the best make-out nooks and crannies.

Public sex is hot. But make sure you find public places that are relatively safe.

PHYLLIS CHRISTOPHER

The Broadway tunnel seemed to be a safe place for sex—except for the drivers who couldn't keep their eyes on the road!

Doorways no one knows about. Pathways sandwiched between buildings. One of my favorite places was a stairwell that led to a basement door right outside my workplace. You could have a whole feel-up convergence in the rain without being seen by passersby (yet you could hear them).

As you go out with friends, take notes on what places seem cozy, sleazy, or queer friendly. Which ones have nice, nonintrusive wait staffs, dark corners, enticing lighting (most important), tasty hors d'oeuvres, cheap cocktails, or fancy drinks? Places with yummy appetizers are imperative because you may not want to fill up on a whole meal, yet you'll need a little fuel.

I have a whole menu of places in my head. Find a romantic bar or restaurant where you'll be able to talk without other lesbians lurking over you or stupid, prejudiced straight people glaring. Gay guy places are perfect. I used to take anyone I was trying to seduce to the Lion, a classy joint in an upscale neighborhood. Men of all ages come after work, often with a straight female coworker in tow. Some nights, though, were much more cruisy than that. Even so, it was a nice place to stare into an amour's eyes. The lighting is the best. Lots of candles and mirrors.

You may also want to pick places that say something about you, so if the gal wants you, she can pass the test by going on your turf. For example, my best friends are fags, and in my single days, we left no boy bar unvisited. I knew the places they used for making out and made them my own. I hang with boys, and if you want me, you

The Single Girl-Goddess Checklist:

☑ Babephone
☑ sex toys
☑ safer-sex supplies
☑ a trail
☑ a map
❑ possexibilities
☑ shopping list

gotta go through some testosterone to get me. After the aforementioned Lion, I dragged tricks to the Detour, where the music blares, so no words are possible. Boys grope each other fiercely against chain-link fences and in dark corners. The whole place reeks of man sex. I also took girls through the Tenderloin, one of San Francisco's down-and-out neighborhoods. (Although in the "urbanization of America," even this neighborhood is being invaded by lofties in SUVs searching for the "city experience.") The Tenderloin harbors many gay male hangouts. Many of those hanging out are hustler boys, working girls (that would be "transsexual prostitutes" to those of you not up on the euphemisms), and drag queens (trannies who aren't for sale *too* often).

The bars in the Tenderloin are filled with people trying to sell their wares, the men trying to buy them, those having a celebratory cocktail after the cocksale, and the rest of us just looking for sanctuary in dark bars with cheap drinks and friendly faces. I'd bring strangefucks there to see if they were too sissy or prissy; then, if they didn't run screaming for a taxi, just to have some fun.

By the way, Jackie passed all these tests with butchfloozy colors. Our second date, if you could even call it that, took place at the Polk Gulch. She volunteered to meet me there for a friend's birthday party, not flinching at the address. Matter of fact, she already knew it. A slutstud after my own heart. Then she threw me up against the chain links of the Detour, like the roughest boy trade. Meow.

You might be guessing that I ran in some shady neighborhoods. You're right. By all means, don't go into neighborhoods where *you* don't feel safe. Other than that, let your curiosity take you to new, adventurous terrains.

So, if you unexpectedly find yourself with a gal ready to tango, where will you take her? Find the places that are right for Youtopia.

Dating is Shopping, So Who's in the Mall?
Your Possexibilities

Now you just need to find some potential lustfriends and lovefucks. Here are some ideas for tracking them down and luring them in:
- Move and tell all your friends you need women movers.
- Happen into barbershops and ask for directions.
- Research a medical issue for yourself or a friend by seeking out clinical technicians. The medical industry is filled with queers!!
- Place an ad for a roommate, even though you don't have an extra room. This one has really

worked for a few of my friends. You get to interview women, find out their quirks, likes, and get a taste of their hopes and values. Plus, you get to share yours and see how they react. **Warning:** Don't let anyone into your home unless you have a few people with you. Meet the potential date in a public place first, as you should any stranger.

•Give blood (that medical thing again).

•Go to a sex club. Throw a sex party.

•Throw a "One Degree of Separation Party." Invite your friends and make them invite someone you don't know, whether the person is married or single, boy or girl, gay or straight, or anything in between. It doesn't matter, because even if that person isn't right for you, perhaps you'll meet someone through him or her who *is*. You never know when a friend's friend's friend might be right for you.

•Tip the go-go dancer or buy her a drink.

•Be a go-go dancer.

•Walk your dog or walk a friend's dog. Very effective.

•Trap the UPS or FedEx woman.

Need a date? Become a go-go dancer.

The ultimate fantasy, isn't it? They're so cute in those shorts! Well, many of them aren't available, but many are. (Why do you think they became FedEx women? For the dental plan? More like the poontang plan.)

•Go to the copy shop at midnight. You never know who might be making band fliers, riot posters, pink womanifestos, rave handbills, or the latest 'zine.

•Work at a film festival.

•If you can't work at a film festival, at least volunteer for a friend who needs to flier some of the movie lines. You'll have a captive audience through which to walk, stopping to chat with whomever you choose.

•Do something public. If you're artistic, then do something with your talent. If not, then the rest of us artists love for our friends to help us pass out fliers for our events, work the door, introduce us at our openings, produce our shows, etc. Or get involved with an issue you feel strongly about, such as: breast cancer, religion, political prisoners, gay day. Attend public rallies or demos.

•Go to the mall around closing time when security is walking around and ask the security dyke to walk you to your car.

•Say to a woman cop, "You look like someone who really knows what's going on here," then ask for directions or information.

•Work at a women-owned sex toy store or, better yet, open your own store.

•Take workshops at said store.

•Rent a Harley and advertise it for sale. (This is a variation on a trick used by Blanche on *The Golden Girls*. She was looking for a rich man, so she rented a Cadillac and pretended it was for sale so she could flirt with whomever came to look at it. Remember, don't really sell it!)

•Go to readings and lectures.

The Single Girl-Goddess Checklist:
☑ Babephone
☑ sex toys
☑ safer-sex supplies
☑ a trail
☑ a map
☑ possexibilities
☑ shopping list

•For those in school, don't be shy about exploring student organizations and events.

•Start your own interest group and place an ad for members. The club doesn't have to be political. For example: dykes who hike, butch and femme two-steppers, couch-potato critics, anything!

•Have a yard sale. Not only a great way to meet strangers, but also you can advertise a few queer-flagging items in the newspaper, so your type will stop by (e.g., biker jacket, complete VHS collection of *Ellen,* boxing gloves, poodle skirt—whatever you think your type will be attracted to). Even if you don't have the item, you can still advertise it. Just say, "Gosh, I already sold it, but would you like a soda?"

Here's a blank checklist for you to fill out!

The Single Girl-Goddess Checklist:

❑ Babephone

❑ sex toys

❑ safer-sex supplies

❑ a trail

❑ a map

❑ possexibilities

❑ shopping list

Flirting Revisited: Going Into Warp Speed

So you regularly flirt with the whole solar system, and now you want a particular gal to know she's special. You're saying, "These eyes and this smile are all for you, baby." You're ready to turn up the heat and turn down the sheets. Everyone flirts differently. You probably already have a few of your own tricks. It never hurts to compare notes or to study someone else's style. It's especially good to trade secrets with fags. Men and women often have opposite ways of cruising, so we can really learn from one another.

Flirting at warp speed is all about sending the message that you want her to want you.

The Eyes

The eyes have it—her heart, that is. We've already talked about the effectiveness and potency of eye contact, but if you want to extend your flirtation beyond a friendly disposition, let your eyes tell all. (False eyelashes can work quite dramatically in this situation.) Let's say you're speaking with this creature you want to seduce. Let the pauses in your conversation get longer as you stare into her eyes. But please control yourself a little. Don't look like a St. Bernard begging for a bone.

Body Language

My friend Denise firmly shook the hand of a cute butch, Amy, when it was offered because she didn't want to seem like a wimp, but then as they withdrew hands, she let her nails trail down the palm of the woman who is now her love.

Tilt your head down, letting a lock of hair fall in front of your eyes, then look up with your eyes while leaving your chin slightly down.

Let your body touch your target oh-so-casually. My friend Jenny stood in an audience beside a woman she wanted to seduce and simply let her breast barely rest against her target's arm. Sini, her lucky victim, later said it was sheer torture and she couldn't figure out if Jenni was doing it on purpose or not. When Sini looked back at her, Jenni just smiled—a Cheshire grin, that is.

Verbal Language

Ask questions that can be taken two ways, then raise your eyebrow.

For example, if you're in a job where you wait on people and a possexible gal comes in, say, "And what can I *do for you* today?" When greeting or saying good-bye to someone you like, say,

> **"I knew if I played my Marlon Brando cards right / We'd meet at the top floor / of San Francisco's Holiday Inn Lounge."**
> —from "The Latin-Angel & the Gangster Butch-Gentleman" by Tina D'Elia

"I *really* liked meeting you." We all move so fast nowadays that superficial, speedy transactions have become the norm. Therefore, if you stress a word by saying it slowly or holding eye contact with someone, it's quite noticeable. Your meaning will be clear, yet, if she's not interested, she'll think you were nothing more than kind. You won't have embarrassed yourself at all. In fact, you'll come across as a self-empowered, sincere, captivating woman.

Vamping or; How to Get Her to Cross the Room

Vamping is the ultimate for objects of desire. We want everyone to come to us without us even lifting an eyebrow. Unfortunately, it doesn't always work like that. Can I say, "Girl, you betta *work*"?

Look approachable. You have to aggressively harness this aspect because there's a whole set of assumptions people make about Queens that has nothing to do with you personally. Many dykes will assume you're snotty. Just be your friendly self and many will get over it. The ones who don't are insecure, so you don't need them in your court anyway.

Wear jewelry or an outfit that people can comment on. That way, they'll always have something to talk to you about. Conversely, use someone else's accoutrement as an entry point for your own comments. One night I sat at the bar of a place called the Café, right where folks had to come up for their drinks. Prime location. I got four phone numbers just by talking about jewelry alone. Why didn't I start with another topic? The boys and I made a bet that I couldn't pick up chicks just by talking about jewelry.

Which brings me to competition. A little competition is healthy. The boys and I used to bet on who could get the most kisses, phone numbers, and more! Women especially need to push ourselves to get "out there," no matter the reason. Many times I'd have just sat in a corner talking to *one* girl who could very well turn out to be nonsexible. Instead, I'd keep pushing to meet chick after chick just because I didn't want to lose the bet. In the end I met lots of people, had a blast, and even won the bets (a couple of times).

Invoke your inner fag. Guys definitely have hangups, but their hormones just bulldoze over those insecure moments. They fret over their bodies and their appearance, status, and personality just like we do, but the amount of energy those worries get is relative to how horny the guy is. Guys put themselves out there. And they get rejected big time, but like Brian used to say, "If you have to go through ten rejects to get a live one, then I might as well get through one to ten as fast as I can."

Don't forget to smile. Try this: You already have said "hi" to people you know as you traverse the party, gala, or bar. You order a drink, perch, and chitchat with the bartender or a friend. Be yourself, but just let yourself be *on the outside* a little bit. If you find something your companion says humorous, laugh out loud. Move. Gesture. Look to the vampee sideways, smile as if you're caught off guard, then look back to your friends. Next time you glance in her direction, she'll be heading your way.

Forget Crossing the Room; Just Step on Her Toe

If the seductive vamp doesn't work, don't give up. There's a high road and a low road. Although I most always promote the high road, I'll be the first to admit a babe's gotta do what a babe's gotta do. When I've run out of other opening lines, I've stepped on toes, spilled drinks, "accidentally" thrown baskets of popcorn, bumped, bounced, and bumbled into total strangers. They didn't stay strangers for long! I guess I wouldn't recommend pouring an entire pitcher of beer down a stranger's shirt (that time *was* an accident, I swear), but hey, just a toss of clear liquid such as vodka dries quickly and leads to oh-so-fun ways of you trying to make up for your faux pas. And yes, you clean 'n' sober cuties, club soda works just as well.

✿   ✿   ✿

That should be enough to get you started. Remember that chutzpah and sheer desire mixed with just a pinch of subtlety and sophistication is really all it takes. And enough guts to keep practicing. After a while you'll be able to do it with all but one pinky tied behind your back.

The Appreciation of Expectations
On-the-Date Dos and Don'ts

By the time you get to this section, you're more than fabulous. You're Divafabulicious. You've donned your tiara, taken your place in a brilliant setting, you've spilled your popcorn and picked up a few phone numbers, not to mention given out yours to a few possexibilities. So here's where the dates come in. Oh, you know most everything by now, but I do have a tidbit or two to pass along.

As a Libra, I see the pros and cons of every situation. So when I dole out these suggestions, remember that each potential amour will require her own tweaking of the date rules. For example, cultural and regional differences come into play. How can she pick you up in a car if she's from Queens and has never driven a day in her life? Or the baby butches who aren't yet out of boot camp may need extra patience. They have to learn somewhere along the line. Let your ego and head be your guide. I say "ego" because if someone is disrespecting you, your ego will be knocking on your conscience saying, "Girlfriend, this is not OK." Your head will temper an ego that's unrighteously sore. Your heart, you ask? It needs to stay safely tucked away on the first few dates, so it doesn't get to vote for a while. These guidelines, this whole book, is about you getting the respect you deserve—from yourself and the rest of the solar system.

One more general note before I get into the details of what we can assume from our dates—

oops…Going UP. That's right, I'm stepping up onto that Shar Soapbox again. I just need a moment here about manners. I don't care if I am the last person on Earth to have them, I will still expect each and every person to treat me with the respect and thoughtfulness that having manners demands. I do not want to hear any excuses about feminism (I'm the biggest feminist on the block) or about hippie influence (I've lived in a van and tripped on Haight with the best of them), or about any other lame-ass excuse for recent generations of bad manners. Bullshit, people, bullshit. GO READ *MISS MANNERS*. Some people pretend that manners make you stuffy or snooty. Nothing is further from the truth. It simply means you're prepared, kind, and have respected yourself and others enough to educate yourself about a few social skills!

EXPECT GOOD MANNERS IN YOURSELF AND OTHERS.

Doling Out Some You-ness and Receiving Some Her-ness

Look into her eyes when you communicate, but definitely let your eyes wander to any body part you like. Return your gaze to hers while trying (yet not succeeding) to hide your embarrassment at being caught in your thoughts.

Breathe into her ear.

Don't cut your nails for anyone until after the third date.

If all is going well, leave your mark. Scratches, lipstick prints, hickeys, a bruise here or there. Hickeys left for the world to see really upset some folks. I'm not sure why, but be aware that your girl might be one of those people. Your mark can be a lipstick print on her or on an item left in her car, home, or pocket. Perhaps you're a scratcher or a biter; I suppose you'll know the right time for that. The key to good marks is that they're genuine in the moment. Your amour du jour will know if you're faking a scream of passion just to excuse your nails ripping down her arm.

Walk about five steps ahead of her when ascending stairs.

Don't detail your past relationships or take her on a tour through your dirty laundry. That's for moms and therapists.

Read a newspaper or two during the weeks you have dates. I know it sounds clichéd, but please, if we just went to war, you'll want to know about it. Conversation, you know.

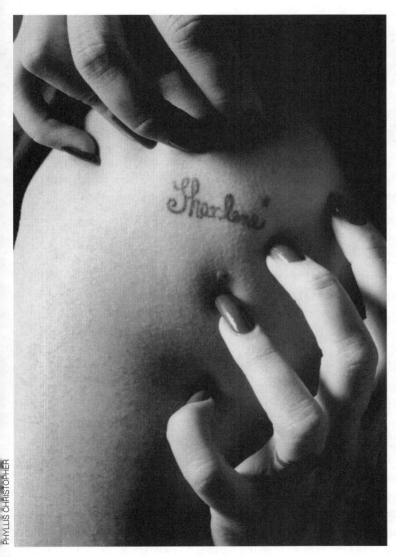

Don't cut your nails until after the third date.

When asked what you would like to do on a date, be prepared. Make a mental list of your likes and dislikes. Don't ramble it off like a three-year-old doing the ABCs. Say it seductively, slowly, and thoughtfully so that she has time to bite on one of the items that interests her as well.

Wrap your arm through hers when walking. A note to butch-loving femmes: In the olden days, the butch walked on the outside of the sidewalk to protect her girl from dirt, splashes, and traffic. These days we sometimes need more protection from what lurks in doorways, so she may choose the inside occasionally.

Don't go to a movie unless it's an organic part of your mutual interest. Meaning that if the whole reason you got the date was because you two were sharing your obsession with *Star Trek* during your HTML lab, then, of course, that's a perfect reason to go out together. But be sure to schedule enough hours for long discussions over coffee or drinks afterward. Otherwise you'll just sit there next to a stranger for two hours without talking.

Don't go to a loud dyke bar for reasons listed above!

Go to gay and women's events or

other live shows. If you like sports, support women's athletics by attending one of their many games.

Talk about your own latest interests, but have some good questions ready so you'll learn more about *her*. If you're the type to get shy and tongue-tied when you're overstimulated in the moment, jot down some topics you've wanted to talk to her about *before* the date (while you're still calm) and keep your list in your purse. Sneak a peek at it now and then (when she's off to the rest room or you are) to help you keep on track.

Don't go cruising some other chick while you're on a date. One thing I learned from Karlyn Lotney (a.k.a. Fairy Butch): A spike heel in the sternum is worth two on the dance floor. You gotta concentrate on what's on your plate. You can always come back to the restaurant for somethin' else tomorrow.

Getting the First Kiss

"Thy lips, O my spouse, drop like the honeycomb; honey and milk are under my tongue."
—Song of Solomon 4:11

Hopefully, she's your OoD dream come true and has swept you off your feet. Or maybe she teased *you* into grabbing the broom. Now you want to get past that first kiss so you'll know she's really yours. See my suggestions in the "Jumping the Gender Fence" sections in Part VI. Simply ask/tell your possexibility that your lips are on the move. Of course, you can just lean forward and *do it*. Then, finally, there is that age-old tactic of just getting drunk. My friend Elle and I always drank together, then I moved away and she got sober. She lusted after an old boss of ours for an entire year without making any moves. She constantly called me frustrated to say, "How does anybody do the first kiss without alcohol?" She'd scream, "The 13th step is *missing*!" It's difficult, but definitely doable. You'll just have to swallow your nerves, let the dreaminess of your gut shine through your eyes so you do indeed look drunk— drunk with lust—and say, "Being this close to you is intoxicating," then kiss her.

If you don't have a problem with alcohol, don't sweat having a drink to loosen up. For Divine's sake, though, don't get so loaded that you're a sloppy kisser or pathetic fuck. That's gross and insulting to everyone, yourself included.

Regarding when to have sex: Some people say if you eat all the dough there's no room for cookies, and many times that's true and you need cookies, but don't you sometimes just want the dough?

Expecting Something of Her

If she's the one instigating the date (i.e., picking you up, courting you), here's what you can reasonably expect:

Expect her to be well-dressed. You agonized over your appearance; why shouldn't she?

Expect her to be on time, and punish her if she's not (provided she didn't call or have a good reason such as a flat tire). Once I wouldn't buzz a date into my building because she was late without good cause, making her wait outside for me (as I took my time to leave). At first she didn't think I was serious and laughed into the intercom. Soon she stopped laughing and was never late again.

Expect her to bring an offering. Southern hospitality dictates that you never come to someone's house without an offering, even if it's just a daisy you picked along the way. For a date, though, it should be more like chocolate, flowers, strawberries, bath beads, or wine. I also like glossy fetish magazines or Barbie trinkets.

Expect her to compliment you. My rule is that she has to compliment me at least twice during the course of the evening or she's history.

Expect her to be well-manicured and to wash her hands.

Expect her to have at least the same toys that you have in your box, if not more.

Expect her to own lube and latex.

Expect her to be well-groomed: body odor controlled, teeth brushed, etc.

Expect her to give you all of her attention.

Your Femme Dollars:
Who Pays for Whom?

When one of you has obviously instigated the date, that person pays. For example, you say, "I would love to take you out sometime." That's obvious.

The less obvious: She says, "There's a crabfest on the pier on Sunday. Would you like to go with me?" Maybe her tone of voice clearly indicates that she's asking you on a date. If you're still unsure, simply smile and say, "Are you asking me on a date?" If she says yes, she picks up the tab. But in those circumstances the one who accepts still offers to pay for a smaller item, such as dessert or coffee. If you do go to the pier, you may get her a balloon or some little treat. She in turn may, in good manners, refuse your offers, saying, "I'm taking you out."

The "Murky Tester" Date: This isn't really a date. One or both of you wants to know if you even want to go on a date. She invites you to go out with her friends to a group event. Or you say, "Hey, let's get coffee some-time." In cases such as these, you go Dutch.

If you're going on a date with an old-fashioned butch, she will plan on paying. Let her. After the second date, if you know she's not made of money, absolutely demand to take her out. Pull out feminism, gender-bending—anything—as an excuse. If you really like her, you won't want her going broke over you the first month. If she refuses, demand that she come to your place for a home-cooked meal (or an ordered-out one, but don't tell or she'll want to pay. Bury those containers, put the food in serving dishes, and reheat in your oven).

In general, try to be obvious. Then you'll know what's up. Don't demand clarification when she's asked you to attend her Super Bowl party with all her brothers, but do when she's asked you to the opening of the Queer Film Fest. As for you, if you're asking someone out, say, "I want to take you out."

That'll clear it up.

The Prospects of Tradition: Assuming the Butch

"You know something, stud," I told her, "you're a pretty nice girl for a guy."
—from "The Latin-Angel & the Gangster Butch-Gentleman," by Tina D'Elia

I've polled many of my BL (butch-loving) femme friends to see what they expect from a butch date. Here's what they said, plus a few of my own. Expect…

For her to drive or arrange transportation. It's acceptable for her to suggest walking on a clear, warm evening through safe streets.

For her to pick up the check (see "Your Femme Dollars" in this chapter).

For her to unlock your door. My friend Veronica was left *standing in the rain* while her supposed-butch date went around to the driver's side and unlocked her own door first. Tradition says that the butch unlocks your door and assists you, closes your door, then walks around the car and unlocks her own door. Unlocking doors, in other words, is the butch or male protocol. One small example of how butch and femme have transformed masculine/feminine roles is that now we consider it nice for the butch to unlock your door; you wait until she's just about at her door, then reach over and unlock her door for her (unless you're in restrictive clothing). The pause allows for her to see your beautiful hand in motion, lets her know not to use her key, and, depending on how far you bend, might give her a glimpse of your cleavage too.

Expect her not to be a cad about your outfit. Hello, we're dykes. We wear whatever we want. My friend Vicki was standing in line when a butch said loudly, "You're not wearing anything under that slip." Not only was it rude to say that in front of her friends and other dykes, but also it could have endangered her because they were on a public street where skanky men were walking by. In this case, the person wasn't Vicki's date, thank God, but all butches bear a public responsibility to all femmes not to bring attention to our sexiness unless we're in a safe place.

Expect her to help you with your coat, get your drinks, and inquire into your level of comfort.

Expect her to not be wearing girly underwear 'neath that full-boy drag exterior. Unless, of course, she's kinky.

The first few times you're together sexually (which is not to say the first date), expect her to attend to you first; she comes second—no matter who's the "bottom" or who's the "top."

Billie's Rules

When I polled my friends regarding their date expectations, my girlsistergirlfriend Billie showed up not only with demands for her dates but also this list for what she expected out of herself as well:

Clean manicure—no chipped polish!

Specifics cared for—no runs in her stockings, ill-matched undies, etc.

She plans on being "fully on," well-thought-out so that she goes with the event and her date.

She expects "perfect diction" for herself, meaning she communicates clearly. She recommends "directness and clarity over image and attitude."

She cares for her manners mindfully, and she assumes her date will.

As long as she and her date have chemistry and interest, when it comes to carnal feasting, she expects to come screaming and fully enjoy herself. She points out that this is as much in her hands as any lover's.

Finally, she says, "I expect for them to be impressed."

How could I have said that any better?! No matter how many of Billie's self-rules you take on, I suggest you make a similar list. What do you assume for your best behavior? That, after all, is what you're aiming for.

Laying Down the Laws

In the end, what's important is for you to have a good time. Your expectations for your dates will become second nature as you personalize them. These suggestions aren't meant to make you stiff. The whole point is for you to feel well taken care of and important. If you're preoccupied with who's picking up the check, you'll miss out on getting to know your date—the real measure of whether you want to go out with her again.

You can always expect, plan for, or hope for anything. You won't always get it, but aim high. Some people say, "If you have no expectations, you can't be let down." OK, whatever. Instead, I say, "If you don't shoot for the stars, you'll never kiss the moon."

There's Another Way to be Single
Being a Mistress—Not the Whip-Wielding Kind!

The ethics of this one could be debated until the cows come home in bustiers! I'm not only a proponent of nonmonogamy, but I also teach classes on it. In these seminars, I lecture, preach, and basically shove my policy of "honesty above all else" down people's throats. So, knowing that, how can I include this section? Well, the whole world works on the system of reincarnating the heterosexual marriage, even though the original smacks of slavery and ownership. Even the hets themselves have been trying to change this model for decades. That model is set up for dalliances, so if you fall off the "we're creating a new world" bandwagon for a few weeks and have a good old-fashioned affair, who am I to condemn you?

Regularly seeing a taken woman supplies you with security and freedom. You have the security of knowing that you, for now at least, have a regular sex partner and affection supplier while maintaining the freedom to do as you please. (Um, if you promised a married woman that you would be true to her, all I have to say is "get a cure." You need to run, not walk, to a therapist and tell her you need the Codependent, Low-Self-Esteem Tonic #1.) Since I never assume that marriage means monogamy, I'm referring not just to freedom to sex anyone you please but freedom from the worries of commitment, the brainache of negotiation, and the wrestle of possessiveness.

You'll rock her world, then be able to write your dissertation uninterrupted. You can fuck her until she's a love-soaked jellyfish, then have the whole bed to yourself and the cats.

To her, you're shiny new, a fantasy come to life. Who'd have thought she'd gotten you? The affair itself is a naughty no-no, so that raises the hot factor instantly. The fact that you can't have her morning, noon, and night makes any moment you have with her special, stolen, and explosive.

> **BRAINACHE:** brayn·ayk, noun: (1) a condition in which one's thinking mechanisms hurt from too much processing over nothing; (2) person who instigates processing over nothing, as in *She's a brainache;* (3) thoughts that are convoluted from too much processing over subjects not yet determined to be nothing, as in *This argument is giving me a brainache.*

A Candid Tutorial for the Other Woman

Always assume you'll never ever get a branded woman to yourself.

Don't let yourself seriously want her to be your woman. Of course, you might daydream about what it would be like if you two got together. Those daydreams are special, arousing, and fun. But when you get seriously pissed that you two are not together on Passover, there's something wrong.

Let her come and go on her time, but don't run your life by her schedule. Make your plans. If you happen to be free when she is, great. Do you have any days that you'll be at home cleaning, working, or reading a book that can be interrupted? Let her know those days. At the same time, sincerely do your stuff without expecting her to appear.

Sometimes we date a taken woman simply because we lust after her. But we may find ourselves doing it over and over again. Being the other woman means you have freedom. It means you're the one who trips her trigger, not because the wife is so blasé but because married life can be so damned routine at times. You're breaking the rules, and so by nature you're keeping it exciting. You like the chase and you love a challenge. You want to make someone *break the rules* for you.

If your OoD radar comes on (thus, you can feel a branded woman desiring you) and you want her to go for it, Jess, a wife-borrowing expert, advises you to not process the situation. It's an easy trap to fall into. She's worried, so she tries to bend your ear about it. She processes enough at home with the wife; she doesn't need to do that with you. Also, if you process with her too much, *you* are taking it too seriously. The more you two agonize over the liaison, the more she's reminded that she has a girlfriend—a girlfriend that she's about to cheat on. Jess says just get into her lap. Be physical and don't talk too much. Reach around to rub her shoulders from the front. "Fall asleep" on her shoulder, nestling in her neck. When she turns to look at you, she'll meet your lips. She wants the whole situation to be one of those times where "one thing just led to another." Let her have her innocent excuse. When she inevitably says, "I shouldn't be doing this," don't say anything. If she means those words, she'll get up and out of there on her own.

Frankly, if you are so hard up for affection that you are chasing another gal's catch, then I think you need to get out and about more. I know, I know. I've done it myself. Just remember this isn't *Melrose Place.* The point is to get what you want and *nobody gets hurt.* That includes you. **Warning:** Don't set yourself up for heartbreak or for running into a homicidal spouse!

No matter how much fun Jess has tasting the taken-woman sampler kit, she always says the problem with being the other woman is that there's always another woman. Sooner or later, you might decide to wield a brand of your own.

Another Way to Be the Other Woman: Leasin' Some Lovin'

You can choose to be involved with one or more partners of a couple in another way by being open, honest, and not hiding behind secrets. Dating a couple or even one member of a secure couple can be one of the most delightful ways a single gal can soak up attention and affection. But don't date fucked-up couples. That said, in general, couples have high levels of intimacy, so they know their sexual responses, they know their limitations, and therefore know where they want to branch out. If wifey number 1 doesn't like to give head, wifey number 2 can get it from you while wifey

A prime example of leasin' some lovin'.

number 1 cheers you on. Ever want to be giving and receiving at the same time, but just weren't limber enough? Well, that's the beauty of three-ways: There are plenty of tongues, fingers, and elbows to go around!

"I'm ready to sign up, Shar!"

OK, sweet petunia, here's how to do it. Read up on nonmonogamy. Then find a couple. Ask the couple to pretend that the room they have in their relationship for you is actually a *room* in a house that they're going to lease out. That's right. Their relationship is a house and they can rent a room/space to you. So what are the parameters of that room? What are their boundaries for you? They need to decide without you around, and really hash it out. They must decide on limits and ask themselves where there's room to grow, if any. Can you be autonomous and knock out a wall or repaint without asking? Can you bring anything to the room or is it already furnished? Is this lease month-to-month or yearly?

When the couple knows what the room looks like, they can convey this information to you and you can decide if you want to move in. For example, they know they have room for fun sexual threesomes on the weekends. Next year, when Janine goes to Europe, you'll no longer be invited over. Knowing this, you decide to go for it. Perhaps you know you'll want room to fall in love. And if they don't want that, you'll decide to not see them at all.

Pretending your relationship is a room-for-let troubleshoots possible miscommunication. It isn't foolproof because people's wants and needs change. Everyone just needs to be as honest as they can and provide new information when they have it. Please increase your knowledge about nonmonogamy by reading the books listed in the bibliography. This only scratches the surface of one tiny way to be nonmonogamous.

Part VII

Troubleshooting Manual: Read Me

Sorry, doll, it's not all twinkly stars and space shuttle rides to the moon with free champagne.

Lost in Space:
Sendin' Out an S.O.S.

This is for those of you saying, "Oh, Shar, you're younger than me and living in the Mecca, so of course you can find a date. What about me? I'm over 40, painfully shy, and living in Idaho! Did you hear me? I said, *Idaho*!"

Wow, that's a tough one, but here goes:

(1) Move. What else can I say? Nothing more profound than, "That really sucks." You and your six rottweilers may love the soft grass of a South Carolina hill under your feet, while the locals would rather have you six feet under that grass. ("Bury her, not the dogs. They're good for huntin'.") I know some wonderful queers who live in South Carolina, but if you can't shine there, get out. Before you pack your bags, though, do try to "shine there" first. Cities are overcrowded. If you can make a community where you are, go at it. And invite me for a visit. Remember too that there's safety in numbers; most often, small towns have fewer gays. I wish Jackie and I could live part-time in Arkansas, water-skiing and bar-b-quing with my cool relatives, but we can't. I'll live this life not spending enough time with my mother in exchange for living my life with the least amount of compromise. Jackie and I do not assimilate well. Let's just say we aren't the Uncle

Toms of lesbianism. We have to choose our battles: Examine your values and decide what's really most important to you. If mating is your number 1 priority, you may consider moving. Life presents difficult choices, but you're a Queen, so I know you'll act accordingly. Skip ahead and read "Don't Let Me Start Lovin' Myself!" later in this chapter. If you can do that, perhaps you can stay right where you are!

(2) The age thing. My friend Shoshana said to me last week, "Getting older and being femme isn't easy in this town." Getting older may decrease your possexibilities, but it doesn't eradicate them. Naturally, a lot of my information comes from the experiences of my friends and family—people of all ages. For example, my suggestions for "Who's in the Mall?" came from all of my friends—young and old. Being over 30 doesn't mean it's all over—there are still ways and means to meet women. Start a group. Reach out. Whatever you're doing, let as many people know about it as possible. Go to events, conferences, or retreats that coincide with your life and interests. If you haven't already, get a computer and get online!!! In the information age (that is *now*) there's no reason to be isolated.

(3) Read Carol Queen's *Exhibitionism for the Shy*. Get therapy. Take drugs. Watch *Oprah*. Step on out of yourself and take charge of your future. Be courageous. Courage means you do things you're scared to do. Anyone can live in fear, but a Queen is a heroine. She sees her fear, gives it the evil eye, and takes care of business.

But, but, but, Shar....

Inevitably, when I give advice there's always someone saying she's tried all of my suggestions and none of them have worked. To that person, I say:

(1) Are you being honest with yourself or are you just finding external obstacles instead of looking at yourself? One time a friend who wore Coke-bottle glasses confessed that she wanted to get contacts but was afraid. She said if she got contacts and still didn't have a girlfriend, she wouldn't have anything to blame. She used her thick glasses to protect her feelings.

(2) If you *are* being honest and have tried, maybe you're trying too hard. Are you a control freak? Do you hate silence or stillness, and always have to be actively doing something? I used to believe you have to work hard to achieve anything, but sometimes the opposite is true. One little saying that has helped me out is, "If you can't try harder, try differently."

(3) Become your own best date and best lover.

Don't Let Me Start Lovin' Myself!

It's easy to become your own best lover. Go to your local women-owned sex-toy store or phone (800) Buy-Vibe or log onto the Internet and get yourself some education. Try books such as *Sex for One* or videos such as *Self-Loving*. If you haven't tried a vibrator, try one. Read Joani Blank's *Good Vibrations Guide to Vibrators,* which addresses many of the concerns and questions women have about these love tools. I used to think I had a satisfactory masturbation ritual. Was I wrong! I was sitting on Susie's bed watching her try on fabulous outfits when she discovered I didn't have a vibrator. "What?!" She reached under her bed and threw down a Wahl two-speed. I learned the meaning of inner flight, of seeing stars without a rocket ship. I thought the vibrator was too strong at first, but I'd received some coaching from Susie, so I knew to hang in there. Those little battery jobbies you get from novelty stores do not cut it. Read the Good Vibrations guide, you'll get it.

Instead of looking for someone else to fill you up, fill yourself up until you're overflowing. That overflow will spill onto someone else. But you won't be counting the minutes until it happens, because you'll be screaming to the rafters in ecstasy having a grand time on your own! (Don't worry if your ecstasy isn't that loud at first. It's takes time.)

If you're still saying, "but, but, but," listen, Wendy Whiner, just get out of my class. You aren't getting it, getting what I'm saying. STOP THINKING JUST ABOUT YOURSELF. Oh, I didn't say you weren't charitable. I said, stop thinking about yourself. Get on out of yourself. Do what I'm telling you to do. Smoke some pot. Brew some tea. Make tamales. Relax. Read the flirting chapter over and over and over again.

Meteors and Black Holes: Navigating Around Passion's Pitfalls

No matter how marvelous, delightful, smart, and powerful you are, the chaos of the cosmos can still deliver a full-fledged assault on Youtopia, leaving you unsexed, lonely, and ego-blown. There's no controlling it. I do have a few suggestions, though, for skirting the storm and transforming-meteor shower into a glistening tiara!

> **BOTTOM:** bah·tum, noun: (1) person who responds or reacts positively to sexual leadership; (2) person who receives sexual pleasure from giving oneself physically or mentally to another for that person's sexual gratification; (3) person who receives sexual pleasure. Verb: (1) to receive physical or mental sexual attention; (2) to offer one's body for another's sexual gratification

How to Salvage a Tryst With a Bottom You Didn't Know Was a Bottom!

If you knew what you were getting into—in other words, if scoring a bottom was on your shopping list—then you wouldn't be calling this a problem. This section is for the many women who find themselves *unexpectedly* with a bottom. I'll explain as I go.

I need first to clarify the huge difference between a "Do-Me Queen" and a bottom. Bottoms are out to please in one way or another. Their sensual response is directly wired to at least *believing* they're pleasing you, if not actually doing so. Do-Me Queens' sensual response is linked to their bodies, and they want their bodies done in a certain way. But the term "Do-Me Queen" carries a negative connotation because these girls don't care to lift a finger for your pleasure.

Having cleared the glitter dust on that, let's talk about what happens when you get with a gal you believe is a top but who turns out to be a bottom. I bring this up specifically because I've received dozens upon dozens of comments, complaints, and questions about this phenomenon from women who have experienced it firsthand.

If you're reading this section, I assume you're shopping for someone to meet you in the middle, if not overpower you, in the boudoir. Let's say you meet this chick who seduces you and implies that she's going to do this and that to you. She's going to treat you like a piece of candy. She's the five-year-old who needs a lick of your sugar. But you get her home and she's flat on her back. She flipped like a pancake.

Unless you're experienced and know that Pancake Syndrome exists, you might be really confused. Your little ego could be first in line for a blow. You might frantically wonder, "What changed between the bar and home?! Did I say something? When she felt me up did I feel all wrong?

PANCAKE: pan·cayk, noun: person who professes loudly to lead sexual activities, then unexpectedly becomes passive (i.e., "flips"), desiring her partner(s) to become the leader(s).

What?!" You don't know that it isn't you. It's her. For some reason, she doesn't feel comfortable revealing that she isn't top material—at all—in public. Maybe she's a liar and crazy. Maybe, though, she's just embarrassed or inexperienced at communication. Most likely she doesn't know how to articulate her desires. She really does fancy you. She does. She just doesn't know how to have those feelings *and* have her turn-on, which is to be bossed around, to be servile and submissive, etc. Our culture teaches, especially those who identify with masculinity (i.e., butch women), that if you want to seduce a woman, seduce her. This chick was savvy enough to know how to get you, but she doesn't know what to do with you once she's got you!

So you've got this pancake in a private corner, what do you do? You can return her to the mall or you can decide to cultivate her as a fun, better-than-nothing rompfriend. I've always said, "As an OoD, I want my lover to want me so badly she'll go through me and her both to get me." That's the desire we often hope for, but let's not turn our tresses away from adoration in a different package.

Remember my don't-get-hungry-on-a-mountain story in "Dating As Shopping"? Hello? Is this pancake actually some trail mix?!

Let's go back to the shopping parallel, it's sort of like buying something knowing you're going to have to alter it at home. She may not be marriage material, but can you ever have too many possexible friends?

So you've decided she's not crazy or too weird, that you like her company or need to be fucked—she's just not a top. But we can get over that problem. You can top her into topping you.

This advice lands directly from scenes my friends and I have encountered. It won't work for every bottom[1], 'cuz every bottom won't want it to work!

The following is a power-play scene. If you're versed in S/M, you probably don't need this advice at all. For those of you who aren't, educate yourself in fantasy by reading *Exhibitionism for the Shy* and one of the many S/M books available. Most S/M folks really know how to communicate and articulate their needs. Don't reinvent the safe word; learn from those in the know.

Begin by telling her that you're going to play a pretend game. You will be the queen/boss/mommy/someone in control. Let her know that if she doesn't like the game at a certain point, she can say a safe word and you'll stop pretending. Or she can say "Question" and break character to ask a question if she needs. She can also ask questions in the voice her character would use. Then the games begin.

Tell her to kneel in front of you. Taunt her with your body. Ask her how badly she wants to touch you. Tell her you want her to be a good little boy/girl/slave/whatever works and to do as you say. Tell her that for her to get off, to receive any pleasure from you at all, she must pass a series of tests for you. Then go from there. "Make" her touch you in any way you please. Be sure you get whatever you need and get it for a good long time. Then decide what her reward will be. Maybe it will simply be for her to go home to her vibrator with thoughts of you. Maybe you'll her treat her to your babedick. You're the Queen—you decide.

How to Peg a Psycho—Read Quickly!

I say "quickly" because what if the psychos read this, then change their behavior to keep us guessing? Eek. There's a tiny safeguard against this, though, in that most psychos don't know they're psycho.

So we're discussing all this dating and whatnot, but what about those evil gals who really should be characters on TV's latest nighttime drama? Frankly, you know that heteromania reigns, because if folks really wanted to see some convoluted drama, there would be a *dyke* soap opera on the telly. Nobody can do it like us, I swear.

Who do I define as a dyko-psycho? A Lulu-lickin' Looney Tune? These gals are psychic vampires. They are chronic liars. They may be brilliant scam artists. They have huge mood swings or bad tempers. They often seem too good to be true. Their story is always changing. They know too much about anything and everything.

A psycho may enter your life in several ways. Sometimes you'll meet someone and know right away that she's crazy. It's simply obvious. But often someone wonderful enters your life and you find out a bit too late that she's a little loo-loo. Then, of course, there are the peripheral crazies. Those are folks who seep into your life via your friends; they are your friends' psychos. You're merely secondary energy/blood supply for these psychic vampires, if not farther down the food chain, and are really only their backup host.

Just as there are different ways a crazy can enter your life, there are also different ways people are cracked. There are, however, two basic prototypes: the JC (Just Crazy) and the LBAC (Lying Bullshit-Artist Crazy, pronounced "LaBack"). Even though it's not implied in her name, the JC lies also. She has to, because she doesn't want anyone to know she's crazy. She probably started lying to herself and others years ago; her reality would only be partially "real" to any objective observer or say, you. The LBAC's life also involves these kinds of lies, as well as very active scamming. Read the list below and ask yourself if these events sound familiar.

(1) She seems to know even more than you do on a topic that interests you. You tell her you're learning hang gliding and find out she spent a year in Acapulco hang gliding. You say, "Great, maybe you can show me a few tips." Oh, too bad. You find out she broke her wrist in eight places so unfortunately she can never glide again.

(2) She seems to not only share your attitudes but also has more *you* in her than you do. This soon becomes apparent since almost no one has a one-dimensional attitude on a topic. But the psychos don't know this. They begin to mimic you and will go too far. For example, you've been having one problem after another with your mechanic. You've been polite and have given them the benefit of the doubt for weeks (psycho doesn't know that) and have finally had it with them. She hears you going off on them. Soon after, you notice she has a short temper and copies your "screw you" attitude, but she's doing it all the time. You're thinking, *Jeez, what a hothead.* But she thinks she's being like you. You might not even remember the time you performed the action she's now copying.

(3) She reads way too much into your every action; she makes everything you do relate to her. If you close the door, you hate her. If you eat a piece of cake, you're trying to teach her a lesson. Then you feel the need to explain yourself to her, which leads us to…

(4) You find yourself missing important events because you're processing with her so much. Somehow she makes you miss Sunday family dinner or a football game with your best friend— more than once. Or maybe she out-and-out says, "You spend too much time with them and not enough with me."

(5) One minute you're spending too much time with her and she needs her space; the next you're supposedly ignoring her and are in love with someone else.

(6) She's new in town.

(7) She's filled with hard-luck stories that affect her circumstances but are hard to corroborate. She doesn't have a place to live because her ex-roommate's ex-lover broke in and stole everything they owned and trashed the place so now she lost her deposit and all her furniture. She got fired from her job and blacklisted in her last town because the boss "just didn't like me. I don't know why."

(8) She likes to do stuff "one-on-one." Your friends complain they never see you. Many people get overwhelmed at parties and like one-on-one attention. Most new lovers hide away, making love for hours and exchanging life stories. But, for some reason, with this chick it feels a little different to you. You've suggested meeting people for a drink or a bite to eat and it just never happens. Maybe you've actually ended up canceling plans (see number 4). Also, you do things in ways that just aren't like you. Maybe you've canceled on friends before, but usually you do call and cancel. Now you just don't show up or you arrive two hours late to say you can't stay. In other words, she's isolating you.

(9) She's ultrasuave. She pays for way too much at first (or for nothing at all—see number 7). She seems to know *everything* about *everything* fabulous. She says she'll take you to this or that club and get in for free. She knows great restaurants and places with the perfect music. It seems like she's read the fantasy date section of your mind or diary. Of course, many, many, many not-crazy people do this, which adds to their fabulousness. But this woman, she's just a little too sharp. A tad *too* sleek. Almost slippery. She is too much like your fantasy, and something about it doesn't seem real.

(10) This is related to number 9. She's too agreeable. Everything is so smooth.

(11) You catch her lying to someone else. I have a *hard-core* policy on lying, which is much harsher than most people's. Honesty is best the policy. If you see that she can lie easily to someone else, beware: You'll never know if she's lying to you with that same sense of ease.

(12) The crazy eyes. This one I just can't describe in words, but if you see it, you'll hopefully know. It's like you aren't seeing past her eyes; until this moment you didn't realize that with most people you aren't looking at their eyes but into them. The eyes really are windows to the soul or at least a reflection of a person's thoughts, feelings, etc. But with a crazy, you see just the eyes and not a millimeter into her, period. They're flat. Something is moving behind those eyes and you can't see it.

Dyke Sex on the Endangered List

What am I talking about?! Dyke sex seems to be running rampant, doesn't it? Even straight girls are having it, and men are wishing they were women so they could too. But sneak a peak between the sheets and not just between our ears. How much sex are we really having? Is dyke sex the latest trend since parasurfing, or is it on schedule to be the next moa bird or spotted owl?

I get this question over and over again: Is not having sex part and parcel with being in a dyke relationship? Is "lesbian bed death" a myth or reality? I was avoiding putting it that way because the hipper dyke factions don't use that term. The words themselves creep up our stocking seams all the wrong way—just like how women softball players desperately try to pretend they're all straight. We're talking total denial. That's what we urban dykes do. We try to pretend this no-more-sex thing only happens to the suburban dykes and the suburban dykes pretend it only happens to the country dykes and the country dykes know you have to have a girlfriend to have lesbian bed death and they don't have girlfriends (unless they moved out of the city to the country with their girlfriends), which they think only the city dykes have.

Women phrase the question in different ways. First there's the overt method: "Shar, does being a dyke mean any girlfriend I get is only going to rock my bed the first two weeks?" Then there's the more subtle, mumbled innuendo: "So, you and Jackie, you…I mean, of course you two still… Have you two had any *alone* time lately?"

I certainly hope that it isn't our destiny. It hasn't been my past. Jackie and I definitely get it on and, yes, a lot more often than just on anniversaries and birthdays.

Before I reveal my plan for how to keep dyke sex from going extinct, let's examine the reason we're on the endangered list in the first place.

You get together with another woman and have totally hot sex: rolling around for hours, kissing until your faces are raw, fucking until everything else is raw. Maybe this pace keeps up for two weeks, then you're both tired and go without it for a few days. There's always a rationalization or excuse: One of you is sick, there's a work deadline, you haven't seen your best friend in a while, a relative is in town. Whatever the reason, you fall asleep in each other's arms (because, yes, you still hook up that night) instead of between each other's legs. After that you're on a sex schedule that lets in the real world a little more. You answer the phone again, you might cook instead of just eating snacks or ordering out, you actually think about a work problem for a few minutes when you're at home (maybe you hadn't realized you hadn't done that in a while), you do your laundry, reply to your phone messages, sleep, go to a social event, rent a video, put your CDs back in the covers. From there sex starts slipping away, and soon you can't remember the last time you had it.

Oh, we can sit on our heinies countin' up the reasons couples stop having sex until Jesse Helms goes to work wearing a pink rhinestone tiara! Perhaps you don't love each other anymore. Maybe one of you resents the other for a past fight or incident. Life stresses, such as kids, jobs, or family, can also affect libidos. The real-life reasons are endless.

I also have a notion that we've got a lot of evolutionary shit going against us. Just think what state the world would be in if everyone stayed in that first three-month bliss forever. We'd be lying in piles of trash and take-out boxes, the laundry would never get done, and no one would make any money. I think there's some pheromone thing that happens that allows us to get out of bed. Of course, there's no reason not to get back in position after a few chores are done.

When one person does not want to have sex, at least the couple has a starting point. We can ask Lucy, "Why don't you want to have sex with Tori?" But most often the mystery is much harder to decipher, because usually each woman wants to have sex and thinks the couple isn't having sex because her partner doesn't want it. Lucy's best friend is hearing all about her lack of sex with Tori, and Tori's best friend is hearing the same thing about Lucy. Each of them is bemoaning the lack of sex and blaming it on the other one. To top it all off, neither woman is lying and just pointing a finger; they each sincerely think the other has lost interest.

Well, I may not have a psychology degree, but I do have a degree in bedroomology, so I can at least help out with this one. I have my own theories about why women do this strange "I'm in my corner, and she doesn't want to have sex with me" beeswax. I'm not the first to say it has to do with the way we're socialized as women on the issue of sex. Let's be specific, though. Show me 100 couples who don't have sex anymore and I'll show you 200 bottoms. Bottoms mating with bottoms means everyone is waiting to be thrown over the dresser in the heat of passion. We're socialized to all be bottoms. That's right. Think about it. The only sex vocabulary we're given as women is "no." To even have sex, we're waiting for someone else to do something that we can then *not* say no to. When we were growing up, we were waiting (granted, possibly dreading), symbolically at least, on our backs for some boy to make the moves so we could have sex. And isn't that what you're doing now? Waiting for her to make the moves? What kind of power is that? Nevertheless, it's what most women have as an operating system. Girl, upgrade to Top2000 and you'll be getting laid a lot more often.

You may be wondering, *How does anyone become a top if all of us grew up waiting for generic-boy to go to first base?*

Many women are born tops, and that socialization never shakes them from their boots. My Jackie is that way. Even the few years she dated boys in junior high, she never waited for a 13-year-old to know what he wanted or what he was doing. She told him how it was going to be. She saw the power behind knowing how to pleasure people at an early age.

Other women are tops because they relate being a bottom to vulnerability and they certainly do not want to be vulnerable. Some may not want to be vulnerable because they don't like their bodies or because they were abused or raped. That doesn't mean they aren't good tops or aren't—by the time you run into them—sincere tops. I'm just telling you where they're coming from, and, believe me, I've gotten this from the source.

Finally, many tops started out as bottoms or in one of those many positions in between. They try lots of different things, then discover they have a proclivity for it. The lesson for us: There's hope, no matter what your age. You don't have to be born with a top chip in your hard drive. We're socialized in a zillion other ways besides this bottom business, and at a certain point we outgrow many aspects of our socialization. We're all also socialized to think big women are ugly and butch women are freaks. Yet, after coming into dykedom, expanding our horizons and letting our clits do the walking, how many of us discover butch and/or big women are the sexiest chicks of all? These are just two examples. Think of your own. By expanding our horizons, we learn what we truly like.

TOP: noun: (1) party-starter top: sexual aggressor, the partner in a sexual encounter who initiates and guides sex; (2) vanilla top or service top: the partner who physically gives her partner sexual pleasure (regardless of who initiated sex) either in the form of, but not limited to, oral sex or penetration; (3) S/M Top: the person in control of a sensual situation, such as, but not limited to, bondage, flogging, or blindfolding.

Retro Corner: Reciprocation

OK, I know we're blazing into the new millennium, but bear with me as I first ask us to go retro and employ our '90s "think globally, act locally" thinking caps for a minute. Have a social conscience, sister, and help out! Ask yourself, "Your Majesty, what can We do to become more sexually aggressive in Our own corner of the Queendom?" Don't let lesbian sex die! Be a party starter! Fuck a girl today!

Ravage Me, Not My Ego

You *must* be ravaged, courted, and wooed now and then, or your poor little OoD heart might start to take it personally. Even I had emotional trauma from *always* having to be the instigator. You can say to yourself, *It's not in her personality to make the moves. She loves me her way. I shouldn't need her to throw me over the dresser and rip my clothes off in fits of unabashed passion.* Oh, bullshit. All OoDs need (at least occasionally) lovers who simply cannot hold back their overwhelming lust. In the meantime, go make some Lust Karma and affectionize someone today.

Let's go back even further.

What happened to the nice '80s you-do-me-then-I-do-you mentality? There were some big problems with it, and that's why it got dumped. Still, as I examine different folks' sex lives, I can't help wondering if there wouldn't be more free sex going around if sex were treated more like prostitution, as a clear-cut exchange. Let's say it out loud, "You do me, then I'll do you." No lazy fucks. Sex begets sex. If you and your honey are having sex for any reason, chances are you'll keep having more sex. Plus, you'll be sexier to other people because sex begets sex, making you smell, walk, and act differently. Haven't you ever noticed that just about the time you're getting laid, everybody wants you and you're thinking, *Now you want me. Where were you when I was high and dry?*

I was a top with my first girlfriend (although we didn't use that kind of language at all). Still, I wanted her to rev me up, but she just wasn't a kick-start kinda gal. I have an incredible libido, so I got sex the way I know how, which is to go after it. Thus, I played the role of instigator in that relationship, and we had lots of sex.

Willingness and Desire

One of the topics psychotherapist Joann Loulan always goes on about is the difference between willingness and desire. Sometimes you just have to be willing to try something new, and perhaps then your willingness will turn into desire. In other words, if your gal is at least *trying* to spice up your life, then be willing to go there with her. Respond to her advances. Going, "Oh, God. That sounds like the dumbest idea since Dan Quayle tried to write a dictionary," is not the way to flame her fire of lust. Try it; you might like it. If you don't, at you two least shared a vulnerable moment together. And willingly being vulnerable together helps keep you in touch with each other.

Conversely, if you want to try something new, she needs to be willing to go there. Anybody can instigate something new. Even a bottom can still run the scene now and then, so I don't want to hear any excuses. Stop waiting for her to start something. I haven't met a gal yet who couldn't take a little bit of bossing around. Even the absolute stone butches I have been with have let me tie them up and do a little show for them. That's the hardest audience, so anybody else is a piece of cheesecake. If your gal won't even try some of my suggestions, then flag a taxi, darlin', 'cuz you need to *move on*.

"I Think You Like Me More Than I Like You" Syndrome

If I've heard that from one butch, I've heard it from a city of 'em. I can be honest in primal/intimate situations (like when my ass is in air), "being honest" meaning looking into her eyes or just *being there*. I melt into her; it is physical, paraphysical. Because I don't engage my secret protective bubble, I don't avoid eye contact or avoid being melted. In other words, I'm not distant. And, in some women's eyes, distance is in direct proportion to love. You are close, present, intense = you're in love with her. You're far away = not in love. In most sexual situations, I'm honest and let myself be or go wherever I want, or where my feelings take me. I've had women tell me that I'm in love with them when I'm not. My friend Bella has the opposite problem: Women are always telling her they're in love with her, for exactly the same reason. During sex she's present, gives them attention, and allows them to do the same to her, so in their minds that equals love. Conversely, we all know women who have to have distance during sex for reasons that may have nothing to do with their level of affection for partners.

These days it seems more people are being honest and real during sex, which may eventually clear up this problem. When more women see that you can be present during sex and really, really enjoy it, or enjoy your time with another person, and understand that means you're a real, honest, fun person, *and* that there's more than one person like that in town, we can get down to mutual appreciation, chemistry, and compatibility—qualities that strongly affect falling in love.

Defrost This....

My blood boils when I hear "She's an ice queen" or "She's too needy." Are those the only two choices? As if the "Madonna/Whore" complex weren't enough to deal with, now we have the "Wonder Woman/Poster Child" complex. We have to have nerves of steel to move through this world, and when we don't, when we're a tad low, we're called "too needy." You know what? Sometimes we *are* too needy, that "too" being determined by the fact that maybe Ms. Wrong is looking too much like Ms. Great. But if Ms. Wrong is secure and has her own self together, then she can delicately deal with this by not running but rather demanding the status of friendship and asking for a plateau. That's what a good person does. She does not go, "Oh, Julie is so-o-o in love with me. I gotta be mean to her to shake her off or I gotta take off and not answer the phone so I can lose her." No, she says, "You know, Sarah seems a little needy right now. I'll give her what I can give, which is _____." Perhaps she can give you something sexual, but realize that it may not lead to marriage or love. Maybe Ms. Wrong can be *nice* and be a good date by taking Sarah to public events now and then.

Extinguishing a Potential Ego Implosion: Running Defense for a Babefriend

One evening a new femme acquaintance, Dietrich, and I were having a great time sharing stories when the evening took a provocative turn. We were strolling through a film screening in a large women's space when we spotted this butch (we'll call her "Lame") who had treated Dietrich very poorly. Not only was she there, but the minute she saw Dietrich she started overtly coo-cooing in this other girl's ear. Well, luckily, I didn't know this girl from a hill of beans, and since I had just met Dietrich, Lame didn't know me nor from whence I'd come. I was wearing my go-go boots, leggings, and Harley T-shirt with the sleeves rolled up. I looked more tough than usual, but definitely femme. To counteract Lame's little scene, I decided to play tomboy-femme-dyke. I laughed loudly, disrupting the screening and drawing attention to us as I pulled Dietrich tightly to me by the waist. I purred, "Well, if we can't find a seat, baby, let's just make our own movie." Dietrich gasped but then played along with my bravado. She pouted at me, then said, "But don't you want to see the picture? I'll find us a seat." I sat down a couple of rows from Lame and pulled Dietrich onto my lap as I said, "I'll be the one finding a seat for this, and as for what I need to see, well, that's right before my eyes," "Aa-a-ah!" That's what she said as she put her head on my shoulder. I successfully boosted her ego while giving Lame something to think about. Sisters have to stick together.

How to Wash Any Babe Right Outta Your Hair: A Sharspell for the Wrenched Heart

"I don't hate you, but I don't like you. I don't feel anything left for you."
—"Emotional Scars," by The Hail Marys, lyrics by Jackie Strano

Oh, sweet pumpkin, is your little heart bruised or, even worse, totally run over by a haggle of Harleys? Never you mind. Dr. Shar will take care of you. Careful, this is strong medicine. If your case isn't bad, cut the prescription in half.

First off, you have to see that the relationship is over. Perhaps you're in one of those breakups where this is totally clear, but let me dedicate a moment to those who are still hanging on. Girl, order yourself some phonics and read my words: I'm telling you, it's over. Those friends who say, "Oh, maybe she'll come back, didn't mean it, will change her mind, blah blah blah…." They're clueless. Their hearts are in the right place and they love you, so they're just trying to make you feel better. But saying this is like telling someone whose hair caught fire that "it doesn't smell and you can't tell. It looks OK." Bullshit. Cut that shit off and grow some new hair.

Those friends need to tell you what I'm telling you right now: It's sad because it was a good relationship and/or you loved each other and/or you had great sex and/or she took good care of you. And it's good that it's sad. Tears are what we pay for people. It's impossible to buy people with money (we can rent sometimes), but after they're gone or even when we are with someone, they can cost us tears. Tears are all we have to give and it's totally OK, and it's also an honor to just let it flow and pay the price willingly. If she isn't worth tears, then she wasn't worth you.

Sometimes we ruminate for days trying to rationalize a breakup, figure out why someone left, or try to articulate "why it went wrong." Much of the time this is still an effort to control the situation. You couldn't control her or the relationship or even the break-up, but goddamn it, you're going to "figure out *why!*" or what you're going to do next or what you're going say to her, etc. But maybe you need to just let yourself be sad and tell yourself, "Honey, it's over. Time to move on." But to move on we need ritual and cleansing. Back to the burned hair: Like I said, cut it off, but if that's all you do, you'll have a big chunk of your head missing. You'll have to style around it and own it. *That* is the reason I'm here. It's called Diva Intervention. We're gonna get rid of the horrid smell, add some highlights, and give you a brand new do. (P.S. This procedure has been tested repeatedly and is a proven fix when details are heeded.)

Day One

Lock yourself in your house, make a date for 10 P.M. with a friend you can slobber on, tell him/her that you might cancel but to come over no matter what. Tell her that your phone might not work.

Then *pull* the phone out of the wall, put it in a Ziploc bag and seal it, put that one inside of another Ziploc bag and seal it, then put the whole thing in a pan of water, then put it into the freezer.

Run to your nearest store and buy comfort foods: Ben & Jerry's, jarred strawberry or hot fudge sauce, instant mashed potatoes. If you drink, buy a small bottle of tequila and ingredients for margaritas. Also buy some ibuprofen and a large cucumber. Go home.

Take an ibuprofen. Cut the cucumber into one-inch thick slices and place in freezer.

Look at photos of you and your ex together and begin eating ice cream, start crying, get choked up so that you can't eat.

Cry. Say "Why?" out loud a lot. "Why? Why? Why?" (Even if you know why, say it.)

Answer yourself too: "I don't know why, honey, but you'll live." (Butch version: "I don't know why, pardner, but you'll live.")

Cry more, choke down the ice cream even though your mouth is getting that icky feeling. Then put it back in freezer and cry hard, lying down, and go in and out of daydreams.

Turn on the TV.

Eat salty foods, then more ice cream, then stop ice cream by 6 P.M.

Write "I hate you, you motherfuckin' piece of shit" as much as you can, then say "No, I don't!"

I love you!" and rip it up while snot runs down your face. Wipe your face and talk to yourself more, this time in front of the mirror.

Scream "Why?" again.

Around 8 P.M. take one more ibuprofen and drink two glasses of water.

Take a hot bath. Crawl into bed and sleep or meditate until friend shows up at 10 P.M.

Drink with friend. Fake laugh until you get drunk, then cry and get very snot-filled. If you don't drink, just slowly become more and more slobbery and slur your words. Physical alcohol content is not the important factor; it's the slobber effect that counts. Don't hold back. Cry and don't worry if you look like a fool.

Take vitamin C and drink at least two more glasses of water. Fall asleep.

Day Two

Crawl out of bed, take two cucumber slices from freezer, and put them on your eyes for 30 minutes or so while you listen to the TV. Then take them off and watch TV until 3 o'clock.

Take a shower.

Go to a pay phone and call a friend and say, "I have to stay away from the phone. Can I come over?"

Forget about work, rent videos, and do suburban things.

If no friends are home, go to the nearest dime store or variety store and go up and down every aisle pondering as many things as possible: Watch people hurry past you, laugh at their jokes and children, take time to talk slowly to the clerks, and let someone go ahead of you in line. Read magazines in line that you never have before, then comment on them to a stranger.

Finally, go to a record store and buy Diana Ross's *All the Great Hits* (the one with "Mahogany," "Touch Me in the Morning," and "Remember Me") and a blank tape.

Go home and cry in bed only to the degree that seems natural.

Day Three: The Homestretch

Get up, eat oatmeal with lots of honey, cinnamon, soy milk (white stuff of choice), and butter, and drink something hot. Take your hot tea over to the stereo and put on your new Diana Ross CD and tape it. If your version includes lyrics, sit on the floor by your stereo and sing along with Diana.

Tape the CD on two sides of a tape so that you can just turn it over and listen to it again and again. Clean house and listen to it until you know the words by heart, then sing them at the top of your lungs.

Finally, do Diana Ross as frequently as possible. You're on your own now, but Diana will take care of it, and you'll not even think to play her one day, and won't even remember your pain until you dig the tape out to loan it to a friend in need.

Day Four

Defrost the phone.

1. For in-depth advice on top and bottom issues, check out one of the many fabulous books available on the market. I've listed some at the end of this book.

Part IX

3, 2, 1...Blast-Off!

Put on your space suit and fire up your rocket fuel, sweetie.
Launch time is imminent.

Beyond Dating
Living Love Large

So, babycakes, you're the sexy, single femme and you're falling in love. Love is the one thing we all have plenty of. It's not like pie. We don't run out of pieces.

Most of my life, I believed in true love as something I knew some people had. But I firmly believe/d no one should hold out for it. Live life, make it great, and you'll be happy. Wholeheartedly enjoy life with good loves, really great loves, including the love you have for yourself. If you're one of the lucky ones who finds your true love, then your definition of "happy" will be blown out of the water, trust me, but until it happens, as they say, ignorance is bliss. I hate it when real love, first love, or just love is discounted. That's bullshit. Fill yourself up with what you need.

> ## "Everybody say, 'Love!'"
> — RuPaul

You can enjoy "pretty-damn-good love" without feeling like you're settling. How? By caring for yourself and your needs. Live life! Don't follow the bad examples the patriarchy has set before us. Open your eyes and aggressively create the relationships you want. There are plenty of examples

PHYLLIS CHRISTOPHER

Jackie and me living love large.

of differently modeled relationships out there.

Better to have a run in your stockings than to run from your heart.

"We're a revolution baby /Your kinda love makes me crazy / Wild Angels rage against it all / You be my Jesus Girl, I'll be your lizard King / You're the Queen of all my dreams."

—from "Saltlick" by The Hail Marys, lyrics by Jackie Strano

Girl-Goddess Glossary

Do you ever feel, when it comes to dating, that everyone knows some secret code and you didn't get your magic decoder ring when you joined the lesbian dating club? Like, where was the Welcome Wagon? Are you a new Queen and a little unsure of how to air kiss? Are you a thoroughly experienced Diva who wishes she could just throw a book at the next person who responds to your curses of "I forgot my boa!" with "Gee, I didn't know you liked reptiles?" Well, here's your chance. Although I can't decipher the entire lexicon of lesbo lingo, I can offer this handy dating dictionary and overall goddess glossary that contains not only the essentials, such as *stiletto* and *dollar-a-wear*, but also some basic codes and translations. As with any language, you really just need to know a few key phrases such as, "How much is a martini?" and "Where's the powder room?" Please contact me with any additions you may have. This is just the beginning.

Air kiss: the act of kissing while leaving just a smidgen of air between oneself and the recipient of the kiss. Often done to one side of cheek, then the other. Performed to preserve makeup or when one has a cold.

Andro: short for androgynous: (1) folks that are not butch or femme, usually on the boyish side; (2)

a person who doesn't like to call herself "butch" yet everyone knows she is even if she doesn't have the manners to prove it; (3) person whose appearance does not reveal whether s/he is male or female.

Anti-schwing: any event, revelation of personal knowledge, attitude, or emotional or physical condition that really sucks the boner out of a possexible situation. Example: Your friend says, "...and then my cat got diarrhea which reminded my date of her ex's cat so she started crying." You say, "Wow, what an *anti-schwing.*"

Ass-whipped and heartbroken: phrase created in the Den of Perpetual Indulgence to indicate subject had a raucous, carnal time being spanked and more, and happily woke up still single after said event. (*Heartbroken* indicates singlehood, not actual sadness.)

Babedick: a dildo worn by a femme.

Babefriend: a femme friend. Usually in reference to friendship. When a babe is your girlfriend she is just your "babe."

Babelust: desire felt for femmes. Example: "I was so filled with *babelust* that I tied a NYLA stiletto onto a line and threw it into the dance floor just to see who would bite."

Backseat driver: See *topping from the bottom.*

Betty: the babe who rides on the back of a Harley or motorcycle. (See also *butter.*)

Boa: (1) the best way to make friends at a party 'cuz everyone wants to try it on or converse about it; (2) the best accessory to add to any outfit if you want to look like a movie star; (3) a strip of feathers you wear around your neck, duh.

Body modification: (1) wearing size 8 Chanel pumps circa 1953 for six hours when your feet are size 9; (2) the H2O bra; (3) strapping on your favorite babedick; (4) piercing, tattooing, branding or any other permanent alteration of the body.

Body shot: the number one way to start a public orgy. "Giver" licks across the "receiver's" body, leaving a wet trail where she then deposits salt. She sexily shoves a chunk of lime into the receiver's mouth with the pulp facing out. She then licks up the salt, downs a shot of tequila, then sucks the lime from the receiver's mouth ending in a passionate exchange of saliva.

Bottom: (1) a stereotype that seems to be inextricably, yet without foundation, attached to the word "femme"; (2) person who responds/reacts positively to sexual leadership; (3) a person who receives sexual pleasure from giving themselves physically or mentally to another for that person's sexual gratification; (4) person who gets off on being done by her babe/stud.

Butch: the opposite of femme.

Butchcock: a dildo worn by a butch.

Butch diva: the peacock of the butch world. She likes things and people around her to be a certain way—*her* way.

Butch flight: the current trend of butch women becoming men, running to their doctors for hormones and surgery, therefore *fleeing* butchhood. (See also *Butch Flight Anxiety Syndrome*.)

Butch Flight Anxiety Syndrome (a.k.a. BFA Syndrome): a syndrome occurring largely in butch-loving femmes—trace occurrences in butch-loving butches as well—where femme fears she will never find proper dates or lovin' because the number of butch women is quickly dwindling due to butch flight.

Butter: the babe on the back of your bike.

Clit cock: the clitoris, especially when rubbed between breasts or on other body parts or when sucked off.

Combo girl: (1) a gal who embodies both butchness and femme attitude; (2) a gal who readily gives a fucking as much as she gets a fucking.

Come-fuck-me pumps: (1) a better invitation to sex than any bow-tied 'n' naked singing telegram!; (2) heels so high and provocative that they are not actually walked in but rather are worn while lounging in bed seducing another to "come fuck me."

Courtesy call (a.k.a. postcoital communiqué): the call made the day after sex or date to check in. Etiquette dictates that the butch makes the call in a butch/femme situation. The top or the initiator of the date makes the call in Femme^2 (two femmes together) situations or in obvious circumstances such as where there is a great age difference. Courtesy E-mail has now become accepted among many women, although some find it rude.

Daddy: a butch dyke who makes sure her girl is fed, fucked, and well-protected from monsters. The degree to which she is "the boss" of a relationship depends on the players. "Daddy" may be played only in the bedroom or may be a 24/7 way of relating to the world.

'Dess Babe: short for "Goddess Babe."

Diva femme: a woman who wears high-femme drag quite often—if not always—has a commanding presence, and makes anyone other than another *Diva femme* seem like a tomboy by comparison. She is often an explicit top or just a woman who knows what she wants, whether that means finding a woman who can actually top a Diva or leading a slutfriend into pleasuring her. A common problem *Diva femmes* experience is run-ins with pillow queens. (See definition below.) Many a *Diva femme* wants nothing more than for someone to bed her over the garbage can and do her right, but many women don't have the *huevos* to take her on and/or they assume that's not what a Diva wants. (Diva example: Ginger Grant. Next to her, Mary Ann seemed like a farmhand, and Mrs. Howell positively butch.)

Doin' the do: (1) having sex; (2) working the room; (3) working the town: hanging with the in crowd, utilizing as many opportunities for fun, fame, or fabulousness offered in any particular city.

Dollar-a-wear: short for "a *dollar-a-wear* or less." (1) an outfit's purchase price divided by the number of times is it worn. Example: A dress costing $50 has to be worn at least 50 times in order for it to be a dollar-a-wear or less; (2) a shorthand way to refer to rationalizing purchasing an item. Example: "I can make these boots a *dollar-a-wear* in a heartbeat."

Dykedick: a dildo worn by any dyke.

Ecru: a shade of beige. Made famous in editor-author Laura Antoniou's (a.k.a. Sara Adamson's) story, first appearing in *Virgin Territory 2* (Masquerade, 1997).

Ensemble: your whole outfit including your spectacular shoes, 'do, and accessories. (*Always* say "*ensemble*" and avoid saying "outfit.")

Femme: read the book.

Femme bitch top: (1) a femme who holds no prisoners. She dishes out as much pain, humiliation or pleasure as she darn well wants to. For more information listen to the song of the same title by Tribe 8; (2) a stereotype juxtaposing the pillow-queen stereotype. Butches often assume femmes are either passive pillow queens or *femme bitch tops*.

Femme Divine: (1) A remarkably open and insightful movie by Karen Everett; (2) the female spiritual archetype that represents all that is holy and wondrous about femmes

Fuck-you pumps: term made popular by Lily Burana referring to pumps made for walking, stomping, and fucking. Also refers to the woman claiming her high attitude heels for herself and not for any man who may be looking on.

Fugly: (1) being fucking ugly; (2) feeling one's body is fucking ugly; (3) staring into a mirror and perceiving oneself to be fucking ugly, as in *to have the fuglies*.

Fuglies: a severe case of: (1) being unable to get dressed as a result of being or perceiving to be fugly; (2) refusing to leave one's domicile because one feels fugly. (See *fugly*.) Usually occurring in women, often as a part of, but not solely limited to, their menstrual period.

Glamour date: (1) someone you go on a date with in whom you may not be romantically interested but who will dress up and treat you like a queen; (2) going on a fancy date in a public place such as a premiere, drag contest, etc.

Goth: short for Gothic. A great excuse to wear gobs of eyeliner.

Helium heels: describes one's sexual position when she is flat on her back with heels to the ceiling. Can be used instead of the term "Do-me queen." Example: "Oh, girl, she had the worst case of *helium heels*. I liked to never get her off her back." The term may also indicate the desire to have lots of sex such as, "Ooh, chile, I'm puttin' on my *helium heels* this weekend. Mama's gonna get some."

Helping yourself: (1) touching oneself to ensure pleasure during a partnered sex act; (2) the answer to the question, "May I touch myself?" Reply: "Go ahead, help yourself."

Hers-n-Hers: two dykes who dress or look alike.

High-maintenance: a realistic description of cars, people, homes, or animals, meaning that they take a lot of time and care to maintain. Often used as a pejorative term to unrealistically describe femmes in some communities. Example: "Femmes are too *high-maintenance*." The HM phrase has spurred the "*High-Maintenance* Rebellion."

Hoo-hoo: vulva.

Kitten femme: a coquette. Seemingly not too aggressive yet definitely has a little kitty agenda that usually includes some trouble such as getting tied up in Gramma's yarn. *Kitten femmes* are, by definition, vanilla bottoms if not S/M bottoms. They have a tendency to mew, purr, poke their noses into hard-to-reach places, and use body gestures and eye contact to communicate more than words.

Lappaccino: the act of sitting, actively, on a babe's or stud's lap until she is "all whipped up" and "frothing" at the mouth with all the desire she has for you.

Mack daddy: a butch daddy who has got her groove on and knows how to make the ladies feel real fine.

Mack mama: a soulful Diva who does some TCBin' with some TLCin'.

Marabou: fine feathers. *Marabou* boas are the smaller boas that seem to be just fuzzy and do not have distinct feathers.

Merkin: a wig for your pussy. Back in the day, having a bald pussy was not a good thing; it meant you had lost all of your hair because of syphilis or had to shave it because you had crabs or scabies. A working girl certainly didn't want her customers to know that, so she wore a *merkin*.

Mistress mommy: usually an S/M femme top who likes to take care of and discipline bad "boys" or "girls."

Moos: the two peaks of the lips. After applying lipstick in a horizontal motion across the top lip, one must go back with the tip of the lipstick and fill in the *moos*.

Mules: open-toed lounging slippers with no straps across heel. Most often refers to the boudoir slippers that have marabou trim across the toes.

Notsexible: a person, place, or thing that cannot be connected with sexual activity. Example: Your new coworker tries to bond with you by scoping out a cute young file clerk across the room. You say, "Hello? I can't hit it with the boss's 17-year-old daughter! She's definitely *not-sexible.*"

One-night stand: a sexual liaison after which both partners go their separate ways come morning, afternoon, or sunset. Seemingly rare in the lesbian nation, but it does occasionally happen.

Ordering take-out: (1) calling up a phone sex line or a working girl to deliver what you want sexually; (2) when a married nonmonogamous couple doesn't feel like, ahem, cooking for themselves so they call and invite a slutfriend to deliver some fun fetish or sensual service straight to their bedroom door.

Packing: the fine art of wearing a dildo under one's clothing in public. Most often done in male drag so that the dildo looks like a penis, but sometimes done under miniskirts or power slips.

Palmolive moment: when one is caught in the act of doing something she knows she shouldn't be, as in "You're soaking in it."

Pancake: someone who professes loudly to lead sexually activities then unexpectedly becomes passive, desiring partner(s) to become leader, as in "She flipped like a *pancake.*"

Pigboy/girl: (1) person who wallows in the juices of sex like a pig in mud; (2) in the S/M world, someone who just wants more and more.

Pillow queen: a very appreciative bottom who likes to sink her head into her pink satin pillows and moan, moan, moan while she receives pleasure.

Pink: (1) Barbie's aura; (2) my vice; (3) Panther; (4) a pussy state of mind.

Possexible: being a possible opportunity for sex, as in "a *possexible* date" or "This van has *possexiblities.*"

Private moment: (1) when one takes care of bodily elimination processes in private (Femmepress Shar urges that some moments stay private no matter how well you get to know someone. It's not only polite, but also keeps intimacy alive in other areas); (2) when one or two people need to be alone, whether for communication or to avoid overstimulation.

Product: short for a hair product. Often, if you don't like your hair, you just need to find the right product. Usually, but not exclusively, referring to expensive salon brands.

Pump: a closed-toed high heel, cut low just to the beginning of the toes, that also encloses the heel.

Pussycat femme: much like a kitten femme but a little more bossy and a bit more demanding about getting a specific itch scratched. Pussycats want the catnip and a scratching post *now*. They will lounge in the sun for hours after being satisfied, and you'll probably forget they almost took an eye out. Age makes no difference as to whether one is a kitty or a pussycat. Examples: Emma Peel, Catwoman.

Q Babe or QQ Babe: Queen Babe or Queer Babe or Queer Queen Babe. An accurate, savvy alternative to always having to say "femme."

Queendom: where you rule (a.k.a. everywhere).

Reflective Surface Disorder (a.k.a. RSD): disorder in which sufferer is compelled to look for her/his reflection in reflective surfaces such as mirrors or less obvious places such as butter knives, pay phones, coin return slots, toasters, etc. Most often, reflection is desired to check teeth for basil or lips for smudging. Term popularized by presidential candidate Joan Jett Blakk.

Rode hard and put away wet: (1) receiving lots of you-know-what then left in bed without postcoital cuddles and therefore left worn out yet still glowing from the throes of passion; (2) an equestrian term referring to riding horses fast then putting them back in the stable without a brushing or a slow-down walk. As a cowboy friend once said, "Good for people, bad for horses."

Serial monogamy: Oh, please, this needs to be exorcised from all dyke consciousness and behavior.

Service top: a person who physically pleasures another with the intent of getting the partner off.

Shlong: derived from combining "short" and "long." Hairstyle in which the hair is cut short on the sides and long in back. (a.k.a. mullet head, UDC—universal dyke cut, sho-lo, neck warmer, Camaro cut, mud flap, buttrocker hair, and hockey hair).

Slingback: a shoe that has a strap circling behind the heel. May be open-toed or closed, but is most often high-heeled.

Slink: the end-all and be-all of walks. Everything from your waist down sinuates forward, your shoulders wave slightly, and the rest of you glides.

Slut: a person who likes sex. Note: Like "fag," "dyke" etc., *slut* used to be a derogatory word (and still is when employed by the unenlightened) for a woman who has had many sexual experiences.

Slutfriend: similar to "girlfriend" or "boyfriend," only it implies that this person is a friend with whom you share affection but don't mate.

Slut pig: someone who just wants more and more and…you get the idea.

S/M top: a person who leads the sexual scene with more appearance of power and control ("appearance" is the key word because the power is given by the bottom).

SNAG: a Sensitive New-Age Guy. Sometimes a realistic description that has no judgment attached, but often used in a derogatory manner to describe touchy-feely guys who are just a bit too sensitive and understanding of the woman's plight and who give you the creeps.

SNAG in your nylons: coming home to find your bisexual boyfriend in your stockings.

Stick pussy: a penis. Phrasing employed during fantasy play or daily with a bio man who wants to pretend he is a woman. Partner tells him he doesn't have a vagina pussy, he has a stick pussy (a.k.a. swinging pussy).

Stilettos: short for "stiletto-heeled shoes." A stiletto is a sharp, pointed object that is used to poke holes in things; thus, it refers to a shoe with a heel that is skinny, long, and deadly.

Surrogate trophy wife/husband: a date who looks marvelous on the arm but is not a romantic interest.

Sweater bumpers: little items you wear under your sweater to make it look like you have hard nipples.

'Taint: perineum. The area between a woman's pussy and asshole or a man's balls and asshole. "'Taint your pussy, 'taint your ass."

Tea-room queen: a person who has sex in private areas of public places such as the Macy's bathroom.

Tightey whiteys: snug-fitting boy panties (a.k.a. men's "brief" underwear).

Tomboy femme: a she-babe who indulges in manicures *and* skateboards.

Top: See *vanilla, S/M, or service.*

Topping from the bottom: when the gal getting done let's you know exactly how, where, and when she wants it.

Tranny ho: a working girl who was born a boy. (See *working girl*.)

U-Haul: a brand name of moving trucks made popular by the joke, "What does a lesbian bring on the second date? A U-Haul." Refers to the lesbian trend of getting married or moving in together quickly.

Vamp: (1) to seduce or to affect another into seducing you (usually without that person knowing); (2) one who vamps (a.k.a. you!).

Vanilla top: a person who gets off on fucking her babe/stud.

Vulva: women's outer genitalia, not to be confused with vagina, which is the canal inside the body.

Working girl: (1) someone who specializes in delivering hormone adjustment, therapy, and spiritual enlightenment all at the same time; (2) a whore.

Moving on Up

Take the Sharfleet Academy Final Exam to See if You're Ready to Graduate!

Select the answer from those listed that *best* answers the question. Choose only ONE answer unless the question is marked otherwise.

1. Shartopia is:
    (a) in the Mall of America
    (b) the land of getting what you want and making your dreams coming true
    (c) a shareware program
    (d) a famous East Indian harpsichord player

2. Pearlene is:
    (a) a jewelry cleaner
    (b) an all-oyster diet
    (c) a tooth whitener
    (d) Mavis's mother

3. OoD:
   (a) is a foreign car with parts made in Madawaska, Maine
   (b) is short for "Object of Desire"
   (c) stands for "On Our Drums," a men's movement rebirthing circle
   (d) means "yuck" to Generation Y

4. A Queen needs to:
   (Check the answer that *does not* belong)
   (a) claim her royal identity
   (b) polish her skills
   (c) care for herself
   (d) *always* have toe cleavage
   (e) take her place in a fabulous setting

5. Staple guns are for:
   (a) surgeons
   (b) homicidal Kelly Girls
   (c) Multifaceted Handy Queens
   (d) Fakir

6. You should flirt with:
   (a) only people with power
   (b) only people with money
   (c) your ex-girlfriend's new girlfriend
   (d) the whole solar system (except jerks)

7. To maintain a killer ass, you should:
   (a) fuck…a lot
   (b) wear high heels
   (c) take the hills
   (d) all of the above

8. A quality hairdresser:
   (a) encourages wearing a shlong
   (b) ignores your requests because he knows best after all
   (c) knows the latest trend and gives that same 'do to *everybody*
   (d) suggests 'dos that go with your face and that require no more energy than you can give

9. Mark *all* true statements:
   (a) You should always indulge yourself in getting ready.
   (b) The Matron Saint of Eyeliner is Tammy Faye Baker.
   (c) Batgirl's hideaway was behind her stove.
   (d) You must advertise on the outside what's on the inside.
   (e) Shar hates luscious violet eye shadow.
   (f) Lipstick should be put on last.
   (g) You soften chapped lips in a warm shower and with Vaseline.
   (h) Quitting some store-bought beauty product can pay off.

10. Mark *all* false statements
    (a) Boobs should be strapped down and hidden from sight!
    (b) Standing up straight will only get you in trouble!
    (c) You should buy outfits exactly as they appear on the store mannequin.
    (d) Monica Lewinsky showed her BVDs to President Clinton.
    (e) Only skinny girls can wear thongs or G-strings.
    (f) Garter belts and stockings are a lovely way to frame your ass.
    (g) Wearing lingerie is the perfect way to feel sexy and be naked all at the same time.
    (h) Queens can wear dramatic elements such as boas, jewels, fun fur, and sequins.

11. Fill in the blanks on the following questions regarding shoes:
    (a) You are a goddess and your shoes are the _ _ _ _ _ .
    (b) To avoid breaking your elbow, be careful in this kind of shoe: _ _ _ _ _ _ _ _ _ _ _ _ _.
    (c) If your feet hurt, all you need is a _ _ _ _ _ and a _ _ _ _.
    (d) Fucking in heels requires balance, _ _ _ _ _, determination, and quality heels.

12. The greatest inhibitor to being sexy is:
    (a) not feeling sexy
    (b) wearing a size 14
    (c) not knowing where your mojo is
    (d) not owning shares in Eve.com

13. To get laid you should, among other things:
    (a) whine really loudly in public, "Why-y-y can't I get la-a-aid?"
    (b) think sex is a disgusting act reserved only for creating a male heir
    (c) oil yourself up, masturbate for hours, and roll sensuous images through your mind
    (d) reserve showering for birthdays and major holidays

14. *Most* femmes who date femmes enjoy:
    (Check the *incorrect* answer.)
    (a) putting makeup on each other
    (b) running through flowy curtains naked to the *Baywatch* sound track
    (c) having hard-core sex for hours on end
    (d) partaking in fashion phone sex

15. To train a baby butch, encourage her to:
    (a) spit in public
    (b) open the door for you
    (c) say femmes are dumb sluts who'll just leave you for a man
    (d) ask you, "Why can't you just wear jeans?"

16. Single femmes:
    (a) have all sold their souls to the devil
    (b) are so boring nobody will ever date them
    (c) never have a lonely night
    (d) are fabulous without having to answer to anybody else

17. True or False? The best way to find true love is to change your personality with each person you date, hopefully after you steal their diary to find out what they're really looking for in a mate.

18. Which is *not* a step of dating as shopping?
    (a) wanting something
    (b) buying a gift certificate to U-Haul for your latest lay
    (c) deciding where to start looking
    (d) getting ready
    (e) knowing you want something

19. If you meet a possexible babe while you're out with someone else, what is the *most* dog-awful thing to do?
    (a) ignore the new girl
    (b) work your place of employment slyly into the conversation
    (c) get drunk and make out with the new girl right then and there
    (d) clap your hands, saying, "OK, who's up for a three-way. I get done first! Called it!"

20. Circle the false statement:
    (a) You should *never* spill a drink on a babe in an effort to meet her.
    (b) Invoking your inner fag helps women bulldoze over insecure moments.
    (c) Smiling sweetly works wonders for getting a stud to cross the room.
    (d) Maintaining eye contact even when conversation pauses shows you may be romantically interested.

21. On a date you should:
    (a) pick boogers and mutter to yourself
    (b) list every form of therapy you've ever had, all the voices you hear, and your favorite way to get rid of warts
    (c) wrap your arm through hers when walking
    (d) stare at all the other cute women who walk by

22. Sometimes women pick an aspect of themselves that society deems "unattractive" (such as wearing eyeglasses or being heavy) to:
    (a) hide behind as an excuse for not meeting people
    (b) turn into a positive, sexy trait
    (c) start a really cool magazine about
    (d) all of the above

23. If you find yourself in a relationship where you and your partner aren't having sex you should:
    (a) run for the hills
    (b) go retro and try the "You do me and I'll do you" motto to see if it fires up desire
    (c) never initiate new ways of having sex; you might miss *Nightline,* after all
    (d) stop kissing her and touching her altogether, 'cuz like, why bother?

24. If you really enjoy yourself during sex, it means:
    (a) you're *deeply* in love with whomever you're sexing
    (b) duh—you're a lascivious slut who should be burned at the stake
    (c) you're in touch with your body and feelings when you have sex
    (d) you don't know how to run a business

25. True or False? You are a Goddess who deserves to create original relationships that meet your needs and that let you to be the best *you* you can be.

Time to Tally!

Give yourself one point for each correct answer. For questions that have more than one answer (such as question 9), give yourself one point for each correct answer you checked.

1. b
2. d
3. b
4. d
5. c
6. d
7. d
8. d
9. a, d, f, g, h
(Note: If you answered (b), you were wrong. Tammy Faye is NOT The Matron Saint of Eyeliner. This was a tricky one. The Matron Saint of Eyeliner is Endora from the *Bewitched* TV series.)
10. a, b, c, d, e
11. Fill-in-the-blanks:
(a) You are a goddess and your shoes are the a l t a r .

(b) To avoid breaking your elbow, be careful in this kind of shoe: B i r k e n s t o c k s.

(c) If your feet hurt, all you need is a p e r c h and a p o s e.

(d) Fucking in heels requires balance, g r a c e, determination, and quality heels.

12. a

13. c

14. b

15. b

16. d

17. FALSE!

18. b

19. c

(Note: Getting drunk and making out with someone else is sloppy and hurts everyone's feelings. Answer (a) is not very nice but acceptable. Answer (b) is the best way to leave her a trail to find you, although if she assumes you're dating someone, she might not track you. And (d) may not go over that well, but, hey, it's honest, inclusive, and works for me.)

20. a

21. c

22. d

23. b

24. c

25. TRUE! You are a Goddess who deserves to create original relationships that meet your needs and lets you to be the best *you* you can be.

How'd you do?

Below 20 points: Femme Flunkie. You need to hire a tutor immediately and write out each chapter in eyeliner! Have some patience and work through each section word for word. If you still flunk the exam after taking it three times, you need to reread the "Butch Boot Camp" section and ask yourself if that's where you *really* belong. Good luck.

20-23: Debbie Dolittle. Dust off that dunce cap; someone needs summer school. Do you think a tiara is an Italian dessert? Do you not believe you're a Queen? Don't you like velvet, berries, and love? Go over the questions you missed carefully. Maybe you need to act out my suggestions, practice in front of mirrors where appropriate, etc.

24-27: Haphazard Princess. Listen up, my wayward Diva, were you cruising the stud outside the window when you were supposed to paying attention in class? This may be satisfactory in gym class but not here, little missy. Reread the chapters to all the questions you got wrong and apply lipstick at the same time. I'm sure you'll be fine.

28-31: Dollface Diva. Oh, sweetie, of course you graduate, but you could have made me just a teensy bit more proud. Go through the answers you missed and spot the areas in which you'd like to boost your Goddess know-how. Maybe we just disagreed about drunk make-out sessions, or you got technical about baby butches spitting. In any case, you'll find your way around the universe with no problem!

32-35: Extreme Queen! You're Divafabulicious, a Goddess Extraordinaire! Better than that, you know it and you know what to do with it. Congratulations. You graduate with honors. Throw away your compass—the universe is yours!

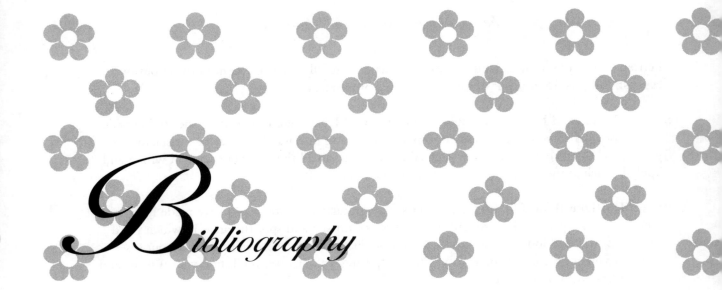

Bibliography

This is not a full bibliography—just a few favorites on the following topics. Although I've organized them by subject, most cover many issues.

Femme-centric Essays and Fiction

Allison, D. (1994). *Skin: Talking About Sex, Class, and Literature.* Ithaca, NY: Firebrand Books. (Get your hands on everything this woman has written!)

Harris, L., and Crocker, E. (1997). *Femme: Feminists, Lesbians, and Bad Girls.* New York: Routledge.

Nestle, J. (1998). *A Fragile Union.* San Francisco: Cleis Press.

Nestle, J. (Ed.). (1992). *The Persistent Desire: A Femme-Butch Reader.* Los Angeles: Alyson Publications.

Nestle, J. (1987). *A Restricted Country.* Ithaca, NY: Firebrand Books.

Newman, L. (Ed.). (1995). *The Femme Mystique.* Los Angeles: Alyson Publications.

Butch-centric Essays and Fiction

Arobateau, R.J. (1995). *Lucy and Mickey.* New York: Masquerade Books. (Red is a self-publishing, prolific, cult-favorite, working-class, trans-butch god. For other works from one of our own national treasures, write to: 484 Lake Park Ave., PMB 228, Oakland, CA 94610.)

Burana, L., Rosen, R., and Due, L. (Eds.). (1994). *Dagger: On Butch Women.* San Francisco: Cleis Press.

Califia, P. (1997). *Diesel Fuel: Passionate Poetry.* New York: Masquerade Books.

Feinberg, L. (1993). *Stone Butch Blues.* Ithaca, NY: Firebrand Books.

Erotic Essays and Fiction

Antoniou, L. (1993, 1995, 1998). *Leatherwomen I, II, & III.* New York: Masquerade Books.

Bright, S. (Ed.). (1993–2000). *Best American Erotica* series. New York: Simon & Schuster.

Bright, S., Blank, J., and Sheiner, M. (Eds.). (1988-present). The *Herotica* series. San Francisco: Down There Press.

Califia, P., and Sweeney, R. (Eds.). (1996). *The Second Coming: A Leatherdyke Reader.* Los Angeles: Alyson Publications.

Foster, N. (Ed.). (1999). *Electric: Best Lesbian Erotic Fiction.* Los Angeles: Alyson Publications.

Lynch, L. (1985). *The Swashbuckler.* Tallahassee, FL: Naiad Press. (For romance novels with butch-femme themes, Naiad is your place.)

Preston, J. (1992). *Flesh and the Word.* New York: Masquerade Books.

Preston, J. (1992). *Tales of the Dark Lord.* New York: Masquerade Books.

Rednour, S. (Ed.). (1995, 1997). *Virgin Territory I & II.* New York: Masquerade Books.

Taormino, T. (Ed.). (1998–2000). *Best Lesbian Erotica* series. San Francisco: Cleis Press.

"How-To" and Reference Books

Califia, P. (1998). *The Lesbian S/M Safety Manual.* Los Angeles: Alyson Publications.

Califia, P. (1993). *Sensuous Magic: A Guide for Adventurous Couples.* New York: Masquerade Books.

Eaton, D., and Liszt, C. (1994). *The Bottoming Book: How to Get Terrible Things Done to You.* San Francisco: Wonderful Greenery Press.

Eaton, D., and Liszt, C. (1998). *The Ethical Slut: A Guide to Infinite Sexual Possibilities.* San Francisco: Wonderful Greenery Press.

Eaton, D., and Liszt, C. (1995). *The Topping Book: or Getting Good at Being Bad.* San Francisco: Wonderful Greenery Press.

Hall, M. (1998). *The Lesbian Love Companion: How to Survive Everything From Heartthrob to Heartbreak.* HarperSanFrancisco.

Newman, F. (1999). *The Whole Lesbian Sex Book: A Passionate Guide for All of Us.* San Francisco: Cleis Press.

Haines, S. (1999). *The Survivor's Guide to Sex: How to Have an Empowered Sex Life After Child Sexual Abuse.* San Francisco: Cleis Press.

Martin, J. (Rev. 1998). *Miss Manners' Guide to Excruciatingly Correct Behavior.* New York: Warner Books.

Queen, C. (1995). *Exhibitionism for the Shy: Show Off, Dress Up, and Talk Hot.* San Francisco: Down There Press.

West, C. (1996). *Lesbian Polyfidelity.* San Francisco: Booklegger Press.

Fabulous Must-Haves

Bornstein, K. (1998). *My Gender Workbook: How to Become a Real Man, a Real Woman, the Real You, or Something Else Entirely.* New York: Routledge.

Bright, S. (1999). *Full Exposure: Opening Up to Sexual Creativity and Erotic Expression.* Harper San Francisco.

Bright, S., and Posener, J. (Eds.). (1996). *Nothing But the Girl: The Blatant Lesbian Image.* London: Freedom Editions. (A must for every coffee table. Just read all of Susie's books! They are easy to find at your local bookstore or on Amazon.com)

Bright, S. (1990). *Susie Sexpert's Lesbian Sex World.* San Francisco: Cleis Press.

Pallington, J. (1999). *Lipstick : A Celebration of the World's Favorite Cosmetic.* New York: St. Martin's Press.

Queen, C. (1998). *The Leather Daddy and the Femme.* San Francisco: Cleis Press. (Read all of Carol's books too!)

Ragas, M.C., and Kozlowski, K. *Read My Lips: A Cultural History of Lipstick.* San Francisco: Chronicle Books.

RuPaul. (1995). *Lettin' it All Hang Out.* New York: Hyperion Books.

Videos

Bend Over Boyfriend #1 & #2. (1998, 1999). (Anal sex education). S.I.R. Video Productions. For more information, contact www.sirvideo.com.

Hard Love & How to Fuck in High Heels. (2000). (Dyke porn). S.I.R. Video Productions. For more information, contact www.sirvideo.com.

How to Female Ejaculate. (1992). (Sex education). Fatale Video.

Sluts and Goddesses. (1992). (Starring Annie Sprinkle). For more information, contact www.heck.com/annie/.

Online Resources

Good Vibrations, www.goodvibes.com. (The famous sex-toy store based in San Francisco).

Real Dykes.com, www.realdykes.com. (Hot pictures, hot stories, regular columns, for dykes, by dykes, major butch/femme sex stuff too).

Toys in Babeland, www.babeland.com. (Dyke-owned sex-toy store).

Vixen Creations, www.vixencreations.com. (Woman-owned silicone-dildo factory based in San Francisco).